Field Marshal

SAM MANEKSHAW

Soldiering with Dignity

Field Marshal
SAM MANEKSHAW
Soldiering with Dignity

Lieutenant General
Depinder Singh, PVSM, VSM

REVISED AND UPDATED EDITION

NATRAJ PUBLISHERS
New Delhi • Dehradun

First published 2002
Revised edition 2013

Natraj Publishers
17, Rajpur Road,
Dehra Dun 248 001
INDIA
Tel: 0091-135-2654584, 2653382
Fax: 0091-135-2749914, 2651108
www.natrajbooks.com

Production & Layout: Kumar Raman

Published by Upendra Arora for Natraj Publishers, Publications Division, and printed at Saksham Enterprises, New Delhi.

To
my mother, my wife and my daughter,
the three ladies whose love makes me what I am

Acknowledgments

The author and the publishers thank: Director, Public Relations, Ministry of Defence, Government of India, New Delhi; Commandant, Indian Military Academy, Dehra Dun; Commandant, 58 Gorkha Training Centre, Shillong, and Major General T.S. Choudhri for making available photographs for the book and Mrs. Penelope A. Kohli of Open University, UK, for editorial assistance.

Contents

Prologue   xi
Introduction   xiii

Chapter 1
The Early Years   1

Chapter 2
Move to Delhi   17

Chapter 3
Military Assistant to the Army Chief   33

Chapter 4
The Business of Command   57

Chapter 5
Reorganisation   83

Chapter 6
Travelling with the Chief   105

Chapter 7
Prelude to War   123

Chapter 8
The War   153

Chapter 9
Aftermath   181

Chapter 10
Making Way for New Beginnings 205

Chapter 11
The Nilgiris 215

Chapter 12
Valhalla 225

Appendix I 233
Appendix II 235
Appendix III 255
Appendix IV 257
Appendix V 258
Index 261

Prologue

It is 15th January 1973 and the traditional Army Day Parade has just ended. The cream-coloured Impala flying the flag of India's Chief of Army Staff and displaying the five stars of her first Field Marshal comes to a halt behind the saluting dais. The Chief turns and, returning the salutes of the Western Army Commander and the General Officer Commanding Delhi Area, gets in. The car rolls away.

Ahead of us is a Military Police jeep with a large red flag to warn traffic: this is followed by four red-turbanned Military Policemen on motorcycles with two similar outriders following the car. The cavalcade speeds along Palam Marg, crosses the Ring Road to flash down Sardar Patel Marg, slows to turn right along Wellington Crescent, then along South Avenue to Rajpath where, opposite Gate Number 4 of South Block, that monument in red sandstone by Lutyens, we halt. He jumps out, as sprightly as ever, a wave to the assembled crowd and he walks at his usual brisk, firm pace that has lost none of its youthful bounce into South Block: a smile for the lady receptionist and he goes up the stairs, two at a time, to his office.

At the stroke of twelve midday, the Chief of Army Staff Designate, Lt Gen GG Bewoor, PVSM, enters. He is welcomed with a smiling handshake and then, as television cameras whir and flashlights pop, is led to the chair from where he will, in future, conduct the Army's affairs.

A last lingering look and, followed by the Principal Staff Officers, General Bewoor, Mrs. Manekshaw with their two daughters, Sherry and Maja, and my wife who has taken the liberty of dropping by to witness this occasion, he walks down the steps and out of Gate Number 4 where, appropriately, a guard of honour formed by the 2nd Battalion The 8th Gorkha Rifles pays its compliments to the outgoing Army Chief. I say "appropriately" because he is also the Colonel of that Regiment.

The Guard of Honour over, he walks through a huge crowd that has gathered—clerks, peons, guards, casual onlookers— waving and smiling as he always does, trying unsuccessfully to hide the profound sorrow that fills his heart at saying farewell to the Service to which he has given so much and from which he has undoubtedly received much more; shaking hands with whomsoever can get past me and the ADC, then into an ancient black Dodge that now proudly displays the five stars of a Field Marshal and, for the first time, a Field Marshal's flag. As the door closes on him a civilian next to me mutters, "He has fought his last battle." I murmur back audibly, "No, he still has many fields to conquer."

Army Headquarters has just bid farewell to the outgoing Army Chief, Field Marshal Sam Manekshaw, MC.

Introduction

In September 1973, while sitting huddled on a lonely mountain top in the cold Himalayas, with time hanging heavily on my hands, I finally decided to accept the advice numerous friends had been giving me—to put down on paper an account of the period I spent at Army Headquarters as Military Assistant to the Chief of Army Staff, Field Marshal Sam Manekshaw, Padma Vibhushan, Padma Bhushan, Military Cross. It took me exactly one year to complete this account which should indicate that even brigadiers in the Indian Army do occasionally have to pay some attention to their primary work of soldiering.

This is a personal account of what I saw and what I felt. The reader must forgive me, therefore, if during it I tend to drag the 'I' in a bit too frequently. The account concerns a significant period of change, the years 1969 to 1973, when many momentous events occurred including the decisive military victory over Pakistan that not only resulted in the emergence of Bangladesh, but also, more importantly, irrevocably wiped out the bitter memories of the national humiliation of 1962. Above all, the account concerns a man, the Field Marshal, with whom I was privileged to serve through these years in a capacity which can only be termed as close; during this period, the respect, affection and admiration I had for him rose to a degree where I came to regard him as nothing short of infallible. If, therefore, during the course of this narrative I occasionally tend to eulogize, I seek forgiveness for that too.

This book, describing my four years' association with the Field Marshal, is a small tribute to a man who was great by any standard; it is not meant to be, nor can it be yet, a full and objective biography; that will have to wait until posterity can assess in more exact perspective the role of this man in the calamitous days leading up to and ending with victory for Indian arms in December 1971.

The Manekshaw qualities that I have attempted to portray make up the formidable combination required for success: a prodigious capacity for work, a fascinating reconteur with charm and persistence, an irreverence towards red tape, an iron determination, an eye for detail plus a strategic mind that embraced all, yet imbibed the essence, and, above all, a shrewd, sympathetic and sincere ability in man-management that came naturally.

Sam Manekshaw, over the years, gathered around himself an aura of greatness, a charisma. Yet, popular as he was, he, too, had his detractors. While among his friends and well-wishers many myths have grown about his virtues, of his stature as a man, about his character and about his performance, his detractors claimed exactly the opposite. It is not my intention to get involved in an argument with either; my purpose is simply to narrate certain facts as I saw them and leave it to the reader to judge whether myth or detraction is correct. It is my hope that, during the course of this pleasant and to me rewarding exercise, a true picture may emerge of the man who, as Army Chief and Chairman, Chiefs of Staff Committee, played a significant role in changing the geographical face of the Subcontinent and, in the process, gave to the Army, by the time he left it, a little more dignity and pride than it possessed when he became its Chief of Staff.

I have relied entirely on memory while narrating the gist of the four years I spent in Army Headquarters. Naturally, help was sought and, I must acknowledge, readily and promptly provided to fill in the details.

The matter of giving the book a name took some time. Many names were considered and discarded till finally I decided that the name should reflect the Field Marshal's ideas on soldiering generally. And then his words to me one day which were in effect that if, during his tenure as Chief, he could instill a little more dignity in the Army he would consider his job well done, gave me the title I wanted, "Soldiering with Dignity".

The manuscript was sent to the Field Marshal during 1975 with a request to correct and approve it. The reply was characteristically prompt and generous, stating that it would take time but I should expect masses of red ink. Some months later he wrote to say that publication should be delayed as "the present is not the opportune time". The draft stayed with him until it was returned to me in 1996 with permission to get it published. Since considerable time had elapsed between 1973 and 1996, I thought it appropriate to update the manuscript rather than leave it in its original form. This process has been done, partially by additions in the main text where appropriate, and by the addition of a postscript.

1

The Early Years

The man eventually destined to be free India's first Field
Marshal was born on 3rd April 1914 at Amritsar. How did
a Parsi couple settle for the holy city of the Sikhs? I once asked
him and was told that in 1899, his father recently qualified as a
doctor and just married, could make no professional headway in
Bombay, and was advised to try his luck at Lahore in the Punjab.
With his young wife, he set off by train for Lahore. The long,
dusty and hot journey took five days and by the end of it, his
young wife, who had never left the comforts and civilization of
Bombay, was in hysterics and cried to go back. Poor Doctor
Manekshaw did all he could to comfort her, but as the train
steamed into Amritsar, with her first sight of the Sikhs the young
bride screamed her lungs out and refused to go any further. So
they left the train at Amritsar, and there they stayed for forty-five
years.

The Manekshaws had six children, four boys and two girls,
and Sam was the fifth child. Sam had his schooling at Nainital's

Sherwood College. Just before he assumed the appointment of Army Chief, he visited his Alma Mater and, in a brief but very witty speech to the staff and students, remarked that the debt he owed to Sherwood was very big indeed; because it was there, amidst lovely surroundings, being bullied and, in turn, bullying and ragging and quarrelling with neighbours, that he really learnt to fight.*

After completing his schooling, he should have gone to England to pursue higher studies; this was the promise made to him by his father but, fortunately for the Indian Army, Doctor Manekshaw felt that this particular son was far too young to be on his own in a foreign country, even with his two elder brothers already studying there. So he was admitted to the Hindu Sabha College, Amritsar. If he had gone abroad, he often reminisces, he would have become a doctor. "What doctor?" I queried, and was told "Gynaecologist."

In 1969 he paid his first visit to Amritsar after a gap of many years. The reception he got there was fantastic; he was mobbed wherever he went and, no matter how quiet I thought I had kept an engagement, word would leak out and there would be huge crowds to cheer him, shake his hand or just talk to him. On a quiet afternoon with most formal functions behind us, we drove out almost furtively to see the house where he was born. We were in civilian clothes and the driver had been instructed not to display star plates or flag; consequently, we were able to sneak into the house without attracting attention. He showed me, at the entrance, a eucalyptus tree that his father had planted the day Sam was born. "Its grown taller than you," I informed him as he posed beside it for a photograph. The young lady who opened the door to my knock was a bit startled when she heard my request to see the interior. The inhabitants of Amritsar are a

---

*Excerpt from the speech he gave on the occasion is given at Appendix I.

warm and kind-hearted people, however, and without much ado or fuss, permission was given for us to go round. While he explained the changes that had occurred and the alterations that had been made over the years, the young lady accompanying us, perhaps to ensure that her kindness did not end in our making away with the family silver, recognized him, word was passed immediately, and the whole family was around him pressing us with tea, snacks and much kindness. "Never turn away a visitor from your house," the old lady informed us, "for you never know when God will come a-visiting."

After a stint in Hindu College, he applied for and was accepted for entry into the first batch of the newly opened Indian Military Academy at Dehradun for training Indians for commissioned rank in the British Indian Army. He received his commission on 4th February 1934 and, after an attachment as was the practice then with a British Infantry Battalion, the 2nd Battalion the Royal Scots, he joined the 4th Battalion, 12 Frontier Force Regiment, commonly called the 54th Sikhs. He often reminisced about this period and I recall two incidents that he used to narrate. The first pertained to the annual confidential report every officer gets once a year. His first report, he says, was a model of brevity "this officer, I beg his pardon, this man, may one day become an officer". Obviously the officer of the 30s was not as sensitive as the present day officer; an endorsement of a similar nature today would assuredly result in representations and appeals.

The second pertained to wearing dark glasses. I once asked him why he never wore them even during snowstorms and he explained that, as a young officer, he had bought himself a pair of rather high priced Crookes lenses and, as he was walking down the road one day sporting his newly acquired glasses, he passed his Commanding Officer, a crusty old soldier, who was returning from parade on horseback. The old man dismounted, beckoned him over and plucking off the glasses before a startled Sam Manekshaw could utter a word, threw them down on the road and ground them into pieces with his boot. He said, "I have been thirty years in your country and have never worn dark glasses; they are the surest way to ruin your eyes." He then re-mounted and rode away, leaving a very shaken and despondent young man who has never worn dark glasses since that day.

Much later, in 1973, when he visited the United Kingdom at the invitation of his friend, General (now Field Marshal) Sir Michael Carver, he was asked his preference regarding places he would like to visit. There was only one request. Could he visit the 2nd Battalion, Royal Scots? This was arranged, and he presented the Officers Mess of that Battalion his favourite memento, a silver Khukri. A couple of weeks after his visit to the battalion, he received a letter from the Colonel of the Regiment, Major General W. T. Campbell, CBE, which bears reproduction below, because of its historical significance.

"I have just returned home from a visit to Edinburgh and our Regimental headquarters, where I was so delighted to see the beautiful Kukri which you have so kindly presented to us as a reminder of your association with the Regiment. It is now proudly displayed in one of our showcases with an appropriate description.

When at R.H.Q., Duncan Eykyn drew my attention to an important 'double' which you have achieved for the Regiment through your promotion. We already have the distinction of having had the first Field Marshal in the British Army, when it was bestowed in 1736 by King George II upon George Hamilton, the 1st Earl of Orkney who was then Colonel of the Regiment, and now I hope you will permit us to claim this 'double'. I thought that you might be interested in this remarkable coincidence."

During the 1971 war with Pakistan, he used to maintain a careful watch over the activities of his old Battalion, the 54th Sikhs, and one could discern not a little pride when the briefing officer would recount some incident or action where that Battalion had done well. "I should like to see one of my 8th Gorkha Battalions fighting the 4/12 Frontier Force Regiment," he would remark.

In 1937, at a social gathering in Lahore he met his future wife, Silloo Bode; they fell in love and were married on 22nd April 1939. Silloo was a graduate of Bombay's renowned Elphinstone College and also studied at the JJ School of Arts there. A voracious reader, a gifted painter and an extremely intelligent and interesting conversationalist, she made an admirable wife and a wonderful mother.

The outbreak of the Second World War saw the 4/12 Frontier Force Regiment in action in Burma with the famed 17 Infantry Division. Sam was separated from his family for over three years and this separation was the cause of a celebrated example he was later to give while answering questions put to him in his capacity as Chief of Army Staff by the Pay Commission. The question, which triggered off the reply was, why should the Army continue to get separation allowance? This, to clarify, is a token sum every officer and enlisted man gets when his unit moves to a non-family station thus necessitating separation. I say "token" because the name is a misnomer; whereas it is meant to cover the expenditure incurred in running two establishments, the amount paid is, in fact, a pittance. For example, an officer used to get just seventy rupees a month and the men an even smaller amount. The answer to explain the need was, "After my marriage, I went off to war and didn't see my wife for three long years, and when I returned I found I had a brand-new daughter, and the only reason I am sure the child is mine is because she looks just like me." Needless to say, the pay commission broke up in laughter, but went away convinced. The separation allowance continues.

On 22nd February 1942, occurred the much publicised event when Sam was wounded. The retreat through the Burma jungle

ended abruptly for him on 22nd February 1942, when seven
bullets from a Japanese machine gun whipped through his body.
The young captain who had just led two companies in the
courageous capture of a vital hill was awarded the Military Cross.
"We made an immediate recommendation," a senior officer
explained, "because you can't award a dead man the Military
Cross." His orderly, Sher Singh, evacuated him to the Regimental
Aid Post where the regimental medical Officer, Captain GM Diwan,
treated him overruling his protestations that the Doctor treat
other patients first. Sam was evacuated to the Hospital at Pegu
where he was operated upon, and then evacuated further to
Rangoon, from where he sailed for India in one of the last ships
to leave that port before it fell to the Japanese. He still carries the
scars of this wound and I am not quite sure whether it is that or
regular exercise that keeps his stomach in—to the envy of people
much younger than him.

I was to see a great deal of Sher Singh during my tenure in
Delhi. He and some other grizzled old veterans of the 4/12 Frontier
Force Regiment were frequent visitors to Army House and South
Block. The entire staff, including all guards and sentries, had
strict orders that if a man said he was from the 54th Sikhs he was
to be led straight to the Chief, whatever the time or whatever the
Chief happened to be doing. I shudder to think of the
consequences if a couple of serving personnel of 54th Sikhs (in
its new avatar) had decided to pay a call in 1971.

Consequently, these gentlemen would turn up whenever it
suited them with a string of requests that ranged from wanting a
bag of sugar for a daughter's marriage (easy to solve) to asking that
a relative or friend's relative be given immediate out-of-turn
promotion. When I patiently attempted to explain the
impossibility of the latter request and others like it, the worthy
would bristle and inform me: "In the British time if the Jangi Lat
gave an order it was executed without question." No amount of

explanation that times had changed and that such Nadirshahi orders would now invite representations which could not possibly be answered, would pacify them and they would go away and complain to the Chief about the incapable and unhelpful Colonel Sahib he had from the Gorkhas. I got the impression, somehow, that they felt that a Colonel from the 54th Sikhs might perhaps have done better.

The war over, saw Sam working in the Military Operations Directorate at Army Headquarters, first as a General Staff Officer Grade I, and later as the Director of Military Operations. It was from here that he oversaw the fighting that broke out between India and Pakistan, over Kashmir, the two nations that until so recently had been one. It was also under his direct supervision, when the cease-fire was declared, that the famous line called the Cease Fire Line was drawn. Many, many years later, by a strange coincidence, while he was Chief of Army Staff, it was he whose brainchild it was to scrap the Cease Fire Line and call it the Line of Actual Control—but more about this later.

Sam and Thimayya, then a Major General, were selected to be military advisers to the Indian Delegation to the UN, then led by Sir BN Rau. They spent a pleasant 2½ months in Paris where the session was held. Much later when ZA Bhutto led a Pakistani delegation to New Delhi for talks on Kashmir, he was selected yet again to be part of the Indian Delegation. His most vivid memory of the event was of the first day when Mr. Swaran Singh, then Foreign Minister, made the introductory remarks and carried on for over 2 hours talking about everything else except Kashmir. Finally, Mr. Bhutto asked for a break and remarked to his aides in an aside, "Let us give them Kashmir before my bladder bursts."

A lecture tour of Australia followed to acquaint the Australian public with India generally and the Indian Army in particular. I recall two incidents that he used to recount about this tour. In one, after he had laid it on really heavily about how good the

Indian Army was, about its achievements and its triumphs, a grizzled old Australian stood up and stated:

"Colonel, I appreciate all you've said about how good the Indian Army is but I wouldn't want you to go away thinking that we Australians are anything less, in fact we are very proud of ourselves and our ancestors."

Pat came the reply, "So you should be. After all, the ancestors were selected by the finest judges in England."

The second incident occurred as, dressed in an immaculately cut suit and wearing a camel-haired overcoat, he was about to catch a taxi in Sydney. A group of Australians, who had obviously imbibed freely, started discussing within his hearing what nationality he could be. One gay spark concluded that he must be a f–Limey, to which he got the instant retort, "You buggers can't even do that!"

While he was still with the Military Operations Directorate, he was promoted to the rank of Brigadier and appointed Director, Military Operations. This appointment, incidentally, was upgraded first to Major General and more recently to Lieutenant General and is now termed Director General Military Operations. In consequence of this promotion, Sam missed the sine-qua-non of infantry soldiering, namely, command of an infantry battalion. However, the fact that despite this discrepancy he rose to the rank of Field Marshal merely proves the point that every rule has an exception.

He was appointed Colonel of the 8th Gorkha Rifles in 1953. The Indian Army follows the British system of having regiments each with a varying number of battalions. These battalions are then grouped within brigades to form tactical formations. The Regiment remains a sort of home, and is not to be confused with the regiment of some armies like the United States, where it is the actual tactical unit. Colonels of Regiments are selected by vote; each battalion recommends a name and the Commandant of the Regimental Centre, the head of the family as it were, compiles recommendations and then sends the selected name to Army Headquarters. The Colonel of the Regiment acts as a father figure, ostensibly to co-ordinate regimental activities and traditions, but actually to look after regimental interests by way of choice posting and good peace stations for battalions and officers of the regiment. Naturally, therefore, if a regiment has an up-and-coming officer for colonel, its interests are better tended. In consequence, the 8th Gorkha Rifles have had an excellent innings since 1953.

Promotions followed in rapid succession and 1959 saw Sam as commandant of the Defence Services Staff College. There his outspoken frankness got him into trouble with the Defence Minister, V.K. Krishna Menon and his protege of the time, the late Lieutenant General B.M. Kaul and a Court of Inquiry was ordered against him. Despite persistent questioning I could never ascertain from him the reasons and the facts that led to a situation where the Indian Army could have lost its most brilliant up-and-coming General Officer: he just refused to talk, calling the entire episode just another phase. However, he did shed light on this incident in a talk delivered to the DSSC on 11th November 1998.* Be that as it may, the Court of Inquiry that was convened with the late Lieutenant General Daulet Singh, then Western Army Commander, as Presiding Officer, exonerated Sam, but before a formal No Case could be announced, fate intervened in the shape of the Chinese hordes that swept over what we had always considered the impregnable Himalayas. The Indian Army, that proud, disciplined and distinguished force that had fought and triumphed in practically every battlefield of the world, was outmatched, outmanoeuvered and outfought; its remnants streamed back dazed and humiliated leaving among the lush green

---

*Extract from the speech he delivered at the DSSC on 11 November 1998 is given at Appendix II.

mountains of the North Eastern Frontier Agency and the stark white of Ladakh its dead, its wounded and its pride.

The North Eastern Frontier Agency, now called Arunachal Pradesh, was where we suffered our worst defeat, and it was to 4 Corps that providence ironically decreed and Army Headquarters ordered Sam Manekshaw to succeed Lieutenant General B.M. Kaul, the man who had almost ruined his professional career. He took over 4 Corps on 28th November 1962 on promotion to Lieutenant General, and the same day addressed a conference of what must surely have been a very shaken group of staff officers. He entered the room with his usual jaunty step, looked as if he were meeting each eye trained on him and said, "Gentleman, I have arrived! There will be no more withdrawals in 4 Corps, thank you," and walked out. But the charisma that surrounds the man and about which I shall dwell at greater length later, had preceded him and soldier and officer alike knew that the 'chosen one' had arrived and henceforth all would be well. It was as if the dark and oppressive atmosphere had suddenly been illuminated and Sam was the bearer of the light.

After he had left the Staff College, one of the many distinguished and learned speakers who visit that Institution to address the students, remarked on the way Sam had borne himself during his inquisition led by Krishna Menon and Kaul. In the process he expressed eloquently what many others wished to say and what practically everyone had noticed. He was sorry, he said, that his friend Sam Manekshaw was not in his customary place in the audience because he would have liked him to hear this. Anyone can be great in success; only a truly great man can retain the aura of greatness in adversity. This was the lesson he had learnt from Sam Manekshaw, and he would be happy if this was the lesson students at this eminent institution carried with them when they left Wellington rather than trying to imbibe knowledge from pedantic talks such as his.

On 4th December 1963 Sam took over as Army Commander in the west, the second rung from the top. One of his brigade commanders was H.S.Yadav, the man who had been the principal prosecution witness in the case cooked up against him in 1961. At a party in an Officers Mess in Kashmir one evening, talk veered round to Yadav, and the senior brass, knowing the background and not averse to making a few points with the Army Commander, started on what each planned to do to catch or embarrass Yadav. The Army Commander heard this for some moments and then butted in ("before I got sick" as he told me later) with "Look chaps, professionally, Kim Yadav is head and shoulders above most of you, so forget about trying to catch him out. He just lacks character and there is nothing anyone of you can do about that."

In 1960 I served under Kim Yadav as an instructor in the Jungle Warfare School, in Clement Town, which he commanded. I found him to be an outstanding teacher, egoistic yet humane.

At a meeting in Delhi a few months later, Chavan, then Defence Minister, asked him his views on which Army Command Sam considered most important, challenging and threatened. Eastern, said Sam, as it had the Chinese in the North, East Pakistan in the South and on its flank insurgency rampant in Nagaland and the Mizo Hills and, if all that was not enough to fill the hands of the incumbent, the troubled state of West Bengal certainly would. Chavan thought over the answer for a few moments and then asked if Sam would like to accept the challenge of taking over that Command. He accepted immediately and the following morning was asked to do so formally by the Army Chief, General JN Choudhury. He found himself, on 16th November 1964, packing up from the beautiful, bracing heights of Shimla to the steaming but warmly affectionate atmosphere of Calcutta.

Eastern Army had to keep one wary eye directed north on the Chinese; another eye had to be kept on erstwhile East Pakistan which lay in its gut; it had to fight insurgency in Nagaland which later spread to the Mizo Hills, and finally it had to watch over the politically volatile states of Assam and West Bengal. It was, therefore, no bed of roses, and the job of lower formations was not facilitated by the Army Commander's personally coming on the telephone every now and then and 'grilling' staff officers and commanders with endless questions about detail. I remember an occasion in Shillong where I once asked the senior staff officer at Headquarters why he was looking a bit off-colour. He told me that he had just finished a telephone conversation with the Army Commander who had wanted answers to so many questions that, "I am now in orbit".

His mastery of detail was fantastic and, as I was to learn later, he could quote an answer given verbally or in writing months previously to correct someone who was saying something else. A battalion employed in the Mizo Hills, paying perhaps a little more attention to the welfare of its troops and, in the process, a little less than desirable to the operational side, received a rude reminder that 'someone up there' was watching, very keenly, every move that was made. A parcel of bangles was delivered to the Commanding Officer with the compliments of the Army Commander with a cryptic note: "If you are avoiding contact with the hostile give these to your men to wear." Needless to say, the next few weeks saw a flurry of activity by this Battalion resulting in another, more soothing message: 'send the bangles back'.

On another occasion, 5 Mountain Division was celebrating its raising day in 1967 in a non-family area, and some officers had been permitted to invite their families to participate in the celebrations. To everybody's horror, just about then, instructions issued by Headquarters Eastern Command were received, intimating that no officer's families would be permitted into field areas as such licence could be resented by the men. Most families had already moved by the time this instruction, a general one and not meant exclusively for 5 Mountain Division, was received. The General Officer Commanding, Major General Onkar Singh Kalkat, PVSM decided to bell the cat and explain the position to the Army Commander in the hope that he might relent. Accordingly, he made a telephone call and gave the necessary explanations. There was a pause at the other end and then:

"Okay, Onkar, let the families come in but make quite sure that husband and wife sleep apart."

General Kalkat never did explain how he enforced that order. Incidentally, my wife and I had also been invited to these celebrations and we had driven across from Shillong. The Army Commander was there too, and after seeing me he asked General Kalkat, while being driven around by the latter, whether I had chances of 'making brigadier'. Obviously, my profile which he had seen earlier at Shillong had not impressed him.

He was officiating as Army Chief in 1967 when the Chinese had their first clash with the Indian Army since 1962. This occurred at the 14000-foot high pass, Nathu La, in Sikkim where the Chinese learnt to their cost that the Indian Army of 1967 was a different kettle of fish from that of 1962. He was summoned to a meeting of the Cabinet where, as he recalled later, everyone present at the meeting was vying with the others to present to the Prime Minister his grasp of the situation and offering one suggestion after another as to what should be done. After hearing most of the speakers, the Prime Minister enquired whether the officiating Army Chief, until then a silent spectator, had something to say. "I am afraid they are enacting Hamlet without the Prince," he said. "I will now tell you exactly what has happened, and how I intend to deal with the situation." He then proceeded to do so.

During his tenure as Army Commander in the East, insurgency was contained in Naga Hills and Mizo Hills, now called Nagaland and Mizoram respectively. Many innovations were tried out in both areas, and all these collectively allied to the remarkable endurance, bravery and perseverance of the troops deployed there, helped to bring about a situation giving the local populace more confidence in the Security Forces than in the militants despite the campaign of terror unleashed by the latter. Intelligence flowed in and, in consequence, there was very little the terrorists did or planned which the Security Forces did not know about. The culmination was the capture of Mowu Angami, the self-styled Commander-in-Chief of the insurgent army in Nagaland, and his band who had just returned from China.

Bengal in those days was a very troubled state where anarchy was prevalent, and law and order was almost on the way out. Sam was travelling to Dum Dum Airport, Calcutta, once when he found the road blocked for traffic by a huge crowd being harangued by one person. The outrider and the staff officer accompanying him both advised a detour, but this would have meant running away and would have been noticed by the locals. So he got out of his staff car instead, and started walking up to the speaker who, he discovered to his disquiet as he approached, was a "huge fellow, well over six feet tall". Anyway, hiding his mounting uneasiness, he put his hand out and announced, "I am Sam Manekshaw." This unsettled the other person somewhat as he had probably anticipated an argument. He, too, put his hand out and mumbled his name. He was then asked to clear the road, as otherwise "I shall miss my plane". The speaker, by now completely confused, hastened to obey, and the last glimpse the Army Commander had of his latest acquaintance was of that worthy helping to clear the road.

He was in those days, as he claimed later, a veritable "one man employment exchange" and the numbers of ex-servicemen, officers and men, he managed to fix up in jobs with industrialist friends was legion. In fact he could secure more openings for officers and men while in Calcutta than he could as Chief of Army Staff in

Delhi, leading to a remark, one day some years later in the latter city, "I could do more in Calcutta for ex-servicemen."

By then Sam Manekshaw had become one of the most popular and well-known officers in the Indian Army. Stories of the many admirable qualities he possessed and did not hesitate to display were legion. Always an unconventional dresser, he once met Lieutenant General Kulwant Singh, at that time Commanding Western Army and an awe-inspiring man, in a jacket that could be best described as a cross between a regulation shirt and bush shirt. When the Army Commander pointed this out he was asked: "Have you come to see my formation or my dress?" While he could stand up to his superiors, he always stood by his subordinates. Service with him, it was rumoured, was certain to bring rewards in its wake. But, helpful as he was, he never consciously helped a subordinate at the cost of someone else. In other words, "No throat was cut."

I once asked him if he was aware of the jealousy his so-called favourites aroused among others. He replied that he was aware of this but as his "favourites" were all competent officers he defied anyone to point a finger at them as far as their professional competence was concerned. On another occasion I asked him why he could not 'see through' the slick types who fawned and flattered him, and why he acceded to their requests. "Oh, I see through them all right," he replied. "I detest them, but I make use of them."

He was human and approachable to a fault. Once, so a story goes, while he was a Corps Commander, a junior officer on his staff asked for some leave, and the request was turned down by the officer's immediate superior. The officer then tried the indirect approach and made his problem known to the Corps Commander who called the man's immediate superior the next day and said, "Look, I have had a letter from this youngster's father asking that the boy be sent on a spot of leave as there is some family problem to sort out. I am sure we can spare the bugger for a few days, let him go, we won't miss him." The officer got his leave; no feathers were ruffled and everyone was happy, which brings us to his next great quality, the ability to run a very happy and contented team. His professional qualities ensured that the team was also a competent one. He was believed to finish his own work in an hour and spend the remainder of the time walking from one office to another, sitting down with the harried junior staff and helping them sort out the problems they were working on.

They said he never raised his voice, but even a mild reproving look from him with a, "Sweetheart, this won't do", was enough to shake the stoutest heart. Sharply critical, but always constructively so, there was nothing his eye ever missed or his fantastically retentive memory ever forgot. He forgave easily, being basically a kind man. While he was Chief of Army Staff, at an "at Home" he attended in Rashtrapati Bhavan, as the guests came out into the Mogul Gardens he found himself walking beside Mr. V.K Krishna Menon, of whom mention has been made earlier. Polite to a fault, he wished Mr. Menon the time of day and also enquired how the latter was progressing health-wise. He then turned to Mrs. Manekshaw, who was also walking in line, and asked her: "Darling, you remember Mr. Menon?"

Mrs. Manekshaw, not quite as forgiving as her spouse, at least on this occasion, replied brusquely: "No, I don't."

In short, a brilliant mind and a thorough gentleman. Most of these stories, I was to learn later, were true and consequently contact with the real Sam Manekshaw only tended to confirm all the good that one had heard about him.

For his adroit handling of all the difficult and diverse problems Eastern Army faced, and so successfully overcame, he was awarded the Padma Bhushan in 1968.

2

Move to Delhi

I first met Sam Manekshaw at a dinner in the Officers' Mess of the 58 Gorkha Training Centre in Dehradun. This was in 1954 when I was a recently posted-in captain and he was a brigadier. I remember that dinner vividly because, as the junior-most officer in the Mess, I sat on his right at the formal dinner and the only remark that passed between us was his question, "Which is your Battalion?" and my reply, "The 4th Battalion." Apart from this, throughout the evening, and it was a long evening as anyone who has attended an 8th Gorkha regimental guest night will testify, the only time I opened my mouth was to shovel some food in; he never kept quiet.

My first meeting with Mrs. Manekshaw occurred in a far more informal manner. It happened like this: while attending the Defence Services Staff College Course at Wellington in 1963, I came home at about midnight after a stag dinner. My wife and some other ladies, to keep themselves occupied and, I suppose, out of greater mischief, had got together at our house for some cards and supper. They broke off on my return. Two ladies, who lived some distance away, had shared a car and they had hardly driven a furlong or so when the engine coughed and stopped. They tried tinkering with it for a while, but then gave up and came knocking at our door to ask for a lift. The dinner I had attended had been in formal mess attire: this dress, though extremely smart and flashy, is certainly not comfortable. In consequence, the guests had no sooner bid us good night than I had hastened to take it off and so, by the time the two ladies returned, I was in my night clothes.

On hearing of their predicament, I slipped on my dressing gown and drove them to their place in my car. While returning, I found to my horror that I was out of petrol and now it was my car's turn to splutter and stall. I was driving up an incline when I stopped and as I had spotted a stationary car parked just where the incline started, I coasted back to seek help. There wasn't anybody around but, on my calling, I observed someone approaching through the gloom. On coming closer I discovered that it was Mrs. Manekshaw, and her first question, as I tried to get back hurriedly into my car to ovecome my embarrassment at being discovered on the road in a dressing gown, was, "Have you any spare petrol?" I couldn't hide my amusement and burst out laughing. She laughed, too, when I told her why my car had stopped.

In 1972, when visiting Calcutta, the Chief called on the Governor of the time, Mr. AL Dias. By coincidence, during this period, the entire Dias family which included daughters-in-law, sons-in-law and grandchildren had gathered in Calcutta. They are a very informal and close family and, after the call was over and we got into the car and drove off, the Chief turned to me and remarked on the informality, affection and cheerfulness that we had just witnessed, and the warm hospitality we had enjoyed. By then I had known the Manekshaw family for over three years, and so could honestly reply that whereas the family we had just seen were certainly a very happy one, his family, too, was not only a rare sight but also a heart-warming one.

The Manekshaws were a very close family with perfect rapport existing among them. The two daughters, Sherry and Maja, often call him Sam and Mrs. Manekshaw, was Silloo. Later, when grandchildren appeared, they, too, took up the custom of calling him Sam. It did one's heart good to spend some time with the family and see the humorous repartee, understanding, love and affection each had for the others. The puckish sense of humour is best illustrated by a story he used to narrate. Sherry and Maja were studying in Shimla and on one of his visits to see them, he took them to see a movie. The daughters' friend had also accompanied the party. Sam got a shock when, as soon as the film started, a small hand slipped into his. Bubbling laughter from the daughters solved the mystery; they had instructed the friend on what she had to do as their father expected this!

There were a few other meetings over the years and then, in 1966, my Battalion moved to Shillong which lies in the territorial jurisdiction of Eastern Command of which he was Army Commander. I assumed command in March 1967, and he was scheduled to pay us his first visit soon afterwards. I took full advantage of the impending visit to get the red-tape-bound and slow-moving authorities to provide all sorts of benefits for my Battalion with a very simple expedient: I merely had word passed round that the Army Commander was visiting us in his capacity as Colonel of the Regiment and would be spending all his time with the Battalion. This spurred the Military Engineering Service as nothing else could, and lights were miraculously provided where previously there were none, potholes on main roads that had broken many a shock absorber were filled up overnight, and dirty buildings immediately had their first coat of whitewash in years. At the last minute, the visit was cancelled. In my letter to him asking that he must visit us again soon, I mentioned how sorry we all were at the cancellation. Tongue in cheek, I could not help adding that, unfortunate though this was, it would help me bully the authorities once again when he did decide to visit. He visited us soon after this and, with a smile, reminded me about my remark and told me that he would instruct his Assistant Military Secretary to issue a tour programme showing him on a visit to the Battalion every month, and added, "get the maximum advantage out of it". I can now report, that I did.

There were other visits and, at each one, as I came to know him a little better, I had a sneaking suspicion that he was quietly giving me the once-over. On one such visit, during a dinner at the local Area Headquarters Officers' Mess, he put his arm around my shoulder and, taking me up to the General Officer Commanding, asked me to his face, "Sweetheart, tell me, are these people looking after you?" I stammered some sort of a reply to the effect that the Battalion was being looked after but this didn't convince him, so he darted off and within a few seconds was back with my wife to whom he addressed the same question. She, quite uninhibited by military protocol, replied without batting an eyelid, "No. They are not providing an electric connection in our family welfare centre." The Family Welfare Centre got its electric connection the next day, and I got a lot of dirty looks.

On another occasion, in my Officers' Mess, he sat down to write his name in our Visitors' Book. A lady, Diljit Jagtiani, the wife of one of my majors, Kumar Jagtiani, handed him the silver pen lying on the inkstand next to the Visitors' Book. In accepting the pen he remarked "I bet, it won't write", to find the wager promptly taken by the lady with, "I bet it will". Miraculously, because pens of officers' messes are notoriously out of ink, it did write. He returned to Calcutta the next morning and, within two days, there came a present for the lady—a box of chocolates! While on the subject of visitor's books his orders were that every visitor, irrespective of rank or position, would sign on one line, not one page as some visitors insisted on doing.

Fort William in Calcutta has an infantry battalion, both to provide guards and duties for the Command Headquarters and also, should the need arise, for purposes of internal security. He had got the 2nd Battalion of his Regiment to Calcutta for this purpose, and there was nothing that they could not get out of him, so fond was he of them. The only demand he made upon them was that, occasionally, he would drop into the guard room at his house in the morning to sample a bite of breakfast which the men normally eat, 'puri' and plain potato curry.

Once, on a visit to Shillong, he came with a bandaged foot as he had earlier hurt himself slipping down some steps at Calcutta. At a party, he refused to walk down a few steps to receive some fairly senior people there, pleading that he had an injured foot. Just as he was about to walk away, however, after meeting everyone, he espied a sentry of my Battalion positioned at the bottom of the steps. Without a word he hobbled down, shook hands with the sentry, patted him on the back and, after sharing a joke with him, hobbled up to rejoin the party.

It was in Calcutta in 1968 that his Regiment did him proud when two of the battalions representing different formations were locked in combat to decide who would win the Eastern Command Football Championship. My Battalion fortunately won, and it was a great honour for me to receive the championship trophy from him. Later, after he had taken over as Army Chief, he was to preside over an even happier occasion when the Gorkha Brigade football team won the blue riband of Indian soccer, The Durand Championship, and received the trophies and prizes from him, in New Delhi.

Thirteenth May each year is celebrated in my Battalion as the anniversary of a battle fought at a remote village called Taungdaw in Burma during the Second World War. In 1967, I had invited two British Army Officers, Lieutenant General (now General) Sir Walter Walker and Lieutenant Colonel (now Brigadier) Peter Meyers who had been commanding the Battalion and Company respectively in 1945, to visit us. They had accepted and as General Walker was an old friend of my Army Commander from the days when both had served in the Military Operations Directorate in Delhi, the latter had helped in finalising all the formalities that are involved when a foreigner visits.

I had hoped that the Army Commander would also attend, but was reminded of his thoughtfulness when he declined my invitation explaining that, as chief guest, Walter Walker must get all the honours; if he attended, too, considerable attention would naturally be deflected. With characteristic grace, however, he offered to visit us, "to give the Military Engineering Service a slight nudge", as he put it, a week earlier. He did so, and I can now report that the nudge had its effect.

Many visits later came his last one in October 1968 just before the Battalion was to move from the idyllic surroundings of Shillong to the forbidding heights of Joshimath on the Uttar Pradesh-Tibet border. It was at a dinner at Raj Bhavan with that accomplished and charming couple, the B.K. Nehrus, playing host that his Assistant Military Secretary, Dini Mistry an old friend from the days in Palampur when he was commanding an infantry battalion of the 5th Gorkha Rifles in the Brigade where I was Brigade Major, took me up to the Army Commander and stated: "Sir, Depi has done about two years in command; why don't you take him as a GSOI in Headquarters, Eastern Command?" The suggestion was certainly not of my asking, but I got a short piercing look, perhaps to confirm whether or not I had instigated the request; reassured from my face that I had not, a smile and he said, "Why GSO I, Diniyar? There are better appointments for him!" Mystified and not a little embarrassed, I made polite noises and withdrew. Later that same evening, he took me aside and said, "As you know I am

in the running to be Chief-of-Army-Staff when General PP
Kumaramanglam retires in May 1969. Should the Government
decide to make me Chief, will you be Military Assistant?"

There flashed through my mind the story of Field Marshal
Wavell, when he first rose to general rank, asking Bernard Ferguson,
of Chindit fame and an officer of his regiment, the Black Watch,
to be his first ADC and the latter's replying that as he had never
done ADC before he might not be able to make a success of the
job. Wavell's classic reply was that as he had never had an ADC
before, it was his fervent hope that he didn't fail the ADC. The
second thought that flashed through my mind was that if I did
reply like Ferguson, the answer I was almost certain to get was on
the lines that I should not worry, as he would see me through.
Prudently, therefore, I thanked him for the offer and said, "Of
course I agree." In parting, there was no word about keeping the
offer to myself but he did say, "Up to now it has always been my
kismet and now it is yours and mine together."

This little episode should, I feel, suffice to serve as an
introduction to the man. When he gave his confidence, he gave
it without any reservation, fully. He was a fatalist, a firm believer
that what has to happen, will happen; worrying will riot alter the
inevitable. An egoist, yet humble, possessing the most charming
manners, and a stickler for proprieties.

For some unaccountable reason the Government delayed taking
a decision over the appointment of a successor to General
Kumaramanglam. The result was that by March 1969 all sorts of
rumours were afloat—an unhealthy trend. In mid-March, while
instructing at an officers' course in Bareilly I learnt that I was
under posting as an instructor to the Defence Services Staff College
at Wellington in the Nilgiris. I called Sam up from Bareilly on
the telephone to apprise him of this and to ask that this posting
order be cancelled. I could sense a slight bitterness in his reply
when he advised me to accept the posting as his own future was

undecided and, "for all you know, they might not make me the Chief." Very confidently I persisted with my request predicting that there was no chance of someone else being appointed. He agreed to have the posting cancelled, and though I heard no more about the Staff College posting, I did have to do plenty of explaining to officers who had overheard my telephone conversation, as the telephone I spoke from had been a public one utilised by all the officers. Why, they asked, was I being foolish enough to refuse a choice posting like that? I could only plead domestic problems, knowing it was an extremely unconvincing reason.

A few days later, however, came the long-awaited announcement that Lieutenant General SHFJ Manekshaw, MC, was to be the next Chief of Army Staff. My letter of congratulations elicited a short note thanking me for my felicitations and ending with, "Your confidence in me appears to have been well founded; see you soon in New Delhi."

Later, in Delhi, he was to tell me how Mrs. Manekshaw, ever serene, had received the tidings about his appointment. He was in his office at Fort William, Calcutta, when the news was conveyed to him by General Kumaramanglam. He hastened home and told Mrs. Manekshaw who happened, at that time, to be reading in bed. Without taking her eyes off the book she was reading, she muttered a brief "congratulations". Irked, he asked her if that was the only reaction she could display. To which came the classic retort: "Sam, whom else do you think they could have made Chief?" In retelling this incident to others, he used to say that while all the deliberations were going on in the Government to decide who would succeed General Kumarmanglam "only two people had absolute confidence in me, my wife and my Military Assistant".

After the announcement I felt free to tell everyone about my next assignment. It made my wife and me a very popular couple overnight. Suddenly, everyone was a close friend, everyone knew all about me, and everyone had just one wee problem which I was asked to solve on arrival in Delhi. Such is human nature! Incidentally, prior to the announcement, whenever I met officers who were known to be favourites of Sam Manekshaw, each one of them would claim that his next posting was to be as Military Assistant to the new Chief. Not unnaturally, after hearing a few such claims, I did start wondering how many military assistants there were eventually going to be. I realized soon that this was "kite-flying" and what someone called "speculative optimism!"

Meanwhile my wife, Balli, had been staying in Dehradun as a separated family. There, she had made an attempt to see the Sub-Area Commander to ask for suitable accommodation but had been given some excuse and brushed off. When news of my new appointment went round Dehradun, the same gentleman dropped by where Balli was staying and offered to allot her "whichever house you like". Another instance of the frailty of human nature.

I asked for and obtained permission to be attached to Army Headquarters before the Chief Designate arrived so that, "I could find my own way in the corridors of South Block without getting lost". Accordingly, after a tearful farewell to my Battalion in Joshimath, the Battalion I had known so long, grown up in and loved so well, I left on 14th May 1969, reporting to Army Headquarters the following day.

In the new surroundings I commenced familiarising myself with my job and the maze of corridors, offices and staff: the conglomerate that is collectively called South Block. Lt Col Prem Chandra, my predecessor, was a wonderful teacher, initiating me very gently into the mysteries of the job with admirable efficiency.

General Kumarmanglam, the Chief of Army Staff, never noted for his conversational abilities, gave me a good example of his reticence. He knew who I was as he met me practically every day whenever he walked into the MA's office but, it was only on the eighth or ninth day that he addressed me to say, "This is a very important job and you must never open your mouth. If you can do that you will be a success here." I thanked him and assured him that I had no intention of ever opening my mouth without reason.

It was a hot, stuffy, windless day that 29th May 1969 as I waited on the tarmac at the Air Force Station, Palam, for the AN 12 aircraft bringing my new boss from Calcutta to Delhi. The plane landed on schedule at 1230 hours, and I went in to receive him. In the same aircraft were his wife and ADC; his baggage and dogs had come in earlier. Aware that unless specific orders to the contrary existed there would be swarms of officers to receive him as everyone pays obeisance to the rising sun, he had issued instructions that only the Lieutenant Colonel, who generally used to be detailed to receive him when he visited Delhi as an Army Commander, and I should receive him. Even the ancient Cadillac that used to be detailed for him during his earlier visits to Delhi was not forgotten, and it was this car that now awaited him. He was housed at Shanti Bhavan, the Military Engineering Service Inspection Bungalow in Delhi Cantonment.

Among his first orders on taking over as Chief was one which stipulated that, thereafter, whenever an Army Commander visited Delhi he would be received by a general officer. Also that proper accommodation must be arranged for the staff officers that accompanied the visiting Army Commander.

Though General Kumaramanglam was to retire on 6th June 1969, the overlap had been organised so that the Chief and Chief Designate were never in-station at the same time except one evening when the staff at Army Headquarters were to bid farewell to the outgoing Chief.

A day or so later my boss travelled to Nainital where his Alma Mater, Sherwood, was celebrating its Founders Day. He had wanted Mrs. Manekshaw to accompany him but when this demand was suggested to the Air Force, they baulked as only Service Chiefs may travel in the VIP Flight accompanied by their lady. I told him about this objection and his answer amounted to what the Watergate transcripts delicately called 'expletive deleted'. Mrs. Manekshaw accompanied him and we never heard any more about the objection.

Meanwhile the Chief was also touring round to say his farewells. On the evening of 30th May 1969 there was a cocktail party in the Defence Services Officers' Institute, Dhaula Kuan, on behalf of Army Headquarters to bid farewell to General Kumaramanglam. It was attended by officers in Delhi of the rank of brigadier and above—my first introduction to so much brass!

Sam made the farewell speech in which he said, looking at Kumaramanglam: "In my religion everything happens in fives: this is the fourth occasion I am taking over from General Kumaramanglam. I trust Sir, that you will now have a very happy retirement and the government gives you a good job so that when the superstition of 'fives' is fulfilled, I shall be on a happy wicket." The previous four occasions he referred to were when he relieved General Kumaramanglam in command of 26 Infantry Division; the Defence Services Staff College; as the commander of the Eastern Army and, finally, as Chief of Army Staff.

General Kumaramanglam in his reply thanked everyone and, in a reference to the present he had just received and which had cost slightly more than what orders specified said, "I know that this beautiful present you have given me costs more than what an officer is permitted to accept. I am entitled to disobey my own orders once in a while, however and so am delighted to accept."

Next day, that is 31st May 1969, General Kumaramanglam accompanied by his wife and staff left for a tour of the South, arranged in such a manner that his last day in service, 6th June 1969, would be spent in Bangalore, his first station of posting after he had received his commission. On the morning of 6th

June 1969 the new Chief came to the office sporting the badges of rank of a General. The badges were in black as he is Colonel of a Rifle Regiment, the 8th Gorkha Rifles. Incidentally, in an ex-officio capacity, he also became colonel of the Brigade of Guards; a custom started by the first Chief, General KM Cariappa who raised this regiment and decreed that the Chief of Army Staff should be colonel.

I put up a draft Special Order of the Day, long winded and worded in rather flowery language, it came back with a line drawn through it and, in his own handwriting, the brusque message, Horatio Nelson style, "I have today taken over as Chief of the Army Staff. I expect everyone to do his duty."

I admit that, once the initial flush of taking up such a coveted appointment had worn off, I was assailed by countless apprehensions, mainly "will I be able to measure up to the new Chief?" The first day in office was sufficient to reassure me that my apprehension was quite groundless because of the qualities of approachability and patience plus shoulders broad enough to accept the mistakes subordinates made in good faith. Sometime in between 1st and 4th June 1969, I recall having asked him what changes he would like to be made in the office. He looked at me steadily and replied, "When a new broom arrives, everyone expects and fears change. We will change all right, but we will do it so gradually that no one will feel it or resent it." He was aware also of the fact that the Army is so obsessively concerned with continuity that it often disregards the need for change. It was an education to see his easy acclimatisation and how he mastered and re-defined the role of COAS.

The Military Engineering Service which constructs and maintains accommodation for the three services, and the Central Public Works Department that maintains most of the accommodation occupied by government officials in Delhi, were the first to feel the new Army Chief's wrath as he took their representatives around Number 4, King George Avenue, commonly known over the years as Army House, to show them the shabby state it was in. For almost four months the new occupants stayed in part of the house (living out of suitcases) while workmen sawed and hammered in the remainder. At last, it was ready and although, thereafter, an occasional rocket was let off, the renovation proved satisfactory and the baggage packed in Calcutta in May 1969, was finally opened up.

I was to learn, in the months ahead, that this was not a personal fetish; whenever he visited formation headquarters and units, he would refuse to see training as "I have seen enough during my service." He would insist instead on seeing "how my troops and my officers live." There, he would go into the minutest detail.

"Why is the light switch so far away from the bed?"

"Can the lettering on the houses not be more neatly done?"

"Why does this room not have a built-in wardrobe?"

"Which clot has designed this house?" This last, much to the mortification of the accompanying chief engineer who, in all probability was the 'clot' referred to.

He was the bane of the constructional engineer's life but a friend of the officer and the soldier. "When the Government has accepted the commitment of providing housing for my officers and my men," he used to remark, "my engineers must ensure that they get the best possible." And he made sure, while he was Chief, that they continued to do so.

While the Army House was being altered and repaired, the garden also received a thorough overhaul. At 5.30 a.m. every morning the new Chief in a sports shirt and shorts would be outside where batmen, servants, gardeners and whoever else could be collared would be running behind him as he raced along at his usual fast pace, giving directions for the day. In the evening, on his return from the office, a quick change into shorts and he would be off checking whether or not the day's chores had been done, and woe betide anybody if they weren't.

The stereo equipment including an amplifier gadget he proudly called his 'brain box' was installed early. Whenever one visited Army House, one would be sure to be greeted with the most exquisite music. He has a fantastic collection of records, cassettes and tapes, and whenever he is at home one of the gadgets would be sure to be playing. Later, after we had been together for some time and he had delivered one of his rockets to me and found me sulking, after a reasonable period of time which was generally about fifteen minutes, he would walk into my office, put his arm around my shoulder and ask how my music collection was progressing. Then, as a peace offering, would come the bait: "I've got this lovely tape, shall I copy it for you?"

This, as he knew, was guaranteed to break the ice so he would depart, happy that his staff officer was sulking no longer.

This consideration manifested itself in other ways, too. Once an officer of the Regiment who rose to be brigadier, Engineer by name (called Enge by his friends) was posted to a brigade in 7 Infantry Division at that time commanded by Major General M.R. Rajwade, VSM, MC, an old favorite of the Chief from Tezpur days where he had served as his Chief Engineer. Enge, for some reason, could not pull on with his new boss and the outcome was inevitable—removal within a couple of months to command another brigade in some other formation. I once asked the Chief whether he was annoyed with Rajwade for sacking Enge thus. No, he replied, he was not annoyed over that aspect because he believed that incompetent subordinates must be disciplined. What had hurt him was that Rajwade had failed to give Enge sufficient time to develop. "A superior," he told me, "must shield a subordinate for six months. It is only after that period, if the subordinate fails to reform, must he be sacked." I remembered that advice when they gave me command of a brigade and I had to 'bring up' new commanding officers. This quality, incidentally, came into play on at least three occasions in cases of officers of the Brigade of Guards, the Regiment of which he was ex-officio colonel. By endorsing his comments in the annual confidential reports even when, in two cases, he was not in the chain of reporting, he set aside the adverse remarks written by the iniating officer and so saved their careers. Two of the three eventually rose to be army commanders.

On 14th June 1969, he took the salute at the Passing Out Parade of the Indian Military Academy, Dehra Dun. A copy of the address is given in Appendix III.

Pipping ceremony by
the President

With the then Prime Minister, Mrs. Indira Gandhi

Guard of Honour by Welsh Guards - 15 April 1973

Padma Vibhushan by the President - OUR NATIONAL HERO

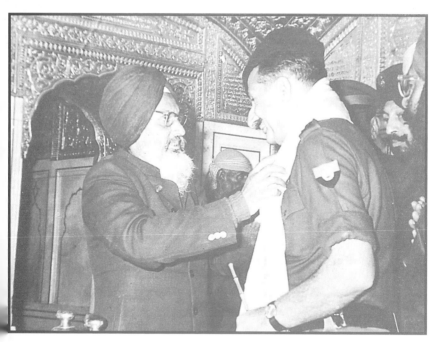

Sam in the Golden Temple

With C-in-C of the
Royal Nepalese Army

Sam at the Indian High Commission in the UK

With His Holiness, the Dalai Lama

With civilians in Bangladesh

Sam somewhere in the Western Sector.
On his left, Major (later Lieutenant) General Jaswant Singh

Some of the PAK ships destroyed by
Indian air raid in CHITTAGONG harbour

Sam on a Buggy

Lt Gen AAK Niazi - Signing the Document of Surrender

Gen SHFJ Manekshaw, COAS, talking to troops in Chhamb Sector

This picture was taken the day Sam put on the Badges of a General

At a Reception. On the left is Capt (Later Maj Gen) SD Sood, ADC

General Sir Walter Walker (Ex CO); Brig Peter Myers (Ex Company Commander),
4/8 GR with families of the Battalion.

The author with General Tikka Khan at Lahore

The President at the Army Day Reception

Sam as GOC in C Eastern Command with the 4/8 GR Football Team

Maj Gen Kalkat, the author, Mrs. Depinder Singh and
General Sir Walter Walker

Sam welcoming the C-in-C of the Royal Nepalese Army and his wife

Sam releasing the author's first book
'IPKF in Sri Lanka'

The author and his wife being welcomed at a Reception

Lt Gen KK Singh,
GOC 1 Corps;
Maj Gen WAG Pinto,
GOC 54 Inf Div;
Brigs Vaidya, Jagat Vohra
with Sam

The author and his wife
with the Defence Attache of
Egypt and his wife

The author's wife
(in the centre)
at one of the Receptions

The author getting the Shiromani Award in 1987
from the then Vice President

The author and his wife

The Chief with a Foreign Officer and Major General MN Batra (extreme left)
and Lieutenant General KS Katoch, MC
the then Vice Chief of Army Staff (second from right)

During periodic Army Commander's conferences, the Assistant Military
Secretaries would get together with the MA for Refreshments.
(L to R), Lieutenant Colonels Venugopal, Muthanna, Sharma
and Medhi Ratta with the author(centre). Venugopal and Sharma were later,
in December 1971, to win well deserved Mahavir Chakras.

3

Military Assistant
to the Army Chief

A rmy Headquarters is organized into five broad branches to conform to staff functioning, viz., General Staff, Adjutant General, Quarter-Master General, Master General of Ordnance and Military Secretary. Each branch has a varying number of directorates functioning under it. The COAS has his own secretariat which functions with a small staff under the Military Assistant (MA) to the COAS. I suppose it is the first two letters which used to lead some people to ask me what subject I had majored in or what master's degree I boasted. In fact, my scholastic education ended when I did my Senior Cambridge. The MA is, in the words of the Book, "In charge of the COAS Secretariat". This sounds simple; in fact, it is a vastly complicated job requiring the utmost patience, long hours and considerable perseverance and tact.

All correspondence that the Chief sees passes through the MA. With a boss like mine, it meant reading every letter in detail and assimilating its contents as he was quite capable of calling me in and asking for a clarification or even, "tell me, lovely, what is this all about?" In the beginning, illiterate as I was, I attempted a broad-brush reply. This was quickly corrected when I found the file being closed and handed over to me with a curt, "Read it." On the first or second day I had inquired whether he would like me to act as a mere post office and keep passing on dutifully all the mass of paper that we received or whether he expected me, correctly, to use my knowledge and experience, which admittedly was not much, and vet these papers so that only a selection was passed on and the remainder disposed off; also, whether I could air my own views on notes and correspondence passed to him. He had agreed with me saying simply, "I like a man to have his own views, and to express them."

Consequently, most papers going to the Chief would contain an attached suggestion or criticism from me on a small slip of paper. The idea was that, on its return journey, I could retrieve the note from the file and the chief's comments would appear to be his own. To my horror I once found that a file with my remarks containing suggestions completely at variance with the original, had been passed on directly to the Principal Staff Officer concerned with a note from the Chief, "The MA has made a good suggestion, examine." Tactfully, I had to explain that expressing my views on notes sent by General Officers and their getting to know of it would not exactly endear me to them. After that, much to my relief, if my view or suggestion was accepted, the note would be worded as being from the Chief.

My next job was to fix all appointments for the Chief. This proved an onerous task as the number of requests for appointments and interviews was colossal. There would be requests for attendance at social functions, requests by people who wished to come and *pay my respects*—a term he hated—"he wants to call and make some request" he would say. Then there were official meetings and functions, visitors who were "in Delhi just for a day", ex-servicemen, some of them regular visitors who came in periodically every month or quarter, especially after the Chief made his widely publicised remark at an Ex-servicemen's Rally: "No one who comes to my door with a request will go away empty handed."

Then there were eight telephones, at least two of which for some unaccountable and frustrating reason would insist on ringing at the same time. Swarms of visitors had to be fended off and queries over the telephone answered, all politely when one really wanted to say something rude and drastic. I used to liken everyday in the office to a day that graduates of the Defence Services Staff College would be familiar with—the telephone battle where the Directing Staff, by painting situations as they would obtain in battle, build up a tremendous amount of tension under which the student has to labour and, hopefully acquit himself creditably. Initially I tried coping with the telephones by attempting recognition by ear-guessing which telephone was ringing by the difference in sound. This, however, proved abortive as every now and then some telephone mechanic would fiddle with a telephone and a sound different from what I was used to would emanate, leaving me as perplexed as ever. Then we became modern, technology took over and every telephone had a light fitted that would glow whenever it was ringing.

One day the Reception Office rang up to say a Princess of one of our erstwhile states had arrived and wished to see the Chief urgently. The Chief was out of his office at that time, fortunately, and so I could truthfully say so (many were the times when I was not quite so truthful). The Reception Officer then rang back to say that, in that case, the lady wished to see me. I gave my assent and, in a short while, a pretty and well-groomed lady walked in, shook hands with me and asked, "General Sahib, are you interested in the India of a few years hence? If you are, I shall sit down and take five minutes of your time." On my assuring her that I was honestly interested, she sat down and said: "General Sahib, I wanted to see the Army Chief personally, but since he is out, I shall tell you what I want and you can explain it to him." I nodded and also, diffidently, pointed out that I was only a Lieutenant Colonel and not a "General Sahib". "Oh! I can see that," she said, "I know all about badges of rank, but I shall call you General nevertheless because you look like one, and in any case, you ought to be a General."

Flattery, they say, is counterfeit money which, but for vanity, would have no circulation. I am mortal and as vain as the next man and so, not unnaturally, I was all attention. On my asking her to continue and tell me what the problem was, I got a severe jolt when she said, "I have come to ask the Chief to strap on his sword and accompany me to Rashtrapati Bhavan where I want him to drive the present occupant out and install himself there."

It was then that I discovered how loony the lady was. Some quick thinking was necessary for me to get out of that one with a whole skin and so, not knowing whether to laugh or get angry, I told her that there would be a problem to this request as the Chief never carried a sword. I added that I would take her to the Adjutant General who dealt with matters of discipline and so on. Moreover, the incumbent was then a cavalry officer and so could be expected to both have a sword and be ready to accompany her after strapping it on. She went out happily.

Visitors, sometimes, also put me in embarrassing situations. If someone came in unannounced and I felt, from my own judgement, and this very soon became uncannily correct, that he or she was merely a request seeker, I would put the person off by profuse apologies with the most convincing excuses made at my persuasive best explaining how very busy the Chief was at that moment such as he was in a meeting of absolutely earth-shaking dimensions and so on. Meanwhile, I had to keep one wary eye towards his office and my fingers crossed as I lied like a trooper because, restless as he was, he would suddenly pop into my office to give a direction or seek an answer. Whenever he did this, he would finish his business with me and then go to the visitor, put his hand on his (or her) shoulder and say: "Yes, sweetheart, Who are you? What are you? Where are you? Have you come to see me or the MA?"

Needless to say that was the visitor's golden moment. Out would come the mumbled assurance that it was the Chief that was to be seen and, as the visitor was escorted by him into his office, I would be left with a red face cursing all and sundry and then, back to earth, to answer frantic calls to rearrange further engagements. Meanwhile out of his office would come a stream of snappy instructions, "Get the Confidential Dossier of so and so", "Call the Adjutant General", and so on. Incidentally, whenever Field Marshal Cariappa wished to call on the Chief, he would give me a call and fix an appointment. General JN Chaudhari, on the other hand, always barged in unannounced, throwing our schedule completely out of gear.

The business of his calling people "Sweetheart", to those who did not know him well used to cause some embarrassment, as it did to a pretty young lady reporter who came in one day seeking an interview and, on being granted it, came in at the appointed time and date a few days later and started turning red and blue after the Chief called her sweetheart once or twice. She only recovered her poise when, at the conclusion of the interview, the Chief brought her into my office and, addressing me, said, "Sweetheart, will you see this lady out." Hearing this, the lady enquired, "Oh! you call everyone sweetheart? I thought you were being fresh with me." From the twinkle in his eye, I could see a retort coming, but thinking better or probably knowing that it was a press reporter he was talking to, he controlled himself, smiled, and went out.

Well before a meeting or engagement, it was my job to get hold of all relevant files and papers, sift them and then pass on the essential details. I learnt very quickly that no matter how high and mighty the person from whom a paper came, I had to do all the spade work; this happened after a file passed by one of the PSOs was neither flagged correctly nor had all the required details in it. I was summoned into his office as soon as the file was seen and asked, "Have you also joined the conspiracy to drive me nuts?"

All private mail addressed to the Chief also passed through me. I opened all letters except those marked "personal". The aim, of course, was to reduce to the barest minimum the number of letters he had to peruse, but he did grumble on the odd occasion when I inadvertently opened a letter from 'a girl friend'. I used to excuse my action by pleading that I did not want him subjecting himself to the threat of letter bombs by opening letters but he remained unconvinced.

He wanted, and obtained, the most thorough and detailed briefing before a meeting. I once remarked about this and was told that he did it for two reasons. First: bureaucrats who also attended such meetings started with the great advantage of continuity, having been in their jobs for long periods and thus possessing very intimate knowledge of their subject; service officers, on the contrary, were denied this benefit as one did a two or three year stint in the Service Headquarters and then made way for someone else. Second: he had seen, as Director of Military Operations and Director of Military Training, even persons of the calibre of General KS Thimayya led up the garden path, or left chasing a red herring, because they did not go fully prepared. "No one is going to pull the wool over my eyes," he would say.

I remember a story which will indicate his thirst for detail. Once the Chief of Air Staff wrote a note to the Defence Ministry with a copy to each Service Chief giving the gist of some information the Yugoslav Military Attache had passed to him after driving down in his car from Rawalpindi to Delhi, via Lahore. When he saw the note he buzzed me over the intercommunication set and asked: "I thought colonel so and so was a friend of yours." On my assuring him that this was in fact so, he queried, "Then why didn't he give you this information." I informed him that the Attache had given me all this information many days ago and I had dutifully conveyed it to the Director of Military Intelligence. "You didn't think it was important enough to convey to your Chief?" he asked and thus left me with no choice but to say "No. I don't pass insignificant bits of information to my Chief."

During the first few weeks, reading his writing, laced though it was with wit and wisdom, used to pose a problem. To those who haven't seen it, his writing is in very straight lines, each letter separate, upright and very firmly put down. He narrated a story once which describes his writing admirably. It seems that when he was Brigade Major in the North West Frontier Province of undivided India, his Brigade Commander, after the first few days, called him in and told him, "Sam, your writing is quite beautiful, but would you please read out what you've written."

Sometimes strange words and abbreviations would be recorded on notes and files he had seen. One, "ED", mystified everyone till I marched into his office to ask what it meant and was told that it stood for "Extract Digit"—what we in the Army normally call "pull your finger out". On another occasion while we were drafting his biographical sketch and I had put up a draft for his approval, the date of birth, through a typing error, which should have been corrected by me but was not, showed his date of birth as 4th April 1969.

The draft came back approved but with the date of birth sidelined, with the remark: "I must have been an absolutely fantastic genius to have been appointed Chief at the tender age of 3 months."

If, perchance, I have conveyed the impression that everything went like clockwork with my overseeing the entire operation in a cool, calm and detached manner, I have erred. Firstly, though I could successfully hide the disquietude I actually felt, I was in fact like a cat on hot bricks trying desperately to cope with listening politely to a visitor, answering at least two telephones, trying to note the more important parts of the conversation going on, perusing a file the old man wanted "early", a favourite expression of his which really meant, "why haven't you presented it already?" All this probably will explain why at least one of my predecessors ended up with ulcers.

Secondly, appointments on the odd occasions did go awry with the inevitably embarrassing consequences. I was proud of the fact that during my tenure, however, this happened only once. That was when the Director of Ordnance Services dropped in to ask for an appointment for the Chief to address the Senior Ordnance Officers who had assembled in Delhi for a conference. In fixing up the appointment I entered it on the wrong day in my Diary. By the time the actual day arrived, I had fixed up some other meeting and, consequently, it was a pretty mortified MA who apologized to the DOS for this inexcusable slip. Later, I wrote a small note of apology to the Chief and was mollified to receive a gracious reply asking me to forget the incident and, adding by way of consolation, that "it can happen to anyone".

We received anonymous letters by the score every day. It was my job to read these and pass through only those that I knew, from personal knowledge, had some substance. Some of these, with the advantage of more intimate knowledge, the Chief would destroy; others would come out with a note written in his own hand, addressed to the person concerned and marked "Personal and Confidential", stating "I have just received this. I have also heard similar rumours previously. There is no reply." Needless to say, the note must have been a shock to the recipient but, by a strange coincidence, not even on a single occasion did we ever hear a breath of scandal after such a letter. Did the person reform or did he tighten his security? I wonder!

Another incident, much more amusing, occurred when we received a letter one day purporting to be from a Mizo girl alleging that a lieutenant colonel commanding an infantry battalion serving in Mizoram had been intimate with her, had got her pregnant, taken her to Shillong where he had paid for an abortion and was now neglecting her for some other girl. The Chief was very sensitive to this sort of accusation as it lent fuel to the accusatory fire that we were ill-treating the locals in insurgency areas. The letter, therefore, went down to Eastern Command to examine and report. After some days the investigation report turned up and it transpired that the officer concerned had had a vasectomy two years earlier and so, whatever else he did, he certainly could not have made that girl, or any other, pregnant. As one lives and learns, I learnt that day that, apart from birth control, vasectomy has other uses too!

From the Prime Minister's Secretary came a forwarding note one day accompanying, for a change, an anonymous letter complaining of nepotism and favouritism rampant in the Army and alleging, by way of illustration, the case of a recently promoted major general appointed Director Weapons and Equipment (DWE). The Chief read it, called a PA and dictated a reply which wasn't really necessary but went something like this: "The Oxford Dictionary defines 'Nepotism', as 'undue favouritism to relations'. Major General so and so is a caste Hindu and I am an equally high-born Parsi. Therefore, there is no religious relationship. The General Officer is 50 years old and I am 58. Therefore, although I was a precocious child, best medical opinion would rule out paternity in this case. Unfortunately, I have not much scope for nepotism: it is almost too frustrating. The only competent officer from my community is already the professional head of the Army."

We never got an anonymous complaint from that quarter again!

On the subject of DWE, I feel a slight amplification is in order. This appointment was and will always remain extremely sensitive, dealing as it does with the most lucrative of all businesses: weapons and equipment. The gun-runner fraternity exerts enormous pressure on the incumbent enlisting his friends and relatives, officers he has served with or under and so on; all designed to influence decisions in favour of the particular party. Allied to this are the mind-boggling monetary figures involved and you can imagine the pressure to succumb and the strength of character required to withstand it and take objective decisions.

Never was his quality of honesty and simplicity more visibly manifested than when he was being briefed. He detested embellishment and demanded the essence; consequently, long-winded explanations bored him and he would become restless. Then very tactfully, because he could never be impolite, he would lead the briefing officer by asking specific questions so that he found out what he wanted in the concisest possible form.

On a visit to a Border Security Force Headquarters once, a lieutenant colonel of the Army on deputation with the BSF started to brief him on operations conducted by his troops. He gave a masterly exposition, on the map, of how good his troops were; of how effective their actions had been and how demoralised the enemy had become. We heard him out in silence and just as he concluded, I thought that he had got away with it. With misplaced confidence, however, he made the fatal error of ending with, "Now: Sir, if there are any questions, I will be happy to answer them."

The questioning started: three questions and the man was a

blubbering mess, as any man will be who knows he's been caught lying. Then the Chief got up, walked over to the lectern, patted the briefing officer on the back and said, "Sweetheart, you mustn't bluff your Chief. He is on your side; he knows more than you think he does and, finally, he is not a reporter for a cheap thrill-seeking news magazine."

As I have mentioned earlier, numerous ex-servicemen dropped in with requests which would range from *"farmaish"* for an out-of-turn promotion for a relative, to a request for a letter of recommendation from the "Jangi Lat", to an airing of some complaint. On his orders, all such cases had to be investigated and disposed off as expeditiously as possible with the utmost sympathy and tact. Woe betide any of the staff who was reported against by any such visitor when the Chief came out of his office into the corridor and found someone hanging around.

Not all were persons with genuine grievances; an occasional crook would also interpose himself. One rang me up once, introduced himself as a Member of Parliament, and informed me that he was sending ex-serviceman so and so to me and could I please sort out his problem. On my assuring him that we would do all we could to help and asking him to send the person over to me immediately, he rang off. About half an hour later the person concerned arrived, was ushered into my office, showed me his discharge papers which were in order, and then narrated his tale of woe; this was that he had left the Army in 1947 of his own free will after serving for two years, but he was now suffering from Tuberculosis and wanted money and free treatment. I arranged some financial assistance and advised him to go to one of the civil hospitals and seek admission there as he was not entitled to free medical treatment in an Army Hospital. The money given to him was adequate to cover at least six months' treatment. I also gave him a letter of introduction-cum-recommendation. Apparently satisfied, he went away.

About two months later, I received a call from the same Member of Parliament who asked me to see the same ex-serviceman again as he had more problems. On my asking him to send the man over, he thanked me and rang off. A short while later the ex-serviceman appeared and narrated fresh woes. The voice disturbed me, however, until I suddenly realized that it was the same voice that had spoken to me on the telephone. When I threw the accusation at him, he didn't even bother to offer a denial, but admitted the fact right away and pleaded poverty by way of excuse. I had no option but to call the Military Police and hand him over. I don't know what eventually happened to him, but I hope that whatever it was it wasn't too severe. Needless to say, I learnt my lesson and, thereafter, even a Ministerial call invited a check to make certain!

On another occasion a man came in, posing as an ex-serviceman, to complain that the Soldiers, Sailors and Airmen's Board at Jullundur, his hometown, was not paying any attention to his repeated requests and grievances and could he be given financial assistance from the Chief? His papers were in order but his story sounded false. While he sat in my office, I did a quick check only to discover that he was a fake. The Military Police were then summoned to take the man away for handing over to the Police.

Another incident, much more heart-warming and one that really restores one's faith in human nature, occurred when a Jat boy with his wife and child came in and informed me that he had come to tell me his story. If he did not get justice he and his family were off to the River Jamuna to commit suicide. I'd been in the chair for a while by then and so had learnt to be cautious and, in any case, I've always had a sceptical attitude towards would-be suicide cases. I heard his story, however, which was that he had been unjustly tried by his Commanding Officer, punished with discharge from the service and awarded three months' rigorous imprisonment. He had completed his sentence and, on going to his village, was informed by his father that he could not possibly stay in his house after the disgrace the offence he had committed brought to the family; he must, therefore, take his wife and child and leave the village. Something about the way the man narrated his story convinced me of his sincerity; I had the matter investigated and discovered that the man had, in fact, been unjustly punished. The sentence was set aside and the man was reinstated. I never heard from him again, but I hope he proved a good soldier and is happy wherever he is serving.

The staff quickly learnt that everything had to be absolutely immaculate in the office. He has a hawk's eye that misses neither poor turnout in dress, nor a speck of dust or piece of unpolished brass. So every morning my first job was to go round and see that everything was neat and clean, photographs straight, peons correctly dressed, staff shaved (except me, of course) and no long hairstyles. Within the first few weeks he enquired why our part of South Block was not as neat and clean as the External Affairs part. There was, of course, no satisfactory answer and so orders went out for a case to be projected to the Government for authorizing a lieutenant colonel, designated "Welfare Officer, Ministry of Defence", and charged with keeping our portion of South Block clean. Changes were introduced and within a remarkably short time, we were not ashamed to receive visitors in our area. Peons were issued new sets of winter and summer uniforms: when they wore these the first day, I was called out into the corridor, shown the peons who were all lined up, and asked, "Do you call this fitting?" So I had to supervise the fitting, and I must confess that thenceforth every visitor who dropped by complimented me on the smart turnout of the Secretariat Staff.

Papers for his signature had to be absolutely meticulous; pin marks, overwriting, cutting, or words added in the margin were not good enough. A copy of a demi-official letter had to be an original to each addressee; duplicate copies would not do. Consequently we soon found that the one electric typewriter we had in the secretariat was insufficient to meet the heavy demands made upon it, so another one had to be procured.

When he gave a draft for typing, he would be like a child waiting impatiently for a present he knows is on its way. Completely ignoring the fact that the draft was a lengthy one, he would buzz me every half hour to enquire about the progress and my reply that the personal assistants, who were all very competent, were working on it would elicit, "it's such a short draft; why does it take them so long?" So working flat out, the poor personal assistants had to produce a paper that was complete, correct and immaculate. No easy job, but they did it. While he was a great orator whose talks, generally extempore, were a delight to listen to, his dictated notes, too, were equally an education and a pleasure to peruse. Very rarely did I see him alter the first draft. Equally rare was a letter bereft of at least some element of humour. Naturally, therefore, drafts which came to him for approval and signature had to adapt to his style and his very high standard; anything less and there would be a great deal of red ink and a direction to retype. Some of the subordinates whose drafts almost always passed were Lieutenant Generals KK Singh, Menezes and Thapar, and Major General IS Gill.

His penchant for simple language reminds me of a story: Cecil B De-Mille, the great Hollywood Producer-Director, once spoke to his staff about keeping language simple; "if you use the word optimist," he said, "how many people will know that you mean an eye doctor."

Though he was a mesmerising speaker in English and with a barrack room mixture of Hindi and Urdu, the more difficult hindi words would leave him baffled. While reviewing a ceremonial parade of 2/5 GR (FF) in Ferozepur, he mystified the Parade Commander with the words, "Same to you" after the latter had reported the parade was ready for inspection in *shudh* (pure) Hindi. After the parade was over, the Parade Commander inquired about this and was informed that he said what he did after he was called *"Be-sharam"* (shameless). The Parade Commander, of course, had ended his report with the word *"shriman"*. On another occasion, at the 58 Gorkha Training Centre, when the officer conducting a demonstration sought permission to start with, *Pradarshan arambh karne ki anumati chahta hun, shriman* (May I have your permission to start), he got a brisk salute in reply and the words, "I don't know what you said, but you may start."

He was very particular about his stationery and insisted on thick paper. I finally got what I was assured was the thickest in the country, and was also told by the stationers that "anything thicker than this is a card; it cannot be called paper", but even this was accepted most reluctantly. By August 1969, he started worrying about the New Year greeting card, and finally approved a design after the printers almost went mad over the number of mistakes he would be certain to point out in each draft.

A word about staff work. The Ministry of Defence has, over the years, burgeoned to a degree where almost every directorate in the three services' headquarters is duplicated. Consequently, when a case is put to the Minister even if it were signed by the Chief and addressed to the Minister or Secretary, it would descend the ministerial ladder and end up in the dealing section. It used to be customary for the case to sit there for a while whereafter the under-secretary or director would return it to the service headquarters seeking some innocuous explanation. Very soon after Sam took over as Chief, and a case that had originated under his signature came back with a query from some junior bureaucrat, a note accompanied the case to the Defence Secretary to the effect that the only people who could endorse remarks on a file emanating under the Chief's signature were the Secretary and the

Minister. If anyone else's views were sought, these had to be on a ministerial inter-office file. This procedure was scrupulously followed thereafter.

His office was a model of austerity and utilitarian simplicity. Wood-panelled walls with a simple pencil sketch of Gandhi on the wall, and the remainder bare. Behind his chair were two bronze statues of Victoria Cross winners, Havildars Lachhman Gurung of the 4th Battalion of his Regiment, the 8th Gorkha Rifles, and Agan Singh Rai of 2nd Battalion, the 5th Gorkha Rifles. After the Pakistani surrender in East Bengal (now Bangladesh), one of the original copies of the surrender document also adorned the wall. There was a maroon wall-to-wall carpet and simple brown curtains. In one corner was his table with an impressive array of telephones on his right and behind these, trays, for the various papers that went in on his left and, no matter how high the bundle, went out very quickly indeed on his right.

He was particular to the point of being fastidious about dress. He was asked while being interviewed by the Pay Commission why the Army should continue to get a Kit Maintenance Allowance. I am sure the Commission's President wasn't aware of what he was letting himself in for when he posed this perfectly innocent question. The Chief stood up and said, "Yes, I'll answer that one. Would you mind stepping out and standing here by my side?" This, to one of the bureaucrats on the Commission, whereupon that worthy stepped out and stood by the Chief's side.

"Gentlemen," the Chief went on, "behold my dress: See my shirt, see my trousers, see the starch, the perfect ironing, the shine on my belt and shoes, see my haircut, and feel my chin. Now look at this gentleman. See his crumpled bush shirt, the creases in his trousers, look at his shoes: I beg your pardon, he hasn't any shoes, he has chappals and no socks!"

The Pay Commission was in stitches by then, and the President said, "Thank you, Chief, you have made your point."

But the Chief had more ammunition up his sleeve and, in any case, he was not a man to let an opportunity like this slip away, so he continued:

"At lunch time, I will go home, take off my uniform for my batman to straighten out, have a wash and then, after lunch relax by reading a book or listening to music; after this I will put on my uniform, brush my hair and come here for the afternoon session. Now take this gentleman: he will sit on one of these sofas, eat from a tiffin box he is carrying and have a nap in his office. After we finish for the day, I will go home, have a bath, have a whiskey, put on a lounge suit and go to a party. This gentleman will also probably be at the same party, having gone to it straight from here, and wearing the same clothes as now." I do not know exactly what the Pay Commissions recommended in this regard, but the kit maintenance allowance continues.

While on the subject of dress, I recall that one of his first orders after assuming the office of Chief was to effect improvement in the turnout of Army contingents, particularly for the Republic Day Parade. To achieve this, another innovation that was introduced was that contingents were to be formed from Regiments rather than, as was the practice until then, from battalions, thus providing the selectors with more choice. Needless to say, Army Contingents thereafter were smarter and much better turned out.

He always sported a side cap. He would invariaby be asked the reason for this preference and the reply was a simple "I like it; my nose shows up." Woe betide any officer who was seen by him walking around wearing a side cap during working hours. The offender would be called up and informed, "You wear this with your mess dress: only Sam Manekshaw can wear this during office hours."

Hospitality at the Manekshaws was always gracious and lavish.

There would be the most interesting collection of guests, so a party meant meeting people from varied backgrounds and professions; excellent wine and liquor and delicious food, some of which would have been cooked by him as, apart from his many other accomplishments, he was expert in the culinary field. During such engagements, the dress would often be stipulated as "black tie", informal meant a lounge suit, and very seldom did he accept the lesser "open collar". A bush shirt was completely taboo as far as he was concerned and, in fact, any invitation to him specifying the dress as bush shirt was certain to get a "regret" from him. Whenever I wore a bush shirt to a party and, in the Delhi summers, this was the only dress to wear, I had to make quite certain that he wouldn't be going there. He caught me in this shirt one evening. He was out of the house, attending a meeting and, as Mrs. Manekshaw was not well, my wife and I decided to drop in at Army House to see her. After that we were going out for dinner, so I had explained to my wife that we would not stay for more than fifteen minutes to give us enough time to clear out before the Chief returned. At Army House, however, Mrs. Manekshaw refused to let us go, insisting we stay until the Chief came back. When he came in, he took one look at my bush shirt and, turning to my wife, said, "You look gorgeous; why do you agree to go out with this *Junglee* dressed as he is?"

In extending hospitality, the staff of Army House were not forgotten. Once a month or once in two months, all the staff which included the guard, batmen, cook, bearer, gardner, watchman, barber and driver would be guests with Sam and Silloo playing host with gracious ease.

Whatever the occasion, he would be immaculately dressed: sober shades, beautifully tailored clothes and always well groomed. I once asked him the price of a pair of brogues he was wearing and was told, "21 Guineas". On another occasion, he let me into the secret of his immaculate clothing: one of his better suits, from Savile Row, London, was opened in Calcutta and paper cuttings were made of it. Thereafter, whenever a new suit was required, the tailor collected the cloth and the cutting and, hey presto, a remarkably well fitting new suit was in his wardrobe! He advised me to follow this example. Ruefully I reflected on his figure which hadn't changed for ages, then I contemplated my own which changes far too frequently, and reluctantly gave up the idea.

Visitors, both at the office and at home, included members of the Fourth Estate and, initially, a fairly large number of astrologers and palmists. The former almost always received very prompt attention and, knowing the value of a good press, he was extremely courteous, frank and considerate towards them. No matter what the question, no matter how sensitive the topic, the correspondent would get an honest and objective reply. After the interview it was my job to get a copy of the "story", vet it for any inaccuracy that might have crept in and, after showing it to the Chief, return it to the correspondent. Then periodically there would be a session at Army House where, over a whisky and soda, correspondents who had been invited would fire questions and obtain his views which were guaranteed to be refreshingly frank, incisive and full of fun and humour. This excellent rapport with the press continued right up to the last day and led to honest and prompt reporting.

In the first few months, swarms of palmists and astrologers descended upon me to seek an appointment. Some of these were granted but I insisted that the impressions and views the person obtained were for private consumption only and not for publication. I did not deviate from this principle but I must confess that, although the predictions were almost always generously optimistic with hints of further laurels across the horizon, none was really truly accurate.

There was always a large number of photographers, including those from the Ministry of Defence, Public Relations Office, seeking an appointment to photograph the Chief in his house or at some function. At a dinner once the photographer, who had been engaged by the host to cover the evening, kept obliging one guest after another who wished to pose for a photograph beside the Chief. As he was also guzzling whisky as fast as he clicked his shutter, it came as no surprise when he became a little light in spirit. When it struck him that I was, perhaps, the only one present who hadn't asked him for a photograph with the Chief, he came up to me, offered to take a snap, and advised me that he had just two snaps left. To oblige him, as he was becoming quite persistent, I went and stood beside the Chief. Other guests, seeing a photograph in the offing, started to crowd in and I quickly withdrew. That photograph taken, I found the irate photographer besides me again, angry that I had missed such a golden opportunity. "You are very shy," he informed me, and only learnt who I was when, well in his cups a little later, he asked the Chief for an appointment in the office, and was referred to me to "fix it". He was most apologetic.

Assisting me in my chores was a small, select staff of outstanding ability. There were two Civilian Staff Officers, Subramaniam and Ukil, equated with service officers of the rank of major; a Private Secretary, Gupta; three Personal Assistants, Seth, Jain and Nair (later relieved by Satpal); an Office Superintendent, Uppal; two Junior Commissioned Officer Clerks and three civilian clerks. To all these staff members must go tremendous credit as they were the silent, but competent workers who laboured many long hours in the quiet gloom of South Block, unsung, unknown, yet each doing a magnificent job, ever willing to take on work and doing it efficiently, cheerfully and promptly. To them I shall always owe a special debt of gratitude.

Delhi's social life, to say the least, is quite demanding. The number of parties a man of some standing, social and professional, is invited to and expected to attend is astounding. They would strain the stamina of a playboy let alone one who has a full, grinding day ahead the following morning. Here also, quite early, we had fixed our respective schedules: my wife and I only went where we were specifically invited, unlike some other arrangements where the staff officer accompanies his boss irrespective of invitation. The result was that I was free to make my own choice and this we proceeded to do as follows. My wife and I would accept not more than one invitation every evening four days a week. Three evenings were kept free to be at home, to spend time by ourselves or to receive callers.

Quite often the Chief and I would find ourselves at the same party; in such cases he would suddenly appear by my side with someone in tow and tell me to see what the gentleman (or lady) wanted and then, turning to the person concerned with a disarming smile, "Please talk to him as he's the one who does all the work; I merely take the credit."

Then I would spend the next half hour or so listening to some tale of woe, often exaggerated, while trying to delay the person until next morning with the futile suggestion that business was better discussed in the office. This sort of thing was acceptable to my wife, so long as the person concerned wasn't an attractive young lady. The latter, unfortunately, occurred not as often as I should have liked; when it did, my wife's eagle eye would see and she would drift gently alongside to be a spectator; sometimes silent, sometimes active, of further conversation. At the first opportunity she would buttonhole the Chief and complain about his directing attractive females my way to which he would say, "Come on, Balli, give him a chance! Why do you go on bullying the poor man—he gets enough of it from me?"

While on the subject of social engagements, I must narrate an account of a conversation that occurred once between the Chief and an Ambassador's wife. She came gushing up to him at a party and invited him to dinner some days hence. He parried it by asking her to contact me as, "he's the one who tells me where to go: I dare not go anywhere without his permission". At this, the lady took my telephone number and promised to contact me the following morning. Then turning to the Chief again she asked, "General, I'll also arrange a dance that evening; do you like dancing?" The Chief, after a small thoughtful pause, remarked, "No, I am afraid I am not a very good dancer." Then, with a twinkle in his eye he added, "but I make up for that as I hold extremely well."

The lady was still laughing when we left the party.

At parties he was always a striking and popular figure, suave, in beautifully cut clothes, very elegant and handsome. A touch of restlessness was there all the time and, in consequence, he could never be still: he made it a point to meet and talk to everyone and wherever he went he would have a smile and joke. He asked me once if I wanted to be let into the secret of how to keep the wife happy while, at the same time, conversing with 'every pretty girl at a party'. On my nodding assent he proceeded to explain the tactic which was as follows: "As you enter, take your wife's hand and, after the introductions are over, ask her where she would like to sit or stand. Lead her there and make certain that you ask, even before the host asks her, what she would like to have, get her that drink yourself and, after she's had a sip, ask whether it is all right. Then disappear for ten minutes after which you come back to her, fuss again for two minutes and disappear again. Keep repeating this; she'll be happy and so, hopefully, will you."

I don't recall him ever being at a loss for words except once. This was in Dehradun at a Gorkha Brigade Dinner in the 39 Gorkha Training Centre. As usual, he was making the rounds and he came upon a group of ladies in a corner.

He introduced himself, quite needlessly really, as everyone knew who he was. When the ladies started to reciprocate, he stopped one as she gave her name by telling him that he knew her husband.

"How long have you been married?" he asked.

"Two years," she replied and then continued, "but we were living together for about four years before that."

That startled him a bit, but he recovered with a "good for you," and moved on. Another lady was asked:

"How many children do you have?"

"I had a miscarriage some months ago," she replied.

And then, evidently seeing the commiserating look on his face, she added encouragingly, "but I am pregnant again,"

"Call him Sam Bahadur if it's a boy," he remarked as he quickly walked away amid many "Ohs" and "Oohs" from the other ladies. It was a boy and the girl took his advice, calling him Sam.

At another get-together, three ladies, sitting together, introduced themselves as Mrs. Mahajan. After the third one had also given the same surname, he asked "Where is the lucky man?"

On a previous occasion, while he was Eastern Army Commander, he visited Shillong to attend an Investiture Parade at which, the current Chief, General Kumaramanglam, took the salute and gave away the awards. After the Parade, as the Chief followed by his Army Commander went in to tea, they passed a group of ladies who were watching the high and mighty go past with very rapt looks. He paused, fell back behind the Chief and went up to the group, startling them by remarking, "Why are you looking like that at the Chief? Look at me. I am much better looking!"

Some time during September, 1969, an American friend of ours, serving with the U.S. Aid Mission in Delhi, asked if he and his wife could accompany us to Joshimath to celebrate Dussehra with my Battalion. He had heard about a Gorkha Dussehra and saw this as a golden opportunity. I readily agreed and asked him to complete whatever formalities there were. A few days before we were to depart, Jack Kennedy (that was his name) suggested we travel in his car as it was bigger than mine. This made perfect sense to me but, since we were to travel in his car, I thought I should inform the Chief who, until then, was unaware of this development. I explained the whole case, obtained his approval, and was walking out when he called me back and said, "You are like Caesar's wife; you are above suspicion and need not refer such cases to me in future." He had complete trust in his staff.

As mentioned earlier, the fact that the appointment of Military Assistant was such a coveted one, was not lost on others. Consequently, there were numerous requests and approaches made both to the Chief and Mrs. Manekshaw to change the present incumbent. A batch-mate of mine from the IMA, RP Sood, who had joined the Ordnance Corps, was a regular writer to the Chief unabashedly offering himself, quite oblivious of the fact that I read the letter first! On another occasion, a friend of the Manekshaws invited Silloo to visit Dehra Dun with her. On her return when I asked Mrs Manekshaw about the trip, she gave a smile and replied that it was nice but the conversation during the entire trip was directed at suggesting that the hostess' son replace me!

After assuming the appointment of COAS, he directed that we resurrect an old practice of appointing silversmiths and stationers to the Chief. Cooke and Kelvey and New Delhi Stationary Mart were appointed silversmiths and stationers respectively. A copy of the appointment letter to the latter is in Appendix IV.

4

The Business of Command

Some time after he took over as Chief of Army Staff, I asked Sam for his views on what qualities he felt a Chief should possess and how he should discharge his duties. Without hesitation, almost as if he had anticipated the question, he replied that the Chief must be popular, be genuinely interested in the welfare of officers and men, and must not seek a job after retirement. As regards discharge of duties, he made two points. First of all, the Chief must have his finger on the pulse of his service to know exactly what was going on. Second, he must set the pace. Put differently, he needs to have vision and direct his energies to realize that vision.

By 6th June, 1969, when he assumed the appointment of Chief of Army Staff, Sam Manekshaw had displayed an abundance of all these qualities. With his perceptive mind and a constant inquisitiveness he knew everything there was to know about the Army, both its drawbacks and strong points. "You know how I get all my information?" he used to ask, "it's my long nose." I have already remarked on his popularity, which came about through his genuine and sympathetic interest in the welfare of his subordinates, and the ready smile and kind word he had for everyone. He was not a job seeker as he made amply clear from the outset. In any case, both he and Mrs. Manekshaw, in their own right, were extremely wealthy and so were not dependent upon a job for sustenance. As far as popularity went, not only did he relate well to all ranks, he also had an excellent rapport with the Prime Minister and most of the politicians and senior bureaucrats, which ensured benefits to the service.

Consequently, knowing the existing shortcomings, the new Chief's immediate preoccupations on assuming the mantle can be classified under two headings. First, the requirement to better the lot of all ranks by constructing new and more comfortable accommodation, improving existing amenities and introducing new ones and, to quote his words, "to instill in the officer cadre that quality so lacking now—dignity". Second, reorganization, re-equipping and regrouping of the Army to make it more responsive to the threats the country faced.

These were the specific tasks he set himself. In addition was the normal routine into which he established himself with an uncanny ability bearing comparison to a duck's taking to water. This was due, of course, to his having previously occupied the two key appointments of Director of Military Operations and of Military Training and also because he had officiated from Delhi as Chief during absences on tours abroad by his predecessor.

In 1969, Army Headquarters, like the other two services headquarters of the Navy and the Airforce, was trying out summer working hours for the first time. This meant starting work at 7.30 am and working until 1.30 pm six days a week—a schedule which had an advantage for the majority as one had the afternoon and evening off for sports or a siesta as one felt inclined: I myself like the secretariat staff, however, found that this meant working from

7 am up to 7 pm as the Ministry, working the usual 9 to 5 routine, would fix some meeting or the other practically every afternoon. I was new that year and so fell into the trap each time: the next year, when summer hours were repeated it was my turn to insist on the meetings being held in the morning leaving me free to play golf in the heat of the afternoon sun!

Alas, we enjoyed summer hours only during 1969 and 1970. The following year, 1971, with the Pakistani crackdown in the erstwhile East Pakistan and in 1972, owing to the tremendous pressure of work occasioned by the war's aftermath, we stuck to the 9 am to 5 pm schedule. Strangely, the civilian staff at the three Service Headquarters always preferred the winter schedule as, according to them, the summer schedule involved their having to leave the house at about 5 am because of distances; it meant that the wife had to get up much earlier to cook breakfast and a packed lunch; and, finally, it meant standing in the hot and afternoon sun at 2 pm, waiting for a bus to take them home. Valid reasons all, but none that could not be circumvented or could outweigh the advantages of an early closure of office.

When these problems were projected to the new Chief, he ordered with characteristic promptness that they be sorted out. The Delhi Transport Union was requested to help and this they managed with great despatch by organising more bus services to reduce movement time. [Naturally, no relief could be provided to the better half.]

Every Tuesday and Friday morning would commence with what is called the Principal Staff Officers (PSOs) Conference. This meant that the PSOs, which included the Vice Chief of Army Staff, Deputy Chief of Army Staff, Adjutant General, Quartermaster General, Master General of Ordnance, Director General of Medical Services, Engineer in Chief and the Military Secretary, would assemble in the Chief's office at 7.30 am in summer and 9.00 am in winter. Each would sit in his appointed place with the Chief as the head and I, as Secretary, sitting at the foot of the table. Before the conference I would write out on the Chief's writing pad the points I felt he ought to know about or the progress of which was tardy and so required a push. After the conference I would dictate the draft minutes and show these to the Chief. The first few drafts saw an enormous amount of red ink corrections. I learnt quickly, however, and in time the red ink decreased to a trickle. He made it clear from the first meeting that the aim was early action on his decisions, and not the civilian interpretation that meetings were a gathering of people who singly could do nothing and together decided that nothing could be done.

It was during one of the earlier conferences that the Chief raised the point about officers, particularly senior offices, saying "Sir" to civilians. "Be polite and correct," he said, "but never subservient." Only one civilian must be addressed as 'Sir' and that is the Supreme Commander, the President; the remainder were all Mr. Minister or Mr. Secretary and so on. This business of 'correctness' was almost an obsession with him and to us, who had the privilege of close association, it appeared to be a magnificent obsession. On one occasion, as his car came out of his residence, 4 King George Avenue, the Scientific Adviser to the Defence Minister happened to be driving down the road. The Chief's driver, used to the flag and stars giving him right of way, carried on, making the Scientific Adviser's driver swerve and stop to allow the Chief's car passage. He entered the office in a towering rage and, calling in a stenographer, dictated a charming little note of apology to the Scientific Adviser; then I was called in and given a rocket for having given him such a poor driver—quite without reason, I thought, as the driver had come with him from Calcutta. Needless to say the Scientific Adviser was more than mollified, and well he might be because when Sam Manekshaw set out to charm someone, the operation went like a hot knife through butter.

On another occasion he entered the Ministry's Conference Room almost on the heels of the Defence Secretary, Harish Sarin. Officers scheduled to participate in the conference were in the process of settling down, with the usual pre-conference activities of finding their places, taking out their papers, putting away briefcases, last minute reference to notes and so on. It was a warm day and the Secretary, entering through one door, looked at one of the Colonels who was sitting down consulting his notes and said, "You there, open that window!" Before the officer could get up came a sharp 'sit down' from the Chief who had entered through another door at almost the same time. Then, in the silence following his bellow, he turned to the Secretary and said "Mr. Secretary, don't you ever again address one of my officers in that tone of voice. You may say, 'Sam, would you please open that window?' and I will open the window for you. That officer is a Colonel and not you there." Harish Sarin, a very powerful civil servant, mumbled some explanation on the lines that he had meant no offence to which the reply was, "I don't care what you meant, I heard what you said and did not like it." I am sure it must have been a bitter lesson to the Secretary, but it was a necessary one.

Whenever he visited formations and units, and whenever he addressed officers he would tell them quite bluntly, without mincing his words, about all that was wrong with the officer cadre: undesirable qualities that were creeping in, like telling lies, career consciousness resulting in a tendency to put self before the Service, undue sensitiveness resulting in an inability to take a rebuke or advice, subservience, and so on. "If it is in your kismet to go high, no one can stop it," he would say, implying that everyone should do his job and not worry about the impression he created. While on the subject of subservience he would narrate a story about an annual confidential report he wrote once on an officer who did more fawning ("bum sucking" to quote him) than work. "Why this officer has not developed a stammer is incomprehensible to me. I know I shall never suffer from piles."

He would tell them about the tremendous amount of time it took him to go through the numerous petitions which officers were making: representing against a posting, sometimes against remarks inserted by a senior officer in their annual confidential reports, sometimes about what an officer thought was injustice, and so on. This was, in fact, so and whenever an officer's representation came up to him for his decision or for a recommendation, if it was addressed to the Central Government he used to go through the case very painstakingly and give the matter much thought. Most of the Chief's time was taken up in wading through this mass of paper. He would exhort officers not to make such representations as, more often than not, they were a consequence of misinterpretation of an order or a misunderstanding which, apart from creating more work for everyone along the line, solved nothing.

"If someone writes in your annual confidential report that you are a bloody fool," he used to say, "that is his opinion and he is entitled to it, as you are entitled to yours about him, which is probably much worse, but unfortunately you can't say it." Representations addressed to the Central Government used to hurt him very much, quite rightly convinced as he was that there can be no fairer justice than Military Law. He used to question why an officer should need to project a case to the Central Government knowing the efficacy of justice in the Army. He would talk about dedication and what he termed "sharam" (shame) of which he used to say there was a great shortage now. In the old days, he would recall, an officer was called "sahib bahadur": that was because he was a gentleman who was brave in battle and otherwise. We were losing these officer-like qualities and the quality of "sharam"; in consequence we were becoming lesser mortals.

Posting of officers was another irritant that required immediate cure. There were three main objections. First: not enough warning between an officer getting his posting order and actually moving. Second: a feeling that not everything was above board in the matter of choice postings. Third: there was considerable ignorance among the officer class about the guiding rules and principles upon which postings were generally based. All these matters were settled very quickly. In one of the first conferences he chaired in Army Headquarters as Chief, he directed the Military Secretary to give between one and three months' notice to officers prior to a move. At the same time, knowing the underlying reason which had earlier forced the Military Secretary to reduce the warning period (the pulling of strings to get changes made), he also directed that once a posting order was issued, it would not be changed without reference to him.

He settled the matter of patronage in choice postings by issuing directions that henceforth all such postings would be referred to the recently installed computer and a selection would be made from the panel of names the computer produced. To ventilate the Byzantine atmosphere that existed in the Military Secretary's Branch at Army Headquarters, he ordered that all rules governing promotion and posting be widely publicized, both to stop malpractice and to remove complaints based on ignorance. The flow of requests and recommendations never abated, however, but it became possible to overlook them.

The wife of a brigadier, aware that her husband's brother was a secretary level officer in Delhi and so close to the Chief, wrote a personal letter to the latter complaining that her husband, an armored corps officer, had been posted to command an infantry brigade. To add insult to injury, she added, the location was Dhana, an out of the way station in Madhya Pradesh. She got quite a rude reply on the lines that others also served in the Army and commanded infantry brigades with distinction. Despite his directions that no "pull" would be permitted, especially if it came from the Ministry, there was the odd violation based on requests from close friends. Fortuitously, these abberations were few.

Though we have been, and still are, a volunteer Army, it was becoming increasingly apparent in 1969 that we were not attracting the best material for officers or other ranks. This could be for a variety of reasons, the principal one being lack of sufficient attraction in the terms the Service had to offer. A man, now better educated and also a beneficiary of the green revolution, would prefer to stay at home and till his land rather than join the service. Also, other services, including the corporate world, offered far better terms and conditions. I suspect that another reason was the knowledge that the service received respect only during war; during peace the soldier was derided and barely tolerated. In short, an Indian version of Kipling's famous couplet, "It's Tommy this and Tommy that, but it's thank you Mr. Atkins when the band begins to play", was making the rounds of our villages and towns and the youth were taking note of it. Furthermore, the world was becoming increasingly materialistic. Who wanted to join a service where the pay was a pittance and you were subject not only to the laws of the land but also the Army Act?

Hardest hit was the officer cadre: existing deficiencies were being further accentuated by the fact that a large number of officers were seeking premature retirement to enable rehabilitation outside while the going was good. The Government had sought to solve the impasse by lowering entrance standards so that plenty of entrants could qualify: and premature retirement was very rarely granted. More or less the same solutions were applied in the case of other ranks. To the Chief the answer lay not in lowering standards as this meant accepting inferior material, but in improving terms and conditions so that better material, hitherto reluctant to enrol, would be attracted. This view was projected to the Government very quickly. The new Chief's conviction that he was not willing to accept dissatisfied or unwilling workers in the Army was mooted. These must be permitted to go when they so asked as it was better to work shorthanded rather than carry 'passengers'.

Instructions were issued to selected service officers to visit schools, colleges and universities, to address the students telling them what the Army has to offer. They were directed to tell the youth the blunt truth of what they would be in for; no padding was to be given as we did not wish to find a lot of disillusioned youngsters who joined thinking they were in for an easy life. On the other hand, the talks were designed to remove misconceptions that kept the young away. These talks, we were to discover, had a decidedly favourable impact in subsequent years.

In the matter of premature retirement, there was considerable opposition from the Government whose views were that this would mean that we were encouraging further deficiencies in an area where considerable shortage already existed. The second objection was that the Government spent huge sums of money on the training of officers and, if someone could just get up and go whenever he wanted to, it meant wasted expenses. These were, of course, valid reasons, but the Chief insisted on having his own way for the overriding reason that he refused to retain people who were unwilling to serve. Also, as he pointed out, once the officer class knew that premature retirement was there for the asking, requests paradoxically would reduce. This, in fact, is what actually happened: if I remember correctly, the number of officers seeking premature retirement was never more than about 20–30 per year.

Officers in senior rank had very little job security. Retirement for them was based on a tenure system which was ambiguous and operated as it suited the system; the individual never knew when the axe would descend. Until 1969 many general officers, some of them of outstanding ability, were retired at the comparatively young age of 47 or 48. This was rectified after suggesting to the Government and obtaining its approval for the introduction of a system of retirement by age. Now everyone knew that he could serve up to such and such age; extensions beyond that were possible but depended on the officer's performance. This not only provided more security to the officer class but it also encouraged better performance as chances of extension depended upon that.

We Indians have an amazing propensity for discovering relationships to further our causes. Therefore, whenever promotion board proceedings went to the Defence Ministry for approval by the Defence Minister, a certain amount of horse trading would ensue—a consequence of an affected officer finding a relative (or a close friend of a relative) in the ministry to take up the cudgels on his behalf. The method was subtle; the proceedings would be sent back with some observations on a couple of cases which had been cleared by the promotion board. Then a telephone call—clear so and so and we will clear the ones under observation. Previously, the easy way out was taken and acquiescence would be conveyed making everyone happy. This Chief forbade it and if observations were raised, they were suitably answered; if they persisted, he would intervene personally and obtain the minister's approval by arguing that the board's proceedings were completely above board.

In one case, that of Brigadier Inder Vohra, although the Promotion Board had recommended his case, the Chief, in his recommendation, felt that this was not a fit case for promotion. Naturally there was a query as the officer's record was good. The Chief explained to the Defence Secretary that Brigadier Vohra had given evidence against him in the 1962 enquiry. There was nothing adverse on record, but his character mitigated against promotion. When the Defence Secretary expressed his inability to debar the officer under the given circumstances, the Chief gave his assent and the officer was cleared and later promoted—which would not have been possible if the Chief had put down his objection in writing.

The 1962 and 1965 operations had shown the Junior Commissioned Officer rank in a very poor light. There was a formidable school of thought that this class must go as it had outlived the usefulness of being a link between the British Officer in the Indian Army and the soldier in the ranks. The Chief refused to entertain this suggestion for the reasons that, firstly we did not have, nor were we likely to have in the foreseeable future, sufficient numbers of officers to fill all the JCOs vacancies. Secondly, even if we had sufficient numbers of officers, the exchequer could not afford the extra expenditure that would be required. Next, as he put it, until 1947 this was a class that could almost run the Army by itself very well. If this superb class had fallen down in standard now, surely the fault must be that of the present-day officer who had brought up and trained the JCO. Lastly, removal of this class would result in loss of incentive for the enlisted man who would then have only a limited future with very much reduced promotion prospects. The answer lay in giving the JCO more responsibility and making him accountable.

Prior to the end of the financial year 1968–1969, the Army was allotted, on average, Rs. 50 crore for construction works. Each year approximately seven to eight crores was surrendered as unexpended balance, giving rise amongst the younger officers of the day to the joke that the more money a senior commander surrendered, the better became his chances for promotion. Anyway, the new Chief had vastly different ideas and these were quickly made abundantly clear when he directed that henceforth not only would the Army not surrender any allotted amount but would continually ask for more money. He was very conscious of the fact that defence spending is important not only for what it provides, but more for what it prevents. During the course of the next few years, while he remained Chief, he never let the Quartermaster General and Engineer-in-Chief forget this and, in the process, the Army expenditure on construction jumped to Rs. 95 crores and new cantonments mushroomed in places hitherto considered field areas. The first few months were undoubtedly difficult ones for the Quartermaster General and Engineer-in-chief, who not only had to work flat out, but also had to give detailed and plausible explanations every Tuesday and Friday about delays caused by red tape and technical problems. There would be a barrage of questions:

"When will work there commence?" "When will work here conclude?" "Has land been taken over?"

"Have contracts been signed?"

"I visited so and so: why are the buildings there leaking? Why is paint peeling off? Why have electric connections still not been provided?"

Once, while driving past the newly constructed Sardar Patel Marg Service Officers' Quarters, he noticed that the walls of some quarters were showing signs of water seepage. As soon as we returned to the office I reminded him of this, and he rang up the Quartermaster General to enquire whether he had seen this seepage. Naturally, he hadn't. "Take the Engineer-in-Chief," he was ordered, "go and see it and report to me within an hour." Some may question the propriety of sending two general officers on a job such as this, but the Chief was quite clear in his mind that, unless such lapses were checked and someone came down with a heavy hand, officers and men would continue to suffer in silence.

Realising the growing scarcity of land for construction purpose the Chief had issued instructions as soon as he had taken over that henceforth all construction would be of the multi-storey variety rather than the bungalow type of house the Army had been used to in the past. Apart from better utilising the limited land that was available, multi-storeyed flats provided added advantages of security and also less expenditure on maintenance by servants, gardeners and the like. Despite all these obvious advantages, whenever sanction for new construction was sought from the Government, a stiff fight would invariably ensue with the Army pressing for building "up" and the Government insisting that we go in for single or, at most, two-storey houses as building high would result in increased expenditure. Finally, it would take the Chief's personal intervention to win the case by arguing that even if land were available at present, the same happy situation was not likely to remain for long, and also the overriding reason that a marginally increased expenditure now was justifiable because, in the long run, the multistoried flats would be cheaper.

The new cantonments that were coming up all over the country received a great deal of attention from him. On his insistence, each new Cantonment was planned as a self-contained colony with its own shopping centres, playgrounds and parks, cinemas, hospitals and schools. He would insist on broad roads with proper lighting. Another hard fought duel that took place between Army Headquarters and the Government was in the matter of electric wiring. The Chief insisted that all wiring must be underground in keeping with modern trends: the Government on the other hand was equally insistent that wiring must remain overhead, owing to the very high cost of underground wiring. This duel finally ended in a draw as the Government accorded permission for some Cantonments to have underground wiring and others to have overground.

Having set this ball rolling, the Chief then began to tackle the next one of improving the lot of all ranks and ex-servicemen. A case was taken up and Government sanction obtained for including the case of the Services in the Pay Commission. This was a very big step forward as it meant that, for the first time since Independence in 1947, the three Services would be putting their own cases directly to a Pay Commission rather than having to rely, as they had done in the past, on someone else fighting their battles for them. Brig. SK Sinha, one of our most experienced, learned and brilliant officers, was chosen to head the newly created cell in Army Headquarters to prepare and put forward the Army's case. This the cell did in a remarkably efficient fashion, eventually preparing a case that was thorough, logical and feasible. In retrospect one realizes that, in fact, we could have gone further by insisting on the inclusion of one representative from the Defence Services on the panel. Had this been done, and we had the clout to get it accepted at that time, a fine precedent would have been set for the future. Perhaps the excellent rapport that existed then and maybe an assurance that the interests of the Defence Services would be safeguarded, may have played a part in the omission.

Concurrently, various other cases were taken up to introduce little perks and benefits, all designed to make the soldier's life a little happier, more comfortable and inviting. Small things like deficiencies in geysers, fans, or water coolers were ordered to be made good. "By what date will all my troops have fans?" "By what date will all my officers have geysers?" These and similar questions were fired at the PSO concerned and woe betide him if the specified date passed without the work completed. All these were triggered off because of the enormous deficiencies that existed because of the craze to conserve funds and dutifully surrender them at the end of the financial year. Electric connections used to be provided in a most tardy manner, and fans were non-existent where they were no longer a luxury but a necessity. Hospitals and messes that were authorised to have water coolers were without these because someone (who probably had two misappropriated refrigerators in his house) had expressed the view, "Coolers for men? They aren't used to such luxuries, and we will make them soft by providing such gadgets."

The Chief, on the other hand, had his own views and insisted that every man must get his rightful share. If an officer was entitled to hot water, then every officer's quarter must have a geyser, and if a quarter didn't, the Chief wished to know the reason. Pressure was maintained not only on the PSOs at Army headquarters but also on all Army Commanders, and if progress on installation of an item was slow in a particular command, that Army Commander got a piece of his mind, "I am giving you the money, can't you even supervise installation and see that work is completed quickly so that we can go on to something else?" About this time someone suggested that as the state of Tamil Nadu was warm throughout the year, officers posted there could do without geysers. This would also "save us some money". A pretty big explosion occurred when this suggestion was aired, and I doubt if that officer will suggest saving funds ever again.

On another occasion at a PSO's conference, a newly arrived general officer suggested, while on the subject of austerity, that officers of the rank of brigadier give up the privilege of travelling by air-conditioned class and travel only 1st class. He shut up when the Chief stated that he was agreeable to issue this order provided general officers also agreed to give up the privilege voluntarily.

In short, the Chief was a man in a hurry, never satisfied, always looking further ahead for something new to do as soon as the work in hand was completed. He was also kindness personified evidenced by his oft repeated remark: "I can never say no; it is a good thing that I am not a woman."

Ex-servicemen, too, received their share of attention. He attended every Ex-servicemen's Rally he was invited to and would invariably preface his address with, "I am doing what I can for Ex-servicemen, not for somebody else's sake but for my own. I know that, three years hence, I shall be seated where you are now." Medical treatment facilities for ex-servicemen were liberalised: a minimum pension scale was announced: cells were created in

States to provide better job opportunities, and vocational training was started to give training to soldiers about to retire in a vocation of their choice that they could profitably follow in retired life. "I want my men to learn something other than killing," he used to say to emphasize the fact that the skills a soldier, particularly an infantry soldier, learnt were useless after his retirement. He must learn something that would earn him a wage to augment his meagre pension.

Just after he took over as Chief, the Army Horse Show, an annual fixture held on the grounds in front of the Red Fort in Delhi, was organized. He entered on time and, as is his wont, surveyed the spectators with one quick piercing look, to discover that a large number of retired General Officers were seated in the third and fourth rows. He corrected this immediately by asking them all to come to the front with a charming, "Good God, Sir, who has given you a seat there; you won't be able to see a thing. Please come up here." Next morning the Principal Staff Officers received quite a tongue lashing at this indignity to retired officers. "Gentleman," he told them, "if you respect them today, others will respect you when you retire. Secondly, while they were in service, you and I used to vie with each other to bum suck them. Why this sudden change now?" Despite his efforts, however, there was very little improvement, evidenced by other incidents, two of which can be cited here. Early in 1974, a letter was issued by an Area Commander to the effect that retired officers' baggage was being stored in Government accommodation. This was irregular and the officer concerned would be asked to remove it within a specified period. If it is not removed, "it will be thrown out". Next, the Defence Services Officer's Institute, Dhaula Kuan, has some residential quarters utilized, mainly by retired officers. Despite persistent pressure, the Chief had not approved an increase in the occupation charges. A few days after he retired, the charges were hiked.

The Army, too, like other services has never claimed that there are no black sheep: there are a few and some do not look after ex-servicemen when they are in a position to do so. This was proved at an Ex-servicemen's rally we attended in Amritsar, where a retired general who had drifted into politics and was, as that time, with the opposition, got up, and without being asked, launched into a long tirade against the Government. This was quite unnecessary as the Rally was not a political meeting. What upset me was that the longer he talked the more he delayed the next appointment. He shut up, however, when a grizzled old man in the audience arose and sarcastically agreed that, whereas the Government was not doing anything, could the speaker tell the audience what he had done for ex-servicemen while he was Minister with the Government then in power.

Ex-servicemen's rallies also provided humour, as happened at Kohlapur when Lieutenant General SPP Thorat, DSO, a retired officer of unusual eminence enjoying tremendous prestige in his home state, Maharashtra, in welcoming the Chief at a civic reception, praised his warlike qualities and thus invited this retort when the Chief rose to reply to the address of welcome, "General Thorat has been extremely kind to me, but then he has always been very kind. Today, however, he has stated an inaccuracy. I am not really a warlike person; the only warlike person in our family is this lady (pointing at Mrs. Manekshaw)—she fights with me day and night," he concluded amidst uproarious laughter.

Many foreign delegations keep visiting the country. Whenever they do, the Embassy or High Commission concerned gets in touch with the Defence Ministry to seek its agreement to a call on the Minister and the three Service Chiefs. With this approval in its pocket, the next step used to be to contact me and my opposite numbers in the other two Services, the Naval Assistant or the Naval Secretary (in my four years in South Block, I could never quite understand why the Navy needed two officers where one sufficed in the Army) to the Chief of Naval Staff and the Staff Officer to the Chief of Air Staff to fix up appointments. This was invariably agreed upon and so fixed up.

The former procedure had been that the Chief brief the officers from a prepared text, answer one or at the most two questions, and the gathering would then disperse. As usual, this Chief had to decide to conduct his briefing differently. Now the audience was asked to shoot questions and he answered each question. Quite naturally, this delighted the audience and came as a pleasant surprise to them as a delegation normally expects to hear a boring one-sided narration on such visits. All sorts of questions, including some uncomfortable ones, would be asked and they would all be fielded beautifully. Once while conducting a similar session with an American War College team, one of the students, pointing to the border of Jammu and Kashmir, remarked amidst laughter, "In my country we are used to seeing this border shown differently" to which he got the reply, "You'll get used to this one in time, never fear."

Visits by foreign Chiefs were always an interesting interlude. Quite early on we had fixed a drill, and this was generally followed for nearly all such visits. The personage would be received at Palam Airport by the Chief and me, plus the Principal Staff Officers; everyone resplendent with medals, sword, aiguilettes and the works. If the visitor was accompanied by his wife, Mrs. Manekshaw would be there too. The airport formalities would include the inspection of a guard of honour, introductions to the PSOs and some refreshments. As soon as this was over, the visitor and his party would be driven to the Ashoka Hotel where guests of the Indian Government used to be accommodated.

There would be a call on the Chief at the office where gifts were presented with an "informal" exchange of views. When General D'jam, the Iranian Joint Services Chief, visited us the discussions lasted almost three hours, and I think it was from that occasion that a very close and warm friendship developed and endured for many years. The gifts from the Chief used to be delivered beforehand as in accordance with his instructions, we used to place these in the guests' rooms so that they received them immediately upon arrival. The social side would consist of a reception in the Defence Services Officers Institute, Dhaula Kuan, on one evening and a quiet dinner at Army House on the last evening. For the latter, only the chief guest and his wife would be invited. The remainder of the party would be invited to my home where, with a small cross-section of Indian and foreign friends, my wife and I would regale them with an Indian meal consisting of "tandoori food, nan and roomali roti".

During his visit, the late General Bubanj, the Yugoslav Army Chief, visited Nathu La, in Sikkim amongst other places. When he made his final call on the Chief, General Bubanj remarked that our defences at Nathu La compared unfavourably with what he had seen of Chinese defences across the border. This was true of course, and it speaks very highly of this man who could discern our weakness during such a brief visit, and then be frank enough to point it out to his host. Hardly had General Bubanj left before orders were out to rectify matters. A few years later I was posted to Sikkim to see these improved defences and, while living in them, prepare my command to fight from them. I can certify that they do give a tremendous feeling of security convinced as you become that nothing the enemy can do could possibly dislodge us from there.

The Chief had strong views on how the Army should develop to meet the expected challenges of the coming years, how it should be deployed to meet immediate and foreseeable threats, and how it should be armed and equipped. He did not hesitate to put these views across to the political bosses. As far as the distant threat was concerned, he was quite clear that it was from China and it would come through North Burma into Assam preceded by internal security problems. Based on this premise, a case was taken up with Government to point out this threat and the Army's reasons for it; the paper then went on to suggest how we should prepare ourselves to meet the threat. It concluded by tabulating the infrastructure that would be required and the additional troops and formations that were necessary for the task. This paper, I suppose, is still making the rounds and must be stiff with notes such as, "please examine".

While speaking to the National Defence College on the subject of "The Army in the Eighties" he made two significant points. The first pertained to employing the rapidly growing Border Security Force to man the border after grouping it under the Army and possibly calling it the Border Command. With this he felt, rightly, that the Army, deployed as it is all along our borders, could be withdrawn to concentrate on intensive training and so become better prepared for its prime function of striking at any enemy crossing our borders. A start to this was made by the Chief in one sector, and it paid handsome dividends during the 1971 War with Pakistan.

The second point he made was in answer to a question about integration of the three services: the Army, Navy and Air Force, specifically the command aspect. I suspect the questioner was aware of the Chief's views on the subject of having a Chief of Defence Staff or permanent Chairman of the Joint Chiefs of Staff. This was, in brief, that we should not introduce this innovation just then because the Army was a much older and larger service and at all senior levels the corresponding officers in the Navy and Air Force in those days were far junior in commissioned service. This would have meant that whenever an overall commander was appointed, he would have to be from the Army. As the other two services were still developing the soldier commander might inadvertently put a brake on this activity which would be detrimental to the country. So he reasoned that the present was not an opportune time to introduce this system and, in answering the question, suggested that its coming was inevitable, nevertheless, as inter-services integration, economy and the conduct of modern warfare demanded it.

Students at the National Defence College prepare a paper during the ten months or so that they spend at the College on the subject of our country's strategy in the year ahead, and talks such as the one the Chief delivered are designed to give the students food for thought. We were therefore, not amused on learning a few days later that, after the Chief had left the College, the students were instructed by the Commandant to disregard these two aspects in the preparation of the paper.

The Chief was aware that modern warfare demanded missiles, helicopters, more sophisticated equipment and, above all, a more highly educated officer and other ranks. Introduction of modern equipment was undertaken at his insistence by increased production at home and by importing to hasten the changeover and to make up for shortfalls in indigenous production. Financing this bill, however, was always the inhibiting factor, and although the Army achieved the maximum possible, it really wasn't as much as required or desired by the impatient chief.

To realise his dream of a more highly educated Army, he ordered projecting the case to the government for affiliating the Defence Services' educational institutions with the Jawaharlal Nehru University, to equate examinations the serviceman passes with university equivalents. The proposal was to equate graduation at the National Defence Academy with a Bachelor's degree; graduation at the Defence Services Staff College with a Master's degree; and successful completion of the National Defence College with a Ph.D. Likewise, lower examinations could also be equated with corresponding school certificates. This equation would also have an incidental side benefit which was that the retired serviceman could boast of a civil degree, the chief requirement for job seekers in our country. The proposal had not been agreed when he gave up office, but it received a favourable reception and soon received recognition. The Chief also envisioned giving selected officers study leave so that they could, during this period, seek admission to colleges and universities to obtain higher education, to benefit both the service and the individual.

Realising the importance of helicopters in the present-day battlefield, he also had plans prepared for training a larger number of officers on piloting helicopters so that when, financial position permitting, we got more helicopters, trained pilots would be readily available. Unfortunately, these dreams remained dreams as 1971 brought in its wake a different set of problems, with attendant expenditure of a vast magnitude that channelled energies and the meagre resources of the country in another direction.

The Chief used to be asked numerous questions about his views on the advisability; or otherwise, of the country going nuclear. His reply usually followed the pattern of affirming that as a soldier he would always welcome the addition of a new toy in his armoury, as he saw no moral goodness in using inferior weapons if better ones were available. The other side of the coin, however, contained many disadvantages. First and foremost it would mean channelling the energies of a vast number of scientists towards research in this field. This, in turn, meant divesting other fields where scientists were now engaged. Secondly, it meant diverting enormous sums of money to achieve nuclear capability: we could not afford to do this. Thirdly, a nuclear weapon was no use by itself; a carrier was necessary to take and drop it on the designated target. Evolution of a carrier necessitated more research and more money. Lastly, when we had all this "we wouldn't know what to do with it".

Later, after India exploded her first nuclear device on 18th May 1974, he gave an interview to a press correspondent. He was asked to comment on the latest development. In his reply he stated that, whereas one explosion does not give us atomic capability, the most impressive facts of our achievement were that it was done at such low cost and with such admirable secrecy. He further admitted that this would add to our strength as "we are apt to be kicked around" if we are weak.

His views on the position we ought to adopt on our borders was simple. He advocated the forward policy as it gave us tremendous tactical advantage, and also because we were strong enough to sustain it. As an example, he decided to locate a brigade at Tangkar La in North Sikkim. With this force it was possible to pose a threat to the Chinese lines of communication in the Chumbi Valley and thus remove the existing threat to South Sikkim and the Siliguri corridor for ever. Here again we reverted, on his departure, to the old pattern of playing safe for some time. Mercifully, better sense eventually prevailed.

Over the years the standard of cooks in officers' messes had deteriorated sharply. This could be attributed to a variety of reasons, the principal one possibly being the rising cost of living and inability of an underpaid officer to afford good, rich and varied fare. Consequently, when one was invited to a party in an officers' mess one could forecast the cuisine with a reasonable degree of accuracy. It would usually consist of roast chicken, vegetables in some form, and caramel custard. "And not well cooked either," the Chief used to remark. So orders went out to the Quartermaster General to organise special training for mess cooks under highly qualified instructors ("Get them from the Oberoi Intercontinental if need be," he was told) to teach cooks the finer points of the culinary art. The requirement was for variety which should be well cooked. Rich food was not required and, therefore, need not be taught. So the training started and there was a noticeable improvement within a year; at least it became difficult to forecast what one was likely to get.

Visitors to see the Chief, and these as I have mentioned elsewhere, were legion had to be given hospitality in the form of refreshments. Whereas the ones that saw me, unburdened themselves and went on their way after a plain cup of tea, for the ones that met the Chief by appointment, this was not enough. For them all possible varieties of drinks and snacks had to be prepared and served by immaculately dressed waiters. The more important visitors were offered good dry sherry. I almost had a bottle flung at me once when, through an oversight, we offered Bristol Cream (a sweet sherry) rather than the required dry sherry. After March 1971 when Pakistan started its own little war in East Pakistan, and working hours for us lengthened into late evenings, I was ordered to stock up with whisky and brandy, too, in my mini-cellar that I maintained in the office.

This extension of hospitality was not to visitors only. Very soon after he took over, while making the rounds of the Secretariat he noticed some tiffin carriers lying around in which the staff used to bring their lunch from home. He inquired of one of the staff how the food was warmed, and he was informed that this was done on a stove on an individual basis. Promptly came the order for me to buy a food warmer: this was done and the staff could then keep their tiffin carriers in this to be assured of warm food whenever they broke for lunch.

Just after he took over as Chief, he observed at a ceremonial function that his staff officers, which meant the aides and I, did not have all the medals that we should have. I might clarify here that there is inevitably some time lag between the announcement that an individual is entitled to a particular medal and when he actually receives it. In the interim period the practice is to wear just the ribbon. The Chief's latest observation, however, pertained to medals which had been announced some five to seven years earlier. He wished to know the reasons for this inordinate delay, so I passed this point on to the Adjutant General whose task it is to make the announcement and procure the medals.

It was discovered that the requirement of medals for all the three services was being met by production from the Government Mint. Naturally the Mint could not possibly cope with the increasing demand and, therefore, production had severely lagged behind. The Chief was apprised of this and he issued two simple directions. One: present a case to increase production so that all deficiencies are made up within a period of one or two years. Two: If this was not found to be feasible, as it was bound to be, present a case for the raising of a medal manufacturing unit under the Ordnance Corps, so that all requirements could henceforth be met by this unit.

Although the Government did not agree to the raising of a medal manufacturing unit, production was increased, somehow but as even this could not keep pace with the growing demand for new medals introduced after the 1971 war with Pakistan, it was decided to allow the private sector to commence manufacturing medals so that no soldier would have to display a chest full of ribbons without any medals. This was done and, although the availability certainly improved, the quality deteriorated as medals procured from industry started to change colour soon after issue whereas the older ones retained their original bloom. So much for quality control!

The prestige of the Army was always uppermost in his mind. Two incidents admirably illustrate this. An Army commander, a close friend, retired and settled in Delhi, took up some innocuous job with the Delhi administration. This was resented as taking such a job meant demeaning the high office the General had previously occupied. The second incident concerns Bhaiya Rajwade, mention of whom has been made previously. Due to an indifferent report by his Army Commander, Major General Rajwade was not cleared for the next rank. A few months later, the same Army Commander retired and then wrote to the Military Secretary that he had undergraded the General owing to some misunderstanding; he now felt that Rajwade was a fit case for promotion. Since the

Promotion Board proceedings had already been approved by the Government, if correction were to be applied, it meant informing the Government of the change of heart. The Chief was very fond of Rajwade and wanted to help; he baulked at the idea, however, as "people will laugh at us and say that even army commanders have started making mistakes of a serious nature in annual confidential reports".

5

Reorganisation

The first task of a commander on assuming command is to review operational plans in the light of political objectives, operational considerations and available resources. During the 1965 war with Pakistan, Sam Manekshaw was commanding the Eastern Army, idling while Western and Southern Armies fought the enemy because the Government had decided to meet the aggression unleashed against us by confining it to the Western front. On taking over as Chief of Army Staff, the first change he wrought was that in the event of another war with Pakistan, and this would always be a war of Pakistan's seeking, the riposte would not be confined to the West; it would also make its effect felt in the East.

To meet this requirement, and also to counter the great advantage Pakistan has always enjoyed because its peacetime cantonments are located near the international border, whereas ours are located well in the hinterland, plans were rehashed and formations were relocated. Thus, it was ensured that the time taken by us to mobilise for war was considerably reduced and the geographical advantage hitherto enjoyed by Pakistan, minimised. This may sound bellicose but was all, in fact, due to the new Chief's mental make-up and his determination to have everything neat and tidy and meticulously planned so that the mistakes made in 1962 and 1965 were not repeated. "I am a simple infanteer and a Gorkha at that," he used to say, "and I want everything cut and dried. Complicated stuff is for the intellectuals."

This planning, it transpired, was fortunately done just in time as, in 1970, following the hijacking by some Pakistani elements of an Indian Airlines Fokker Friendship aircraft, tension between the two countries mounted and our troops had to be moved to the borders as a reciprocal measure after the Pakistan Army had concentrated there. In consequence, an "eyeball to eyeball" confrontation ensued that could be sparked off at any moment by someone's rashness or stupidity. This confrontation was to continue for some months until the Chief, remembering the old rule which comes into play when a large force is deployed on the brink of conflict, "use it or lose it"; or perhaps tired of waiting for his opposite number in Pakistan to move as he and his government kept saying they would but didn't, informed the Pakistan Commander in Chief that he was commencing withdrawal from the borders unilaterally and would Pakistan like to reciprocate. The reciprocation was not late in coming and, after that, it used to be amusing to see one of our formations withdraw and then learn of the Pakistan Army withdrawing the same number of troops. I wonder who knew more about the other, but I digress from the reorganisation that was started.

Government policy was that the manpower ceiling of 8.5 lakhs was not to be exceeded. Yet, it was necessary to expand if we were to be prepared for a possible war on three fronts, i.e., East and West Pakistan and China. The solution, therefore, was to prune drastically as far as non-essentials were concerned—in essence, to review what we had, and then examine how to reduce the tail to strengthen the teeth.

The next step was to review operational requirements. A threat is assessed in terms of what the enemy can deploy in a particular sector, and to ensure that the requisite quantum of troops is available to counter this. This availability is made possible either by physical presence or by correct positioning. Naturally, no country in the world can ensure the former as the number of soldiers required would be astronomical. Instead, recourse is taken to adopting the latter method and only the most likely threats are countered by the physical presence of troops; lesser threats are countered by a token location of some troops and planning to move in reinforcements when and where needed. This self-created apparent weakness is called the taking of calculated risks in army parlance. This was the second step we had to take.

The review revealed a shortage of formation headquarters without which, in the past, excessive last-minute regrouping was necessary involving moving units to a formation headquarters, or for a formation headquarter to assume command of a new sector and the units located there. This, in turn, resulted in units and headquarters being unfamiliar with each other and with allotted operational tasks. So, as the tail started to shorten, new formation headquarters began to rise.

The elements referred to as "the teeth" in the Army comprise the armoured corps, and the infantry. Almost all terrain along our border with Pakistan except, of course, in the north, is flat and open and, therefore, ideal tank country. Intelligence revealed that Pakistan was busy importing tanks and refurbishing its old stocks. Consequently, it followed that our first priority would be more tanks and, with these, the raising of additional armoured regiments to achieve at least parity with Pakistan, which was busy shouting from its rooftops to a gullible world about India's size dwarfing hers, and completely ignoring the fact that as far as strength in tanks went, it had far more. Indigenous tank production was stepped up, import was resorted to and very soon new armoured regiments started taking their places, in the formations to which they were allotted.

At about this time, the Chief was invited to visit the USSR. During this visit, he witnessed some interesting innovations designed to save track mileage of armoured vehicles, mainly tanks and tracked armoured personnel carriers. This was of tremendous interest to us, because we were finding it increasingly difficult to cope with the excessive wastage of track mileage which the intensive training essential for the new tank crews involved. It was obvious that without training on their tanks and their guns, the crew would not be able to perform efficiently in war. In fact, it was this lack of training that was Pakistan's undoing in the war they had with us in 1965. At that time we discovered numerous tanks left intact by their crew who had decided to vacate in a hurry. The kilometers of these tanks showed a negligible amount of mileage from which it was clear that tank crew had not trained on their tanks.

The innovations noticed were quickly introduced into the Army. These were, one: to have tank simulators giving the crew the "feel" of a tank without actually driving or operating one. The second was to utilize a designated number of tanks for training only, leaving the balance in tip-top condition ready to meet any unforeseen eventuality that arose. This meant that when an armoured or mechanised regiment moved from its peace-time location to a field firing range or a training exercise area, it moved without tracked vehicles as tanks and armoured personnel carriers of the same variety (but in lesser numbers) were pre-positioned in the training area.

He was very conscious of the fact that, quite irrespective of the high rank he had attained, there were still some technicalities where only specialists could provide sound advice. Consequently, while review of the armoured corps was underway, he insisted on associating the General Officer Commanding 1 Armoured Division, Major General Gurbachan Singh, with planning at all stages. This did rub some so-called experts the wrong way but was, in fact, the correct thing to do as 1 Armoured Division, the biggest user of armoured vehicles, would naturally be expected to give correct advice on the problems they faced.

Incidentally, this expansion of the armoured corps also had a side benefit: promotion to the rank of Lieutenant Colonel was slow in this arm because of the excellent material, glamour and the stay in pleasant, peace-time cantonments, attracted. Letters went out to some twenty-one selected officers in the Chief's own hand, pointing out that continuance in the Armoured Corps would result in blocking promotion chances of others plus delaying promotion prospects for the addressees themselves. He suggested that the addressee transfer to the Infantry. Most accepted and were transferred where, without exception, they were promoted and performed admirably.

Light Regiments of the Artillery equipped with heavy mortars were organised on similar lines as regiments equipped with guns possessing a much longer range. Employment of the former did not justify equivalent manpower and, over the vehement protests from the diehards, as tradition in the Army almost violently abhors change, orders were issued for light regiments to shed excess manpower. With this, it was possible to raise additional regiments with lighter calibre and longer range guns, thus vastly increasing the Army's hitting power without undue burden on the exchequer. This aspect of burdening the exchequer always weighed heavily on the Chief and he used to remark quite often, "When it comes to asking or wanting something for the Army, I am like a whore, I am never satisfied. I never forget, however, that I am also an Indian and so have to keep an eye on what we, as a country, can afford and what we cannot."

The Infantry, too, got its share. Additional battalions were raised; some were converted from roles they had been raised for earlier and which were less demanding than the role a normal infantry battalion is required to perform. Deficiencies in weapons and equipment were made up, sometimes by sending notes to the Ministry of Defence such as: "It is becoming increasingly difficult to explain to the men why deficiencies exist in the fields of ..." and so on.

Then he would go prowling around units and formations asking why a certain item was still held. "Get rid of it," he would direct, "if it was authorised in Kitchener's time, there is no reason why we should continue to keep it now." Armoured Personnel Carriers were imported and additional infantry battalions converted to man these. First on the list of such conversions was the 1st Battalion of his Regiment. "Let me see how quickly my gorkhas can wreck these APCs," he used to joke. In the event, his Gorkhas turned out to be excellent drivers and their maintenance state was always the finest.

Firing ranges and the various practices that were fired on them, in Army terminology, "Retention of Efficiency Tests", had hardly changed through the ages. Orders were issued to "modernise" these. This was done in two ways. First, electrification was introduced in the Classification Ranges in a phased manner. With this it was no longer necessary, as in the past, for the person firing to go up to the target every time he fired to see the effect; instead he received the result at the actual firing point, thus saving time. Nor was what we call a "butt party" necessary now. This consisted of a number of men not actually firing, but those who man the target-end of the range, charged with showing the target at designated intervals to enable the person firing to engage it. This was now done electronically, thus saving both manpower and time.

Next, the range courses were amended to make them more realistic and educative. For example, it was pointless having a practice where a rifleman engaged a target from 500 yards or over as no engagement with small arms takes place at that range. Instead, it was essential that he practised shooting at shorter ranges and, more important, engaged targets from one position at different ranges as in war.

Bayonet fighting was made more realistic and easier to learn. The old training tended to teach the man to fight by numbers, each motion separated from the other. This obviously was out-of-tune with reality, as a bayonet fighter cannot afford to start pausing between motions when confronted by an enemy. The requirement was one flowing motion, and this was taught. Training aids were few, and those that were held, antiquated. Orders were issued to introduce the latest training aids in plenty to enable the trainee to imbibe instruction more realistically, economically and quickly. "We have had this physical training equipment since the time of Akbar," he used to say, "how about introducing the latest?" I can't say if the equipment was really that old, but the point was made and the latest equipment started to make its appearance. Gymnasia were constructed to provide better facilities. The Scientific Adviser to the Chief of Army Staff, the very efficient Mr. Duegan, was instructed to produce a set of calisthenics, suitable for Indian climates. He complied, and it proved a boon to office types who could tone up all their muscles with these exercises in a few minutes every morning.

As a consequence of all these conversions, raisings, imports, increased production and so on, the pressure on staff at Army headquarters was enormous. This was maintained by a constant barrage of questions shot all round, all the time. No detail was too small to escape his notice, or once reported to him ever forgotten. So the general officer who came in for a conference on a "morning after the night before", was in for a rough time. Concurrent action was the constant refrain, and if someone was found not playing his part, an explosion was inevitable. By concurrent action was meant tying up all details while the main case was being finalised. If, for example, a case went to the Government asking for sanction to raise an armoured regiment, he expected all personnel and officers for the regiment to be earmarked and warned to be ready to move as soon as the sanction was received: the necessary equipment, stores and vehicles, too, were similarly required to be made ready. The answer, "the case is with the government" as an excuse for not taking all this action, used to infuriate him.

Training was reoriented. For some time it had been obvious that the Army was lacking an institution to train officers for higher command. This was rectified by proposing to the Government and obtaining sanction to start a College of Combat at Mhow in Madhya Pradesh. This entailed the bifurcation of the Infantry School and some training courses that were, until then, run there to be transferred to the College of Combat. A new course called the Higher Command Course to train selected officers in the mysteries of higher command was also started. He went through the syllabi for this course with his usual thoroughness and resisted all efforts to over-work students or grade them at the end of the course, as he realised that both these factors inhibited learning.

Selection to the Defence Services Staff College in Wellington, Nilgiris, an inter-services institution that trains officers of the rank of Major for grade two staff posts, was hitherto by examination. Therefore, an officer who just managed to keep his head above water during his service with troops, but mugged up and did his entrance examination papers well, was assured of a vacancy and Rs. 75 per month as qualification pay (later increased to Rs. 100 per month) after he graduated from the staff college. This was remedied by introducing a system where the examination results plus the showing with troops was totalled and nominations made on that basis.

Formations and units had always had a perpetual crib that too many vacancies on training courses were being thrust upon them, so that a large number of officers were missing from their primary function of commanding troops. This discrepancy was accentuated by the fact that every officer and soldier gets two months' leave each year. All this, in effect, meant that some officers were absent from their posts for anything like four to six months of the year. This was rectified by deleting unnecessary training courses, and rationalising the number of vacancies that would be allotted.

In introducing change or a new innovation, he always sought unanimity from his Army Commanders and Principal Staff Officers. Their views were always solicited when a change was contemplated, and when received had his most careful consideration. He did this, he told me once, so that: "When I leave, the next Chief will not start changing everything we have done. This will happen if he is not consulted; if he is consulted then he will spend his time and energy on improving things, not in lesser matters." There was another, deeper reason. Too often in the past he had to accept changes about which he was neither consulted nor associated. He did not want to repeat this.

With the increased inflow of arms and equipment from abroad, the pestering by gentlemen, I used to jokingly call them "Gun Runners", increased: these were the representatives of foreign firms in some cases, and foreign countries in others, who deal in the sale of arms and equipment of a warlike nature. A lucrative business, I might add, for the gentry in it, as the financial involvements are mind-boggling and run into astronomical figures. There would be requests for appointments: there would be invitations to dinner, "at whichever restaurant you prefer on whichever evening the Chief is free". They would employ every conceivable trick of the trade to bring pressure on the Chief to select their particular item. Relations and close friends would be persuaded to telephone or write; politicians would call or send messages. The Chief made his views quite clear, however; very soon after taking over he told his Principal Staff Officers that he could not care less which country a particular item belonged to or whose pockets were lined in the process, "the principle is and always will be, that the Army will get the best equipment". He refused to deviate from this rule even though, in consequence, there must have been many ruffled feelings. But he knew that what he did was good for the country and the Army. On at least one occasion a gun runner proved to be a blessing in disguise.

We were negotiating with the UK for a particular weapons system, and agreement was reached on practically all aspects of the deal except the time frame. We wanted it quickly and the producer was hedging, expressing his inability to meet this particular requirement of ours. Enter Mr. Gun Runner, a Delhi-based socialite and an ex-Major who met the officials of the Ministry concerned in the producer country and started off by telling them how very friendly he was with the Indian Army Chief, and then went on to say that, if the deal was negotiated through him, he would ensure even more favourable terms than the producers had negotiated. Since the deal was a Government to Government one, the officials naturally refused to discuss the matter and, in fact, for security reasons, even denied all knowledge of the deal. Thereupon the Major lost his temper and went to the extent of saying that, if this were so, he would see to it that this deal fell through, and went to another country that had a similar weapons system. He would get the Indian Army to strike a deal with them. This upset the officials and, hardly had our friend walked out, than they rang up our negotiators and, after telling them about the whole unsavoury incident, agreed to meet our requirement of time. The deal went through. When the incident was reported to the Chief, he laughed and wondered aloud whether to thank the Major or rap his knuckles.

The "Gun Running" business had an unfortunate fallout, too. An old friend, Chibber, was a dealer for one of the European arms producers. He met the Chief on a regular basis and even when he was black-listed by the Defence Ministry and considerable pressure was brought to bear on Sam to terminate the friendship, he refused to do so. To the best of my knowledge, no undue influence was ever exerted by, or on behalf of, the Chief to obtain any contract for Chibber. People in this field, however, have numerous avenues to use, and this must have been done as, despite the ban, contracts did go his way. The friendship endured.

Whenever he visited a formation or unit, I used to take copious notes of all the points raised and problems thrown up. He would invite problems by persisting: "Look, Sweetheart, you must have problems. Even I have problems, so how can I believe you do not have any?" Finally, the officer concerned would open up and tell him his problems and those of his command. These points were then condensed on return to Delhi and raised at the next PSO's conference. Then, knowing that from the following day he would start checking, a veritable commotion would occur at Army Headquarters. As far as the formation or unit visited was concerned, its problems were resolved and deficiencies made up, leaving the officers there in a happy daze.

Despite his other preoccupations, he found time to suggest to the Defence Secretary, KB Lal, (Harish Sarin, his predecessor, had moved to some other assignment by this time as, indeed, had the Defence Minister, Mr. Swaran Singh, replaced by Mr. Jagjivan Ram) that the annual Defence Ministry Report which is presented to Parliament just before it debates the Defence Budget, needed a thorough overhaul. Until then the Report had always been a study in ambiguity, shrouded in secrecy, telling the intelligent reader almost nothing. The suggestion was promptly accepted and, between them, the Chief and the Defence Secretary produced a most illuminating document for the 1972 Defence Debate in

Parliament that provided a wealth of hitherto unpublished detail. It earned approbation from Members of Parliament who, while showering praises on the Report, were quite unaware that the author was sitting in the Speakers Gallery, quietly listening.

Dealing with facts and figures on the one hand and bureaucracy on the other, tends to make staff officers cooped up in South Block oblivious to what is actually happening on the ground. This became apparent quite soon when, knowing from personal experience (confirmed by many others in lower formation headquarters and units), that radio sets were in chronic short supply, the point was put to the staff at Army Headquarters to examine. Within five days a beautifully prepared chart arrived showing the overall requirements and holding. The figures proved that there was no deficiency when I knew for a fact that there was no unit in the Army which was holding its quota of radio equipment. This state of oblivion was quickly remedied. He insisted that Principal Staff Officers and Directors visit units regularly: "Not to enjoy their hospitality, but to ask them what their problems are and then to sort them out. I don't want any witch hunts: the aim is quite simple—help the troops!"

This attitude takes me back to 1964, when he was Army Commander in the West and visiting Palampur in the Kangra Valley where I was Brigade Major. Palampur is a hill station and it is customary for the influx of visitors, commanders and staff officers to reach its peak in summer. After all who wants to visit a hill station in winter when the plains, too, are pleasant enough? So when the Army Commander went around asking when the Chief Engineer had visited, the invariable reply was "about six to seven months ago". The last straw on the proverbial camel's back was when he came upon a barrack whose roof had been blown off during a storm. He asked when this had happened and was told that it was three months earlier. "Who lives there?" he asked next, and was told that some married other ranks used to live there, and were now being housed in tents. I happened to be standing next to him at the time. He turned to me and said, "You are going to get such a rush of visitors that you will be sick of them. But don't let them browbeat you as they are all coming to help, even if their tempers, ruffled after I have had a word with them, indicate otherwise." So it transpired that, in the next few weeks of the middle of winter, Palampur was the silent and startled witness to a constant stream of high-ranking visitors, each vying with the other to be helpful.

Dress, too, came in for some change. With the expansion of the Army after 1962, we had become quite a large army and it was becoming increasingly difficult to remember faces and names. To overcome this, the wearing of name-tags was introduced. To help others get over their initial reluctance to accept change in a society as tradition-bound as the army, he wore the first name-tag, labelled "Sam Manekshaw", himself and insisted that every officer and JCO wore one.

The uniform of the Military Nursing Service Officers was, until then, an apology for a uniform and the girls were, quite naturally, concerned about the shabby appearance they presented. A change was ordered. By coincidence, a friend introduced an Australian who was visiting India at about this time, who was said to be a fashion designer with a boutique in London. The gentleman was asked to suggest a uniform and he produced a pretty glamorous drawing which the Chief and Mrs. Manekshaw approved after its adoption had been recommended by the Matron-in-Chief. The uniform was adopted in 1971. However, the incident had an amusing ending. The fashion designer, after being well wined and dined by the upper crust of Delhi's society and running up a sizeable bill at one of Delhi's leading hotels, suddenly disappeared and subsequent enquiries revealed that the man was an impostor. Whether the hotel recovered its bill, I know not but the gentleman certainly did the Military Nursing Service a favour and I hope that, wherever he is, he reads this to know that the uniform of one branch of the Indian Army is now his creation.

The uniform of the Indian Army is so designed that it is meant primarily for wearing in the field during training and war; it is also, after a bit of starch is added, used for ceremonial purposes. This duality is hard on the soldier who must wear the dress without starch while on training and then with starch when required which is usually at short notice. The matter of providing each soldier with uniform specifically for ceremonial purpose was examined but the financial impact worked out to some astronomical figure which was obviously unacceptable. The proposal was, therefore, hurriedly shelved. Instead, a limited proposal, to issue the infantry battalions stationed in Delhi and other major cities with a new pattern uniform for summer and winter wear, was accepted and implemented.

We are the only country in the world that continues to retain a cavalry regiment, 61 Cavalry. There was during the 'pruning' stage a vociferous body of opinion that suggested that the horse had seen its day, and so we should get rid of this regiment. Guessing, accurately as it transpired, that accepting this would be treading on very sensitive toes and also, that he, an infanteer, would be accused of doing down the cavalry, the Chief very shrewdly decided that 61 Cavalry would henceforth provide the guards of honour at Palam and Rashtrapati Bhavan whenever a foreign dignitary was received. This, he reasoned, would add a touch of much-needed colour, as the men of 61 Cavalry wear distinctive ceremonial attire on such occasions. Furthermore, to silence the critics forever, he became Colonel of 61 Cavalry nipping in the bud any proposal for disbanding this regiment.

Particular as he was about dress, he hated the sight of an officer under an umbrella. During his visits to units, if it was raining, he would refuse offers of a waterproof coat or umbrella and would insist on walking in the rain which caused me the problem of a wet turban and wet hair, both difficult to dry in the rushed programme that invariably lay ahead. In October 1972, on a visit to South Korea, while we were being shown around a National Monument, the tomb of an ancient hero, Admiral Li, it started to rain. The guide, a most efficient young lady, produced some umbrellas and commenced distributing them among the delegation. When she turned to me, she half offered me one and then withdrew it saying with a glance at my turban, "Oh, you have your own umbrella." She relented a little later, however, and let me have one. I was photographed under this and when I showed the picture to the Chief, he turned to me and gave me a right royal rocket for using an umbrella while in uniform.

While these changes in dress were underway, I thought it an opportune time to take advantage and get the uniform of my Regiment, the 8th Gorkha Rifles, standardised. This Regiment, incidentally, has always been famous for the most immaculate turnout and for this reason had earned the title of "Shiny Eighth". The tradition persevered with the Colonel of the Regiment himself setting a fine example. The fly in the ointment was that each battalion had its own peculiarities of dress and all previous efforts to standardise used to be shelved with the remark, "The Government will not agree." Every two years, each Regiment in the Army holds what is called a biennial conference at its regimental centre, attended by all battalion commanders of the regiment and presided over by the Colonel of the Regiment. We held our conference in 1970 at Dehradun, where our Regimental centre, 58 Gorkha Training Centre, was located. I had suggested to all Commanding Officers that they raise the issue of dress. This they did, and pat came the usual reply from the Chief who was presiding, "I don't think the Government would agree." Upon hearing this, I interrupted to state that if the Colonel of the Regiment agreed in principle we could sort out the remaining red tape. He agreed, so it was a simple matter to get the Adjutant

General at Army Headquarters to issue an amendment to the existing dress regulation incorporating whatever we wanted. Now the 8th Gorkha Rifles continue to be shiny, but uniformly shiny with scarlet "pom-poms" in the Gorkha Hat, to scarlet flashes on the shoulders, black leather belt and black brogue shoes for walking out. Imitation, they say, is the sincerest form of flattery: therefore, it was gratifying to see the leather belt and brogue shoes standardised throughout the Army, some years later.

The other supporting arms and services of the Army received new and improved equipment to make up for deficiencies, and to replace antiquated equipment which we had been making do with for ages. The Signal Corps had better radio sets and other communications equipment. The Corps of Engineers received better bridging equipment, mine laying and mine breaching equipment. The Research and Development Organisation, over the activities of which, incidentally, the Chief kept a very careful watch, was directed to produce a special shoe for an infantryman when negotiating a minefield to minimise, if not obviate altogether, the danger of injury if he stepped upon a mine.

The Electrical and Mechanical Engineers had much needed replacements of recovery vehicles. Now, with these, it was possible to recover damaged vehicles where on-the-spot repair was not possible during battle, so that they could be evacuated to workshops in the battle area, repaired quickly and returned to the user. More tank transporters and powerful towing vehicles were procured to save the life of tank tracks which were in acute short supply, and to tow the various types of artillery pieces in service respectively.

In the past, while importing equipment, a major shortcoming in our planning had been that we had not envisaged the problem of spares. Consequently, after some time, the equipment would become a white elephant, needing constant attention and maintenance, but unusable for lack of spares. The new Chief knew about this and always insisted on the requisite spares being procured with the imported equipment. Being a switch from past practice, this was resented by the negotiators, both ours and those of the foreign country concerned, but accepted eventually, with reluctance to our obvious advantage. This became apparent during the 1971 war and its aftermath.

Hospitals also received his attention, but not in the usual manner of additional raisings and so on. There were two aspects that needed improvement. First: all military hospitals were dark, dingy places that more often than not depressed patients rather than providing them comfort and good cheer. Constructional changes were ordered to ensure that wards had more light and, in consequence, became cheery places. A concerted drive to achieve a higher standard of cleanliness was ordered and achieved. Second: why was there a delay for patients awaiting medical attention? This came to light when he visited the Armed Forces Medical Inspection Room at the rear of South Block, and asked a Sepoy how long he had been waiting to see the Doctor on duty. He was given the figure of something like four hours. The Director of Medical Services, Army, was in the Chief's office within the next half-hour and while I know not exactly what transpired, the general's face, when he passed through my office on his way out, indicated that it was drastic. Anyway, a noticeable improvement in this regard was soon evident.

The intelligence services, too, had their share of his perception. Until 1969, these services were their own masters, psuedo-professionals whose incompetence was amply proved during the two conflicts in 1962 and 1965. Immediately after he took over the Army, he started questioning their organisation and function. The Armed Forces were the biggest users of intelligence yet, strangely, they were not represented in the various agencies that had mushroomed over the years to collect and collate intelligence. His argument received a favourable reception, and as soon as the proposal was accepted, service officers were posted to these diverse agencies. The excellent assessments the Defence Services received during the 1971 war with Pakistan bear eloquent testimony both to the wisdom of this step and the efficient work of these officers although posted in a domain that hitherto had remained a mystery to friend and foe.

The Army has many categories of personnel but may be broadly divided into two: combatants and non-combatants. The latter consists of personnel like Mess Cooks, Barbers, Washermen and *Safai Walas*. By virtue of the job they performed, which is self-explanatory, the privileges they enjoyed and the pay they received was less than that enjoyed by the combatants. Yet the non-combatant followed his unit into battle, shared its trials and tribulations, and worked just as hard and was just as honest and diligent as the combatant. Also, on occasions, he was required to use a weapon and fight beside his combat comrade. The Chief sought to have this incongruity removed by combatising the non-combatant, and thereby not only improving his pay and privileges but also opening up better promotion prospects. This case was soon accorded Government approval and the term "non-combatant" was removed from the Army, thus bringing at par privileges, pay and promotion prospects for all ranks.

Not all cases the Chief took up were approved by the Government and in one case at least it was just as well that approval was not accorded. This case pertained to free rations for all officers. I might clarify here that in peace stations only junior commissioned officers and other ranks have always been entitled to free rations. Officers paid for whatever they ate in the officers' mess and the daily messing normally varied between rupees five and nine per day, depending on the station and the officer's eating habits. In a field area the officers also had free rations, and if serving in an area above 9,000 feet or in an area designated as having an uncongenial climate, they were entitled to a slightly more liberal scale of free ration. The new proposal originated with good intentions and envisaged officers in peace-stations getting free rations too. When the matter was examined, however, it was revealed that this would amount to additional expenditure which the Government would not accept. To circumvent this impasse, some bright boy suggested that the extra rations officers and men had in high altitude areas should be reduced to normal field scale as this cut in expenditure would offset the increased expenditure that would accrue by providing free rations to officers in peace areas. I argued vehemently against this proposal, pointing out that the time had come when troops serving in high altitude and uncongenial climate areas should be offered more temptation to serve there: the new proposal envisaged, on the other hand, taking away whatever little inducement was offered. This was bound to be resented and might even end up by an increased number of personnel declining to serve in tough areas. The proposal went to the Government, however, but fortunately it was not approved as its introduction might have benefited a certain number of officers but would have been detrimental to the Army. In 1984, the Government approved a proposal to provide free rations to all officers. There was no reduction in scales authorised to field and high altitude areas.

The Army, as well as the Navy and the Air Force, maintained a small presence in most of our Embassies and High Commissions abroad. This presence takes the form, as far as the Army is concerned, of Military Attaches of the rank of Colonel in most countries and, in the case of the USA, USSR, UK, France and West Germany, of the rank of Brigadier. As a posting abroad seldom comes one's way, it was inevitable that a great deal of patronage crept into the selection procedure. This was very quickly remedied, and the procedure evolved was that the Military Secretary put up a panel of names selected by the computer and selection was made only from this list. A slight variation was also introduced in the training of such officers before they embarked upon their new assignments. The selected officer had to be with Army Headquarters, on attachment for a period that ranged from six to nine months. During this period he and his wife were taught the language of the country where they were going and given an opportunity of travelling extensively around our country to have a more thorough grasp of the country's achievements and our problems and, finally, they were gradually introduced into the social whirl that surrounds a military attache. The method of selection and the new innovation by way of training did, undoubtedly, help and ensured that our representative abroad was a high-calibre officer. This was evident from the excellent reports from this new breed. Despite the stringent selection, rules an odd abberation was inevitable. At the Defence Secretary, KB Lal's request, an officer was posted as Military Attache to France. Poetic justice was dispensed when he soon got into trouble.

Talking of military attaches and their selection brings me to the point that some countries have a system where a military attache, if he has worked well enough, may volunteer for a second or even third tenure. This system has the great advantage that the officer and his wife are settled and proficient in their job which consists mainly of keeping their eyes and ears open during social engagements, knowing precisely what to look for and reporting all this in an objective manner. We, on our part, have decided to stick to the system where an officer does one tenure and then reverts to his main work which is soldiering with troops.

One of the tasks of the Army is to provide assistance to civil authorities when required to do so. As every soldier knows, this is a most distasteful task as requisition for army help is only made when the law-and-order situation has deteriorated to the extent where the civil administration cannot control it. It means a show of force which may even necessitate opening fire on our own countrymen, most of whom are usually misguided people led into mischief by a few vituperative, violent types. Good intentions of the troops in such situations do not easily communicate themselves to the subjects. Self-restraint passes unnoticed and the presence of a sniper in a suburb cannot explain the berserk behaviour of troops that follows.

In 1969, following the split in the Congress Party and the fall of a few state ministries, the law-and-order situation in the country had deteriorated considerably. Consequently, numerous calls were being made upon the army to render aid to civil authorities. Whereas the rendering of such aid during natural calamities and the like is a humanitarian task which the army performs willingly, aid rendered towards maintenance of internal security is anathema to the soldier. Naturally, therefore, following these regular demands, feeling against this task started growing and officers and men were talking about this openly. In early 1970, this growing feeling led the Chief to comment on this aspect in a newspaper interview, and it drew on his devoted head the annoyance and ire of some politicians. The Chief was quite right, however, in drawing attention to this increasing misuse of the army, and he was forced to do so because the politicians failed to play their part. Historically, if the genesis of any militant movement is analysed, it will be seen that the starting point is invariably misgovernance and the non-acceptance of minor, even inconsequential demands. Only then does the snowballing effect start, when quiet and peaceful protest turns into violence. In any case, can one name even one person in authority, whose incompetence and insensitivity led to a deteriorated situation, who was held accountable? How can an aggrieved public be reassured about the good intentions of the government unless they see justice done in the form of the culprit(s) being brought to book. After a brief furore the matter died down but the advantage that accrued was that calls for army help became far fewer.

Perhaps, as a consequence of this, rumours to the effect that the Chief was planning a coup started making the rounds. These must have been taken seriously as, on one occasion, the Prime Minister asked him directly about the veracity of the rumours. According to Sam he re-assured her by quoting a couplet, exact details of which I forget but which went something like "You mind your own business and I will mind mine."

6

Travelling with the Chief

In hindsight, one of the most interesting and educational aspects of my job as Military Assistant was travelling. I could not, unfortunately, accompany the Chief on any of his foreign visits, except when he visited Nepal at the invitation of the Commander-in-Chief of the Royal Nepal Army. But I did accompany him on most of his tours within the country.

Visits to units and formations, accompanying the Chief, were enjoyable occasions. It meant a change from office routine; it meant seeing new places, meeting many old friends there and making new acquaintances; and, from the professional point of view, it meant an opportunity to observe very closely how other units and formations functioned and discharged their duties. Later, after I relinquished this appointment and was posted elsewhere, it used to be perplexing, but a pleasure, to meet so many people who would preface their introduction with, "We met when you came with the Chief to such-and-such place." More than anything else it meant seeing our great country as it really is. This has always been my advice to foreign friends who come to India as tourists or on posting: it is pointless seeing Bombay, Delhi and Srinagar and going back; to see the real India in all its diversity, splendour and beauty one must go to the interior. From the Palace compounds in Gangtok how can one forget the sight of the riot of colour that the rising sun's rays play on Kanchenjunga's snow-capped peaks? King among mountains, it stands alone, brooding and towering in all its awe-inspiring majesty; how can one forget driving through the lush green forests of Arunachal Pradesh where every tree is an orchadium; watching the sunset from Cape Comorin where three seas meet; or flying over the Himalayas to Leh and seeing the snow-covered mountains far below, lined up like soldiers on parade—very grim, terribly forbidding; or to sit in one of our numerous hill stations, a log fire burning in the grate as you see the rain outside driving dusk to darkness at the end of the day. To see these sights is to see so much beauty that, as one very charming girl once told me, one wants to stand and weep. It is all very moving, inexplicably sobering and, above all, indescribably beautiful.

During the first week of every month, I used to seek and obtain the Chief's direction for the visits he wished to make during the following month. A tour programme would then be issued, normally a fortnight in advance, for each visit. Apart from the usual details of dates, timings and places to be visited, there would be an instruction to the effect that command and corps representatives were not required, as the Chief felt that their presence inhibited the free expression of views by units. I prided myself on the fact that, apart from one or two occasions when minor changes were necessary, we never issued an amendment to a tour programme. I realise now, of course, that credit for this must go to the Chief for not changing his mind as do many other senior officers I know. Such alterations, as one who has been on the receiving end knows, mean a complete change of programme with all its allied work. So, for a staff officer it is a small matter to state that his commander will visit an hour later; at the lower formation or unit level it means that all preparations made earlier have been infructuous.

We usually travelled from the Air Force Station, Palam, in one of the Indian Air Force Communication Squadron Flight aircraft which meant an Avro 748 or a TU 104. On a few occasions, when places in the close vicinity of Delhi were to be visited, we went by helicopter which would be either an Allouetee or a MI 4. Very seldom did we travel by train; when we did it meant that the Chief's Saloon would be attached to the appropriate train and detached at his destination.

Not unnaturally, receipt of a programme stating that the Chief was visiting a unit or formation resulted in a flap at that end. In the first few months after I took over, despite the fact that detailed instructions on the subject existed, I used to be bombarded with questions such as: "What would the Chief like to see?" "Would so and so programme be suitable?" "What are his preferences as far as food goes?" "What particular brand of Scotch does he like?" "What cigarettes does he smoke?" "What would Mrs. Manekshaw like to do?" and so on. Endless questions which I answered and, in so doing, tried to convey the reassurance that there must be no panic as the one priceless quality the Chief had was the ability to put the other person, no matter who it was, at ease.

So at the appointed time we would depart: the party usually consisted of Mrs. Manekshaw, an ADC, a PA, an attendant, which meant one of the Gorkha Orderlies, and myself. There would, sometimes, be others who were cadging a lift or proceeding on duty. Everyone would be aboard by the time the Chief and Mrs. Manekshaw arrived. I used to meet them on the tarmac for some last-minute instructions if they were necessary, and then I would run up the steps, followed by Mrs. Manekshaw and lastly, the Chief himself. He would spend the time between getting out of the car and into the aircraft in meeting the pilot, the Air Force Station Duty Officer and sometimes, if he was present, the Air Force Station Commander.

I sat with the Chief and Mrs. Manekshaw in the VIP cabin. As soon as we were airborne (I don't think I ever strapped on a safety belt during the countless miles we did), the attendant would walk in, and the Chief would take off his shirt which would be put on a hangar, next the shoes would come off and in their place would be the cloth slippers that Air India provide on their flights. I then showed them the programme of the visit, he would ask a few questions like names and so on (which, in the beginning, I did not know). Then he would settle down to reading a novel, or get immersed in the files and papers that he had not had time to see in the office, and which I carried with us. Mrs. Manekshaw busied herself in solving crossword puzzles.

The mention of a novel reminds me of an incident that occurred one morning in the North East Frontier Agency as we helicoptered in. He asked me if I ever wondered why he didn't feel cold when we visited the snowy heights. I confessed that I did: whereupon he produced a paperback out of his briefcase, showed me the title, which was of a rather racy and risque novel, and stated that it was reading such material which kept him warm.

Whenever we were out of Delhi for more than two days, the arrangement was that all incoming mail and urgent papers requiring the Chief's signature would be sent to us wherever we were by my most efficient Civilian Staff Officer, Mr. Subramaniam. This mail would be handed to the Chief during flights as, in between, he hardly had a moment to himself.

The ADC carried snacks, not only for us but for the entire aircrew, as the Chief's orders on the subject were explicit: "Every man in the aircraft will get an equitable share of what we carry." The Chief's favourites were potato wafers, chicken patties from the Ashoka or Oberoi Hotels and, I was to learn later, rolled parathas with potatoes inside. Coffee, tea and soft drinks were provided by the aircrew. Once on a 1971 visit to Agartala where he had flown via Guwahati, the return flight was delayed and so we could only take off from Guwahati at about 8 pm The Home Secretary and the Director, Intelligence Bureau, had accompanied the Chief on this trip and they were terribly impressed by the hospitality aboard the plane, when the efficient aide, Shubhi Sood, produced a bottle of whiskey plus sodas and snacks.

Just before we were due to land, his attendant would walk in and straighten out his uniform. As we taxied to the disembarking point he would look out of the window and point out to Mrs. Manekshaw the more important personages that had collected to receive him, and also tell her their appointments. There would also be more intimate detail:

"So and so is a widower, so don't ask him how his wife is."

"So, and, so was with us at so and so; ask him how his wife named Shoba (or whatever) is."

Airport introductions over, we would motor to the place where the Chief and Mrs. Manekshaw were to be accommodated. There the guard would turn out; the Chief would take the salute, inspect the guard, shake hands with the guard commander and order the guard to break off. He disliked frequent turnouts by the guard so, after obtaining his approval, I used to instruct the guard not to turn out during the remaining days of the Chief's stay. Also, the bugler used to be instructed not to sound reveille in the morning as it disturbed Mrs. Manekshaw's sleep. It was my job to instruct the visited unit to arrange separate bedrooms for the Chief and Mrs. Manekshaw because of Mrs. Manekshaw's complaint that, "his snoring keeps me awake". Whenever he stayed as a guest at Raj Bhavan or at a Command House or with some friend, the Chief's flag was never flown in deference to protocol. The host continued to fly his flag.

A quick wash and a cup of tea and we would be off to follow the laid-down programme. This generally meant taking the quarter guard, meeting all officers and JCOs, a visit to the barracks where every man he met would be asked how he was, whether he had any problem—all with a firm handshake and a disarming smile. Sometimes he would meet a man with a bigger moustache than his; this would be remarked upon with "How dare you have a longer moustache than your Chief." Another man would be asked how many children he had and if he gave a number over two it would either be, "I am junior to you" referring to his two daughters, or "you've beaten your Chief". Sometimes, a cookhouse would be visited where invariably the cook would be asked who the better cook was out of him and his wife. The question would be followed by an embarrassed reply usually favouring his better half. During all this time the constant refrain was: "What are your problems? What can I do to help?"

Then with a snappy, "thank you for showing me around", he would walk off to the car at his usual brisk pace with all of us attempting to keep walking without breaking into a trot with varying degrees of success. He would get into the car with a smile, and he would be gone.

Talking of his brisk pace reminds me of when we visited military hospitals. The person there who had the biggest problem keeping up with him would be the Matron. It used to be amusing to see the poor girl trotting along, one hand keeping her hair in place, the other keeping the swirling skirt down, and gasping for breath as she tried desperately to keep up and answer the volley of questions coming from him.

On one visit he asked a lieutenant colonel commanding a unit what the task of his unit was. The officer, probably rattled by the presence of his Chief, perhaps not at his best that day, stumbled and mumbled and fumbled and just could not say anything right. The Chief tried his best, and when he was like this he could be truly excellent, to calm the officer but to no avail. Finally, he put his arm round the officer's shoulder and, patting him on the back, said, "Sweetheart, I am beginning to get the uncomfortable feeling that you are bluffing me." I doubt if that officer had any sleep that night. On another occasion while visiting a battalion of the Garhwal Rifles, he asked the commanding officer what action he took against a man who contracted venereal disease. Venereal disease, as everyone knows, is preventable and so if a man contracts it, a great hue and cry is raised as it means amongst other things that the man has disobeyed orders, his superiors have failed to explain orders, and so on. Anyway, the answer to this question was that disciplinary action would be taken against the man and his head shaved off. "Shave his head off?" The Chief echoed, "Dammit, he didn't do it with his head."

He seldom lost his temper: when he did, it was only after grave provocation, and it would be evident only to us who knew him well. His face would redden and he would look round and say, "I want to be alone with the General (or who ever)." This was the signal for the accompanying officer to withdraw to a safe distance while he lambasted the poor officer who would emerge a little later, completely shaken and terribly distraught. Sometimes the 'rocket' took a less subtle turn. Once while going round an Officer's mess he noticed that the silver was not polished. Officers' messes, usually, take great pride in their collection of mess silver, as this not only adds to the beauty and dignity of the mess, but also has many old, sentimental memories, collected, presented and preserved as all these pieces are over the years. Unclean silver, therefore, is no small affront to the dignity of the mess. He turned to the ADC and, within the hearing of the Commanding Officer and his Brigade and Divisional Commanders, instructed him:

"When we get back to Delhi, send this Regiment a tin of silver polish. They evidently don't have any here."

To the men, he was always a popular and welcome visitor. It was on one such visit that he acquired his name "Sam Bahadur". This happened while visiting the 6th Battalion the 8th Gorkha Rifles, where he asked the Commanding Officer's Stick Orderly if he knew who he (the Chief) was. The stick orderly is the man selected out of the day's quarter guard, possessing the smartest turnout and most impressive presence. Instead of doing duty at the Quarter Guard, he accompanies his commanding officer the whole day or until ordered to break off. Some battalions have a custom that, at the end of the year, details of how many times a man has been selected to be stick orderly during the year are totalled and the winner gets some award. Promptly came the acknowledgement from this one that he did. The next question was whether he knew his (the Chief's) name: this too was acknowledged by the youngster who, when pressed to tell us what it was, replied "Sam Bahadur". From that day the new name caught on and wherever he was amongst troops it was always "Sam Bahadur". "Sam Bahadur" was also the name given to a marching tune composed in his honour by a band-master of the 8th Gorkha Rifles. On 29th January 1973 during Beating of the Retreat by the massed bands in Vijay Chowk, New Delhi, after he had relinquished office, when the Bands emerged to start the show this, appropriately I thought, was the tune they played. On a visit to Nathu La once, he asked a huge, burly Sikh soldier if he had any problems. Everyone present, particularly the man's Commanding Officer, was a little startled to hear the man acknowledge that he did have a problem. When asked by the Chief what it was, I am sure he must have been very moved and delighted to hear the reply in Punjabi that the only problem the man had was that the Chief did not visit them often enough.

There were interesting interludes galore. One I shall always remember was a delightful evening we spent in the Palace at

Jaipur where, over dinner, three interesting hours were spent hearing a scintillating exchange between the Chief and Rajmata Gayatri Devi, our very charming hostess. The subject was politics with the Chief defending and justifying Government policies and actions, and the Rajmata, a staunch Swatantra Party member and almost violently anti-Congress, attacking them. What portfolio would she accept in the Government, assuming that she were offered one, he asked her. Tourism, she replied, as it offers the biggest challenge and has the brightest future. Both of them were highly intelligent and well-informed people and both had razor-sharp brains; she was also very beautiful. It was one of the few occasions when I was sorry that dinner didn't last longer as it made a sobering change from Delhi's night life to be invited to enjoy the generous hospitality of the Jaipur Royals.

Visits to Military Hospitals had to include a cup of tea with officers of the Military Nursing Staff. He would talk to each one, asking her if she had any problems (this always ended up with a request for a radiogram or curtains or carpet; sometimes, if the girl were very brave, all three). He would then ask one girl (not necessarily the prettiest) if she would show him her room. Initially, this used to embarrass the poor girl and the embarrassment would grow more acute if, as you entered, there were some "unmentionables" hung up to dry. Later, word went round and we used to find the girls not only better prepared, but also readier to point out shortcomings such as lack of geysers, fans and so on. All this time the local commander would be biting his nails and looking daggers at the poor girls. He would be assuaged, however, with a smile from the Chief and a remark such as: "They like me, so they talk."

Accommodation was one of his pet subjects and when he went round a unit, the engineer responsible for maintenance or construction nearly always ended up with a rocket. On a visit to Jaipur once, the accompanying engineer, a major, took the rebukes quietly at first and then started answering them politely but firmly. He was right, of course, when he explained his problem such as red tape that caused delay, paucity of funds and the like. The Chief heard him out quietly and we departed. About six months later I was reminded of this incident, which frankly I had forgotten, when on one of the Promotion Board Proceedings which come to the Chief for approval was a hand-written remark in the customary red ink against that very same officer whom the Selection Board had failed by a fractional margin, "This officer had the guts to stand up to me; pass him." How he remembered was beyond me.

I tried to keep afternoons free so that the Chief and Mrs. Manekshaw could relax. On such occasions we would all go sightseeing, or I would accompany Mrs. Manekshaw to a curio or antique shop. She had the most fabulous collection of porcelain China and antiques gathered over many years from all over the world. Many were the long hours, I remember, we spent eyeing what I thought was trash, but what would eventually turn into a masterpiece after she had picked it up and subjected it to her magic. Evenings generally meant a cocktail party followed by dinner. Mrs. Manekshaw always insisted on an early dinner so it was my job to remind the host to serve soup no later than 9.30 pm at the latest. As I, too, detest late nights, this was a most welcome chore.

The following morning the routine would go something like this. As was his custom, the Chief would rise at about 5.00 or 5.30 am irrespective of when he went to bed. Over a cup of tea, he would browse through the morning newspapers which between us (hosts and I) we had to ensure were delivered by this time. Then a change to a sports shirt and slacks and a walk in the garden where more often than not, the gardener would be told where he was going wrong. Then, after a wash and change, breakfast and we would depart for the airport.

On return to Delhi, my first job was to draft charming little thank-you notes to every unit and person whose hospitality or kindness he had enjoyed. Mrs. Manekshaw wrote her own letters, and these were written equally promptly. One letter would go to the Captain of the aircraft or helicopter that flew him, and another would go the officer who had performed the duties of liaison officer during the visit. Each note had to be as if he had written it and, therefore, ingenuity had to be stretched somewhat to produce something that was a combination of grace, appreciation and wit. He never returned a letter, so I suppose I passed muster on this score. Then, all promises he had made, like presents of money, gifts and so on to Nursing Officers, Officers' Messes and the like, had to be honoured very promptly as, if I did not report completion within two days, I had to have a very plausible explanation ready.

Sometimes, during a visit, he would notice something that was not as it should be. That person, too, would get a letter and in this, after appropriate words of appreciation over the hospitality enjoyed, would come the second paragraph starting with the ominous words. "This, however, is not merely a bread-and-butter letter: I am not satisfied with..."

At the start of this Chapter I mentioned that I accompanied the Chief only on his domestic travels. For foreign trips, I was politely told to "man the office" and, so, except for the visit to Nepal, I stayed at home. I did not take very kindly to this but, in retrospect, I realise that, with the pace he set, he did not want the tempo to slacken while he was away. Also, with the piles of mail he used to get, if I was absent as well, the office would be overflowing with letters when we returned. His leaving me behind in this way was, however, eyed by some PSOs with suspicion assuming, wrongly, that I was left to spy upon them. The real job, apart from clearing mail regularly, was to keep him "in the picture", wherever he was, about the latest development (by letter and telephone) and also to keep sending important press cuttings for his perusal. On such occasions, even letters marked "personal" were opened and, I might add, on most occasions even received a reply from me.

Planning foreign trips was a far more complicated affair than organising domestic ones. To start with, the Foreign Office laid down which countries could do with visits from service chiefs and which countries could do without. Invitations from the latter were politely declined; those from the former were processed. Approval was sought from the Ministry of External Affairs through the Ministry of Defence. Once formal approval was obtained, the itinerary at the other end had to be planned. This was a joint effort in which the particular country's Military Attache, our Military Attache in that country and I put our heads together— figuratively speaking as vast distances separated us. We evolved a solution to meet the desire of the hosts to show everything they had and, in the bargain, probably keep the Chief and his entourage awake throughout the visit and my requirement that while seeing the maximum, the Chief had as much spare time as possible to relax and sightsee. A compromise would finally be arrived at but not, I must confess, without sometimes resorting to my biggest clout, "The Chief wants the programme to be like this".

Concurrently, a case would go to the Government to obtain approval of the entourage and the funds required to meet the cost of presents, entertainment and so on. Needless to say, when I went to the Chief to enquire whom he desired included in his party, I used to wait, hopefully, pencil on paper, for him to say "you". This I never heard and, so, who can blame my face for getting longer and longer as visit followed visit and the Military Assistant stayed behind to tend the office.

Incidentally, while on the subject of Government approval for the funds and composition of the party I should mention the predominant role of finance. Once the Defence Minister approved the request, either wholly or by modifying it, the case went to finance. These gentlemen then have the authority to turn down the request as approved by the Minister or seek clarification like "Visit to so and so country was for three days; why is it now necessary to visit this country for four?" or, "during the Chief's visit to so and so, only two officers accompanied him; why is it now necessary for three to go?" Much time and effort would go into answering these queries and numerous others like them. The fact that the visit was due to commence in another few days, and the hosts were sending frantic messages asking exactly who was coming to enable them to do the print and inscriptions, did not help ruffled tempers. Anyway, all details would finally be sorted out and the Chief would depart on schedule leaving a very dejected and forlorn-looking Military Assistant on the runway.

The red tape did not always end with the departure; it sometimes followed me even after the Chief's arrival. One such incident occurred as follows: the Chief, while visiting the USSR, telephoned me with directions that he would be landing at Santa Cruz Airport, Bombay, on a certain date and he wanted an IAF aircraft to pick him up for the journey to Delhi. Accordingly, I fixed up the aircraft and, as the Chief was to arrive at about 3.00 am, we left in the IAF aircraft from Palam at midnight and reached Santa Cruz by 2.00 am. The Chief's flight came in on time; he and his party cleared customs, transferred to the IAF aircraft and we took off for Palam. After a month or so an objection raised by audit was received stating that Lieutenant Colonel Depinder Singh was entitled to travel in an IAF aircraft of the VIP flight only while accompanying the Chief of Army Staff. In the present case he had travelled from Palam to Santa Cruz alone and, in the process, violated existing orders which could result in an audit objection. A cryptic reply that Lieutenant Colonel Depinder Singh committed this unpardonable sin in all good faith: that he had no desire to waste scarce Government funds which commercial travel would have entailed, which was why he had decided to avail himself of the services of an IAF Aircraft that was going empty, elicited no response. Hopefully, the objection lies settled in some obscure file.

Each visit had to be followed up with a detailed report explaining the itinerary: what had been seen, and ending with recommendations such as what we could with profit introduce into the Service, what we could learn, where we could help and so on. The accompanying officers would usually dump a note written illegibly and incoherently in my lap and depart to their duty stations, pleading some excuse or the other, leaving me with the task of deciphering what they had written during the visit one late night after another, and to prepare the detailed report for the Chief's approval. If this wasn't adding insult to injury, what is?

The Nepalese visit occurred in 1972 and we flew into Kathmandu in an IAF aircraft. Advantage was taken of travelling in our own aircraft rather than commercially, as in the past, to carry numerous gifts which, it had been decided, the Chief would give away when he attended an Ex-servicemen's rally at Pokhra in Western Nepal.

In Kathmandu, the Chief decided, over the protestations of the hosts, to see incognito the sights the bazaar and town had to offer. Accordingly, he put on a sports shirt, a pair of jeans and his favourite footwear when dressed thus, a pair of Peshwari Chapplis, and without escort, flag or star plates departed with Mrs. Manekshaw and an ADC. They parked in the town and went into the nearest shop. They were immediately recognized as, in early 1972, memories of the liberation of Bangladesh were fresh in the public memory and here was the liberator in person. Within no time at all, a large crowd had collected, with everyone wanting to shake his hand, talk to him or just collect an autograph. Fortunately the Liaison Officer given to us by the Royal Nepal Army had anticipated something like this, and so was at hand to perform a neat rescue act.

There was an audience with His Majesty, the King of Nepal. The Ambassador, in his briefing, had cautioned us against speaking without being spoken to as it was against protocol. He must have been really startled when the irrepressible Chief asked the Queen, during a lull in the conversation, "Does His Majesty help you in the kitchen?"

The Pokhra visit was even more eventful and memorable as we met numerous veterans of many wars: old friends by the score and it was a pleasure to see them, bent with age but still looking remarkably smart and energetic, wearing their campaign stars and medals with justifiable pride. I wish we could have stayed longer to sit with them and talk of old times, when some of them had played a big role in holding the hand of the young, green subaltern I was then and putting him on the right track to soldiering. So bitten was I by this bug, however, that during my holidays in 1973 I travelled to Pokhra by road, and made up for lost time by trekking in those mountains to my heart's content.

The Nepalese visit had an amusing postscript. During it as is reciprocal practice between India and Nepal, the King of Nepal had presented the Chief with a Nepalese sword called Khandka (not to be confused with the Khukri which is smaller), in an audience and granted him the honorary rank of General in the Royal Nepal Army. On our return, some bureaucrat queried why the Chief had accepted this honour without first obtaining Government approval. Government approval had, of course, been taken but the Chief drafted a reply and it went something like this. "At the audience," he wrote, "the King got up and made the presentation. The Chief had two options, politely accept or rudely decline. He chose the former. Now, the Government has two options, politely keep quiet or show lack of grace and ask that the honour be returned. Could he please be intimated with the Government's desire?" We waited patiently, but no reply ever came forth.

Sometimes, during domestic visits, we travelled by train. This, as I have mentioned before, happened all too seldom as it was a pleasant, relaxing form of travel. The Army Chief boasts of a railway saloon all to himself. It contains a drawing-cum-dining room with a kitchenette attached to one side and, on the opposite side there were four coupes. The saloon would be attached to a convenient train and detached at our destination where one would be woken up at the appointed time even if the saloon had come in earlier. The advantages, as far as the Chief was concerned, were that he got more time to relax and he could easily taste his favourite dish, alu and puri, that vendors at railway stations sell.

The mention of alu puri reminds me of another incident that occurred earlier. Just after I took up my appointment as MA, we invited the Chief and Mrs. Maneksaw for dinner. It is no small event to have a Chief and his wife in your house for a meal. Quite naturally, therefore, Balli and I were in a panic. Balli prepared all she and the cook had to with a great deal of loving care. To play safe she also got some kulchas, which are similar to puris, as a stand-by in case the *tandoori nans* (chapatis) we were making at home did not turn out well. Now when you buy kulchas, some shops also give you *alu* (potato) curry free. At the last minute, Balli decided to add these to the table, too. I suspect it was just to add to the number of dishes displayed! Anyway, when the Chief came in, he surveyed all the dishes and then with a gleeful, "my favourite", pounced on the kulchas and alu. And that was all he ate, much to our mortification which kept increasing as he wouldn't stop praising that dish.

To cover all his travel expenses while touring within the country, each Service Chief is allotted a yearly grant, called the tour grant, which amounted in those days to about Rs. 25,000 in the case of the Army. The Navy and Air Force being smaller received marginally smaller grants. In addition to this grant, the Chief used to get an allowance of Rs. 500 per month for entertainment organised at home. So, before a tour, I used to draw the required cash to cover expenses we were likely to incur. These consisted of paying for board and lodging, and tips to servants and staff that waited on the Chief. In accordance with the Chief's orders, the tips used to be on the high side. I was to discover later that, after he relinquished office and ceased to draw a tour grant, his tipping was just as lavish even when he paid it from his own pocket. Before we boarded the plane, it was my job to tip the driver who had driven the Chief around.

Sometime in 1971, when austerity was the order of the day, some financial wizard floated a suggestion that the tour grant could be decreased. Nothing more was heard of this suggestion, however, after we replied that the tour grant was mainly for tipping servants and the like, and if a decrease was contemplated, it would be the subordinate class who would be hurt. Nevertheless, since some money used to be left over at the end of the year, I suggested we utilize this to purchase and present sterling silver trophies to battalions of the Regiment. Each battalion of the Regiment had at least one.

Whenever the Chief visited an Ex-servicemen's rally, we used to draw between Rs. 7,000 and 10,000 cash from the welfare funds maintained by the Adjutant General, and I would pack Rs. 50 in some envelopes and Rs. 100 in others. These would be thrust into the Chief's pockets when, after the rally, he met the ex-servicemen and their families over a cup of tea. He would go on dispensing as fast as I replenished and, in the process, a photographer once snapped my hand entering the Chief's pocket. The copy he sent me had a cute caption, "Whose hand is picking the Chief's pocket?"

Travelling to and from Palam would be enlivened by questions like, "Why do Indian women have such big bottoms?" (They don't wear high heels) "How would you resolve the problems of Calcutta?" (More housing and public utilities). "Have Indians no shame?" (On seeing the common spectacle of men urinating or defecating on the road.)

7

Prelude to War

In 1947 when the British Government handed over the power it had wielded in the subcontinent, it did so to two entities, namely, India and a new State called Pakistan. The latter in turn was, by virtue of geography, further sub-divided into two separate wings called West Pakistan and East Pakistan. East Pakistan, surrounded to the East, North and West by India and to the South by the Bay of Bengal, was separated from its Western wing, where the capital of the new state was located and wherein lay all the power, by approximately a thousand miles of Indian territory. By sea the distance was even greater, Karachi to Chittagong being 2,900 miles.

During the 1965 conflict with Pakistan, the Indian Army made no aggressive move against East Pakistan for the reason that India did not want to escalate the war but had desired, instead, to keep it at a level where Pakistan would see reason. Nevertheless, considerable Indian opinion, both civil and military, maintained that we should have undertaken offensive operations against East Pakistan for no other reason than to deny its territory to the insurgents in Nagaland, and later, in Mizoram. Insurgents from these two areas crossed over into East Pakistan whenever they found the going getting too hot. There they not only found sanctuary that was "out of bounds" to Indian Security Forces, but were also provided with facilities for training, monetary aid, arms and ammunition. Thus replenished and rested, they returned to their villages to continue their depredations. In view of the Government's decision to leave East Pakistan untouched, however, this shade of opinion could not prevail.

Discontent had been simmering in East Pakistan for many years. And well it might because of the repressive tactics of the West Pakistanis and ruthless exploitation of the eastern wing by the western. Above all, the feeling grew that the majority, a population of 75 million, were being treated as second-rate citizens by a minority of 55 million whose only claim to power lay in the fact that they were born in the western wing. The Pakistan Government did not help matters when they raised a few bogeys over the years, the most notorious being what came to be called the Agartala Conspiracy Case wherein some East Pakistanis were alleged to be involved with India in a plot to overthrow the government.

This, allied to the political events that followed the holding of Pakistan's first elections, created a situation where confrontation became inevitable. Now, either General Yahya Khan who had assumed power in Pakistan through a coup on 26th March, 1969, had to permit the Eastern Wing to form the government as the regional party of East Pakistan, the Awami League, had won an absolute majority in the National Assembly or an attempt had to be made, employing the military and the various police agencies that were available, to curb the growing aspirations for equality of the inhabitants of East Pakistan. What the West Pakistani could not understand and what the East Pakistani will never forget is that it was the former's arrogance and greed which created an irreparable rift, and the crackdown was but the last act in a play moving towards its tragic and inevitable conclusion.

Consequently, when the Pakistan Army cracked down on the province on 25th March 1971 it came as no great surprise, though the severity with which the army struck certainly did. The Chief was in Pune that day, and I had to ring him up to tell him that the Prime Minister wished to see him as soon as he could return. He started back within the hour and the meeting was fixed for 10.30 pm in the Army Headquarters Operations Room. Some officers who had cadged a lift to Pune and Bombay were gallivanting around there when this sudden change of plans took place. They had to be left behind and they made the return journey by train, ruefully, at their own expense.

The Prime Minister, Mrs. Indira Gandhi, escorted by the Defence Minister, Mr. Jagjivan Ram, and the Chief who had met her at the entrance to South Block entered on time. She seated herself, looked round at those of us who were present, then at the maps, very composed, very confident. She smiled at the Chief and asked him to start. He gave a succinct account of the background to the events leading to the crackdown and then gave the intelligence picture (as known at the time) of the strength and dispositions of Pakistan's Armed Forces in the East and the broad dispositions of the Indian Army at the time.

The Prime Minister stated that the people of East Pakistan were going through a traumatic period and we should come to their assistance immediately. The Chief replied that he was conscious of the necessity for this political requirement, but militarily he was not ready, as most formations and units were well dispersed, far away from their peace-time locations and depots, performing election duties. Time was required to concentrate them, equip the troops, carry out forward stocking and prepare for the task in hand. Furthermore, at that particular point in time, as far as the world was concerned, it was Pakistan's domestic issue. The Prime Minister then enquired if there was anything else we could do to relieve pressure on the East Pakistanis. The Chief smiled and replied that despite his earlier requests, he had not been allowed to raise a force of *"badmashes"* (crooks). There was some further discussion, and then another of her enigmatic smiles which appeared to be directed at everyone present, then a "Thank you, good night", and she walked out.

The decision to postpone intervention was discussed again a few days later at a cabinet meeting where many ministers demanded immediate intervention. The Chief's was the lone voice advocating patience for the reasons enumerated above and others which are listed here. Finally the Prime Minister, who had listened patiently, ordered that the cabinet meet again later in the day to reconsider the issue. After the others had left, the Chief asked the Prime Minister whether he should claim insanity and resign. She rejected the offer, telling him he was absolutely right. While thanking the Prime Minister for her support, the Chief stated that he could guarantee capture of East Pakistan in two weeks provided he was given a free hand. To another query from the Prime Minister about time required to get ready, the Chief replied that it had to be after the monsoons, ideally late November as that would also eliminate the Chinese threat. While travelling back to the office he narrated all this to me and added that he was at one time apprehensive that I might have had to make the return journey alone. The re-convened cabinet meeting, later that day incidentally, confirmed his decision.*

To those of us who were fortunate enough to be privy to these developments, it came as a big surprise when, after some time, ugly rumours started to make the rounds that the Army

---

* A detailed and personal narration of the discussion that took place is contained in a talk he delivered at the Defence Services staff college on 11 November 1998. This is given in Appendix II.

had developed cold feet and so had refused Cabinet orders to intercede immediately. This was a fantastic insinuation and it is amazing what a large number of gullible people there were who swallowed it. Firstly, it was incorrect as there was absolutely no truth at all in the whole story. Secondly, there can never be any question in India, with the democratic values it cherishes and follows, for an Army Chief to flout a Cabinet decision of this magnitude. He can certainly express disapproval and, if he disagrees with the reconsidered decision, he is at liberty to ask to be relieved. He cannot disobey an order and stay in office. Anyway, there was some avoidable unpleasantness, which was not eased when one of the Ministers in the Government, who was known to have remarked upon this, addressed the Chief, at the flag-hoisting ceremony that takes place on the ramparts of the Red Fort in Delhi on 15th August each year, and joked that this year (1971) the Chief's guns (meaning the artillery guns that fire the salute) were firing with extra vigour. The Chief replied that he was surprised at this, having heard earlier that the Army was supposed to have developed cold feet.

Immediately after the conference in the Operations Room on 25th March 1971, was over, I escorted the Chief to Army House. Not much was said on the way as I did not wish to intrude into his thoughts at that time. Knowing him I was quite certain that despite all the worries and problems that now confronted him, he would change immediately on reaching home, get into bed and, as soon as his head touched the pillow, go to sleep. Therefore, I was quite surprised to hear next morning that what the Chief, in fact, did was change into a T-shirt and jeans, get into his private car, roll down the windows and drive himself along the Palam road, "to get a breath of fresh air", as he explained to me later.

Plans to meet various contingencies that could arise in East Pakistan had, of course, been exercising the minds of the general staff over the years. Lest this remark be misconstrued, let me hasten to amplify that it would be an imprudent general staff and, indeed, a poor army that failed to do this much. Initial plans called for a purely defensive strategy, in that the main threat was appreciated to be in the cutting of the Siliguri corridor, that narrow piece of territory that separates Bengal and Assam. It was apprehended that a combined thrust, south by the Chinese through the Chumbi Valley and north by the Pakistanis through Rangpur, might block communications running east-west.

To this end, therefore, although the Indian Army had a fairly substantial presence in Bengal, it was mainly oriented at this time towards ensuring law and order and a peaceful election. All heavy weapons and, indeed, most of the equipment of these formations had been left behind in peace-time cantonments as it was not required for the task in hand, which was supervising elections. Therefore, the Army was in no position to undertake offensive operations in March 1971 in any case. Weather-wise too, this was a most inopportune time, as the northern passes were opening with the winter snows melting, and pre-monsoon showers were due to commence in May. Politically also, such a move, even if militarily feasible, would have been quite ill-advised as it would have alienated world opinion against us. The problem was then perceived to be an internal one of Pakistan's and the magnitude of the crisis created in India by the refugee influx was yet to be understood by the rest of the world.

After a short interval, the Prime Minister commenced a whirlwind tour of some countries to explain the facts behind Pakistan's crackdown and, more importantly, define the serious repercussions that were in store for us if something was not done quickly to solve the problems. Here, the biggest problem India faced was the refugees fleeing East Pakistan and seeking sanctuary in the neighbouring states of Bengal, Tripura and Assam—all of whom already had their own ethnic tensions. So it was not only the question of numbers of refugees but also where they settled. Some observers were later to deduce from this tour that our intention was to gain more time. This was untrue as the solution India sought was a peaceful one, and the world had to be given the opportunity to persuade Pakistan to stop its repressive actions and relieve India of the enormous pressure increasingly exerted by the refugee influx. The intention, therefore, was not to gain time but an honest attempt to lay before the world precisely what the problems were and also to seek help, assistance and mediation. Regretfully, though opinion swung overwhelmingly in support of India's case, it could not alter Pakistan's policies and actions.

In addition to these pressing problems, the Prime Minister was beset with internal squabbles. This was the time when the Kamraj Plan was being implemented involving the sidelining of many politicial heavyweights. Also, elections were to be held. At this time the Prime Minister would send for the Army Chief, see him in private and, after a cup of tea, see him off without, on most occasions, discussing anything substantive. These meetings naturally spawned speculation that martial law was in the offing. To what extent these rumours pre-empted internal disturbances, I know not; but elections were held in a peaceful atmosphere and Mrs. Gandhi returned to power with a massive majority.

So, while political settlement was hoped for and sought, the armed forces proceeded with their planning and preparations to cater for the eventuality of war, as it required no great prophet to foresee that war was inevitable. Paradoxically, however, while a soldier, General (later Field Marshal) KM Cariappa, a retired Army Chief, warned of the dangers of war and suggested that a political middle way must be sought, it was Jaya Prakash Narayan, that apostle of peace, who advocated war as a solution to this dilemma. The fact that there was agreement between the Prime Minister and the Chief over no-commencement-of-operations before October-November, naturally could not be publicised. Therefore, unremitting pressure was maintained all round for preparations to be completed at the earliest. In any case, Pakistan was at liberty to launch operations whenever it suited that country, and we could not afford to be caught unaware.

It is not my intention to narrate here an account of the detailed preparations that preceded the war; I merely wish to highlight some of the incidents that occurred during this momentous period so that the reader can get a fuller, more objective picture of the events as they occurred and the man about whom this book is written.

Sam Manekshaw, in addition to his appointment as Chief of Army Staff, was also Chairman of the Chiefs of Staff Committee since late 1969, when he took over from the Chief of Naval Staff, Admiral Chatterji, who had retired. Until April 1971, the Chiefs of Staff Committee functioned in the manner in which its composition intended, namely, in compartmentalised sections, each Service Chief minding his own business and refraining from treading on the sensitive toes of others. It required a man with the personality, character and driving charm of Sam Manekshaw to assert in the Committee the position of Chairman and, at governmental level, the position of the Chiefs of Staff Committee itself. This, I might add, was helped immeasureably by the fact that the Chief had extremely cordial relations with the Prime Minister and top bureaucrats of the time and what a galaxy they were: P.N. Haksar, T.N. Kaul, D.P. Dhar, P.N. Dhar, L.P. Singh and others. An equitable share of credit for this must naturally go to the other two service chiefs as well who accepted the dominant position of the Chairman and to the political masters who, accepting the situation, gave the Chairman and the Chiefs of Staff Committee their unstinting support and confidence.

Admiral Nanda, that very popular Chief of Naval Staff, the man who really blooded the Indian Navy and enabled it to win its spurs in battle, described this in his own inimitable and jocular fashion, much later in January 1973 on the occasion of the farewell from the Chiefs of Staff to the outgoing Chairman when he said: "Great credit must, of course, go to Sam for the brilliant leadership he gave to the Chiefs of Staff. We must not forget, however, that equal credit must go to the other two Service Chiefs who accepted this leadership voluntarily."

A word here about the Chiefs of Staff Committee. We have adhered to a system, which was followed by most countries during World War II, of each defence service having a professional head, the senior-most among these by virtue of service as Chief, chairing the Chiefs of Staff Committee. This consists of the other two service chiefs, a secretariat and certain experts in the fields of intelligence and the like. The chairman also represents his own service. The UK and USA, from whom we had inherited this system, have since changed over to other systems where the introduction of bureaucracy between the professional and his political master is deleted. For various reasons, the main one being the misapprehension that the new system will throw up a professional, who is too powerful, we have stuck to the old system where relations between the defence services and the Government depend upon individual relationships rather than, as they should, upon the system as a whole.

Though I have mentioned that relations between the three services Chiefs were cordial, there was some element of tension between Sam and Pratap Lal, the Chief of Air Staff. Perhaps it was due to the different personality traits of the two men: Sam, outgoing, gregarious, informal; whereas Pratap Lal was intellectual, reclusive, formal. Fortunately, this undercurrent never surfaced except on one occasion when, at the behest of the Army Chief, orders were issued directly to Eastern Air Command. The Air Chief reacted angrily and demanded that such a lapse must never occur again. Technically, of course, he was absolutely right even though the lapse was, in fact, a minor abberation, committed in good faith.

After relinquishing office in January 1973, Sam Manekshaw was to refer to the cordial relations that existed between the Government and the Chiefs of Staff Committee. In an interview with Mr. Heikel, then Editor of the influential Egyptian paper, *Al Ahram*, he said, "At the outset, the Prime Minister gave me her directions and then left me completely free to conduct my affairs as I chose. In consequence there was never any interference by or conflict of views with the Government. What more can a soldier ask for?"

Fresh plans were now required to be drawn up to meet the new situation. Briefly, the threat was fourfold. In the west was the main bulk of the Pakistan Armed Forces; all along the northern border stretching from Ladakh to Arunachal Pradesh were the Chinese in Tibet and, in this context, it must be remembered that we had to be on guard all along our borders as the possibility of a Chinese intrusion into Nepal, Sikkim and Bhutan also posed a very live threat to us; in the east was East Pakistan which our intelligence agencies commenced telling us in March 1971 was being reinforced very speedily with men and material from the west; and, finally, there was the continuing threat of insurgency in Nagaland and Mizoram.

Having obtained the broad National direction, the Army Chief's first step was to finalise operational plans. The Army was fortunate to have at the time as Director of Military Operations, the brilliant soldier strategist, K.K. Singh. He and his staff worked many long and, undoubtedly, weary hours to complete the staff work this necessitated. Then, each Army Commander was invited to Delhi, the plans discussed with him, and his views sought on their feasibility. These views naturally received the utmost consideration, and then after due deliberation the Chief would give his decision. One point he was emphatic about was the allotment of troops. He absolutely refused to accept any suggestion which would have a formation with one command until a certain time when it would revert to another command on the development of a particular situation. "I want no horse trading," he would say, "and I want everyone to know exactly what he is to get or not get." The unsaid fact was that, in the fog of war, with every commander crying himself hoarse to emphasise how great the threat opposite him was, it becomes extremely difficult to decide on the fresh allotment of troops. So the plans crystallised, took shape and my long hours in South Block became longer but, now with an aim in view, they were increasingly interesting hours.

The rapid concentration of massive reinforcements into East Pakistan cleared the existing doubt about whether the freedom fighters there would be able to assert themselves without outside assistance. It was apparent that they would not. Therefore, the Army had to be moved up initially to bolster the BSF and then as it became obvious that Pakistan was bent on war, to locations commensurate with tactical plans. It may have comforted some Pakistanis then and may even comfort some now to attribute the trauma of 1971 to Indian machinations, thereby avoiding some unpleasant facts, the most unpalatable being that the crisis was exclusively home grown.

Apart from operational conferences, numerous other conferences were held to increase indigenous production and to decide what equipment must be imported and to lay priorities for such import. Cabinet meetings had to be attended, progress had to be checked and, at the same time, formations which had moved to the border to be ready to meet any threat that materialised, had to be visited to check their operational plans and to understand and sort out their problems. Between April and November 1971, despite the tremendous pressure of work in New Delhi, the Chief visited all formations down to divisional level and most down to brigade level. He would address officers and men on such occasions and, though the outline of his talk would vary to suit the occasion and his mood, three points were always made with a firmness that his unfailing humour and ready wit could never quite mask. "When war breaks out" he would say, "there will be no scavenging. My Army has soldiers in it, not thieves. Secondly, no womanising. I have been all over the world," he would remark with a naughty smile, "and I can say with authority that we have the most beautiful women in the world. Why go to lesser women? Furthermore, our fight is not with their women, it is with their Army. Therefore, when you feel tempted, put your hands in your pockets and think of Sam Manekshaw." This invariably brought the house down. The third point was an exhortation to all ranks to display valour and aggressiveness. With this, he would also tell the troops about what other preparations were afoot, what equipment was being procured, and when they would get it to meet their requirements and to make up for their deficiencies. Here his fantastic memory used to have free rein as he reeled off facts and figures of imports, of dates when ships carrying our requirements left various ports, when these were expected in home ports, and so on.

When he addressed officers separately, a little more bluntness would creep in. He would tell them of the crisis of confidence that was creeping in between subordinates and superiors at practically all levels. He would emphasise the need for developing mutual trust, of telling the truth, irrespective of what the consequence may be, of inculcating the quality of "sharam" by which he implied the facing up to one's obligations and discharging them to the best of one's ability. He would tell them of the incorrect, untruthful and often exaggerated reports he was continuously getting from areas where troops were actively engaged, and how these reports stretched his incredulity and tested his patience, how wrong assessments could be made if one relied on them and the great harm that would inevitably follow if this was done. We learnt that some senior officers resented the tone and content of such talks. However, what mattered was that the message got through; in any case it can be in nobody's mind that the Indian Army is a nursery school where coddling was necessary.

While on the subject of officers, I shall digress to narrate an illuminating incident that highlights his qualities of fair play and honesty. Numerous reports were received that a particular Brigadier was involved in various malpractices. When the case came up to the Chief he spoke to Mr. P.M. Haksar, then Principal Secretary to the Prime Minister, to tell him that he was sending a file which he wanted him to peruse. I took the file to Mr. Haksar who studied it and informed me that, as an administrator himself, he felt that disciplinary action was called for. The reason the Chief wanted Mr. Haksar's advice was that the Brigadier was the younger brother of Lieutenant General B.M. Kaul who, in 1962 had instigated the inquiry against Sam. Now the Chief wanted to ensure that not only was justice done but seen to be done as well.

When visiting, one public relations officer always accompanied the Chief's party to photograph the visit and report on it. On one occasion he spoiled the complete reel in his camera and, as I always carried my own camera with me to take the odd snap, he requested me to hand over the reel in my camera to see if a suitable photograph could be found for publication in the newspapers the following morning. Luckily, one did prove to be good enough and I was delighted to see my effort on the front pages of newspaper dailies the next morning.

During the 1965 war with Pakistan, quite a large number of sackings took place among the senior officers: not all deserved this fate, of course, but, on the other hand, not all were innocent either. Be that as it may, this development did leave a bad taste in every man's mouth. The Chief had been Army Commander in the East then and so had taken, at best, a sympathetic interest in these cases which did not really concern him, as Eastern Army was not involved at that time. He remembered, however, not that he could forget because most of these officers commenced making appeals against earlier decisions when the new chief arrived. That this was always playing on his mind was evident when he addressed officers, particularly the more senior ones thus: "There will be no sacking this time," he would say, "we are all doing the present job for the first time and people are bound to make mistakes. It is the senior's job to correct and to teach and, most important to tolerate. So, don't come to me asking for a subordinate to be sacked, because, if you do, I shall ask what part you played in helping him, and heaven help you if you cannot give me a satisfactory reply."

Having worked in Army Headquarters in many important and sensitive appointments, the Chief was familiar with bureaucratic and political red tape and had learnt how to negotiate the treacherous minefields successfully. Taking full advantage of the old rapport he enjoyed with the Prime Minister, he came to meetings armed with her approval: then it was a simple matter to announce that the Prime Minister had approved the purchase of a hundred tanks (or whatever), and "I leave you to work out the particulars. I shall check back after one week." There was never any delay and, in any case, no bureaucrat was brave enough to risk the Prime Minister's displeasure if there was any slackness. Whilst on the subject of imports I should mention that, in the situation existing then, not all weapon systems we accepted were the best. To give one example, we imported the Grad P Single Barrel Rocket Launcher from the Soviet Union based on the favourable reports the Soviets provided and our evaluation team accepted. After the weapon was received and deployed, it was suddenly discovered that we had no ammunition. When the ammunition was provided, the weapon proved a failure. It was eventually passed on to the Mukti Bahini. The Chief was man enough to confess to the Prime Minister that we had made a mistake and he accepted full responsibility. The Grad P was later replaced by the Grad 21 Multi Barrel Rocket Launcher which proved a great success. In fact, Major General I.S. Gill, the Director of Military Operations, who witnessed the first demonstration, reported to the Chief that he was not sure what effect it would have on the enemy but, "even at the gun end, I was frightened."

At about this time the Chief asked all his army commanders if they were doubtful about the war performance of any particular subordinate. If there were any they could be moved to less taxing appointments. Lieutenant General KP Candeth, the Western Army Commander, named two. The cases of both were examined in detail. Senior officers under whom these two had served previously were also approached for their views. Based on all this, it was decided that Western Army's apprehensions were groundless, and General Candeth was informed accordingly. To his credit the latter accepted this decision, but it is a tribute to his insight that he was, in fact, proved correct on both counts.

During one visit to 15 Corps in Kashmir, there occurred an incident which, to the professional soldier, will speak volumes. When all the formation commanders had been assembled, each one gave his operational plans in turn. When each commander finished his account, the Chief, as was his wont, would ask: "Suppose the enemy attacks in another sector, what offensive plans can you put into action to hurt the enemy?" This question was designed to test two things. One: whether commanders were exercising their minds and not merely sitting back awaiting every detail from "higher up". Two: though our policy is defence-oriented, plans must exist to counter an enemy strike in one or more areas by posing a threat in another and thus making the enemy react. War, after all, is but a game and whosoever can call the tune will win the day. Coming back to the story, it was amusing to hear practically all commanders expressing their inability to take offensive action in view of the presence of an enemy brigade which lay concentrated in the North opposite Uri. This brigade appeared to be posing a threat to every one of our formations in Kashmir and finally led the Chief to inquire humorously whether this was an ordinary infantry brigade or one with the superhuman capability of moving to practically each sector, hitting us, and then being ready to move to another threatened sector.

The moral of the story is the value of concentration: we sadly lacked it in Kashmir until the Chief ordered rectification and it was only after this happened that we became more confident. What is more important, we made the enemy react rather than reacting to what the enemy did, rather like holding a knotted fist behind your back while talking to someone; he never knows what you have inside the fist or what you are going to do with it.

Back in New Delhi unremitting pressure was maintained on Directors and Principal Staff Officers. Endless questions about detail would be fired at them to which he expected instantaneous replies and, what is more, these had to be correct and up-to-date. As the days wore on and the pressure continued to mount, faces became longer, holidays became a distant memory and, to the golfers, a golf outing was remembered with nostalgia only when one went home and saw the golf bag lying unused, gathering dust in the corner. The only man whom the pace just could not touch or change was the Chief himself: he would come in at his customary time of 9.00 am looking spruce, smart and vibrant as ever and he would be looking exactly the same, in fact, even more composed as we finished for the day at about 7.00 or 8.00 pm when he would go home. Throughout this period, I don't ever recall his losing what the Americans so aptly describe as his "cool", his calm imperturbability, his sense of humour and his priceless capacity for giving a spot decision. A touch of irritability would occasionally creep in when he was confronted with delays caused by red tape or incompetence; then the face would redden slightly, the sharp look would become a little more piercing, a brief staccato whiplash and the routine would continue for the rest, while the poor "victim" slunk off to "nurse his wounds". This was of course, the visible face. Nevertheless, the tension was telling on him which was evident from the increasing lines on his face and the rapidly multiplying grey hair at the temples. But who can blame him for this? It is not easy to function knowing that what you do or do not do, affects the very security of your country and the integrity of its territory.

It took him about two months to put his own house in order; he then turned to the other two Services. Their operational plans were scanned in detail and some major changes made. I used to be present at these briefings and he would suggest the change, get it accepted in a most tactful manner, and then stress how very much the change would help the land battle.

The Eastern Army Commander, naturally, came in for considerable grilling. I remember that telephone conversations with him or his staff, and there would be at least one every day, ran for as long as an hour at a time and, throughout questions ranging from "where is so and so unit?" to "what happened to that patrol in Nagaland?" to "what is the progress on the construction of a certain road or runway?" would be fired. One particular telephone conversation deserves mention. This was with the Brigadier General Staff, Eastern Command, Adi Sethna (who later rose to be the Army's Vice Chief of Army Staff). Adi had just finished narrating the exploits of a particular patrol that had "shadowed" a Mizo terrorist group from our territory into East Pakistan. The patrol had located the terrorist camp and, when the terrorists were relaxing, attacked it. The patrol claimed to have killed some terrorists and had destroyed some weapons including one medium machine gun. They had brought back one machine gun barrel and some ammunition. After he completed his narration the Chief asked, "Tell me, Adi, why didn't the Patrol bring the machine gun?" There was a pause at the other end and then Adi replied, "You know, Sir, I've been wondering about this myself." I don't think the tremendous burden that Lieutenant General Jagjit Singh Arora, the Eastern Army Commander, laboured under in those days and the great pressure that was constantly on him has been correctly appreciated by the powers that be; he certainly deserved more than what he got.

Ostensibly to help Eastern Army in the gigantic problem of receiving, screening and moving the millions of refugees that were flowing out of East Pakistan and also to enable the maintenance of a more efficient liaison with the civil agencies involved, a major general, designated Director of Operations, with a small staff was authorised as part of Headquarters Eastern Command. Major General Onkar Singh Kalkat was the first incumbent; later relieved owing to ill health by Major General BN Sarkar. I said "ostensibly" as the main function actually was to maintain liaison with the Mukti Bahini and oversee its operations.

As the intelligence flowed in and the country's frustration at being denied help to overcome our legitimate grievances was made abundantly clear by the Prime Minister in her speeches in India and abroad, the broad strategy to fight the war that now appeared increasingly imminent, emerged. As we did not covet Pakistan territory, operations in the West had to have a defensive bias so as to contain anything Pakistan might do. The massive influx of refugees in the East was causing intolerable strain, both monetarily with millions of extra mouths to feed and, more ominously, economic dislocation and upset racial groupings. For example, there were more refugees in Tripura than locals at one time. Therefore, to get rid of this burden, to fight the most recent and novel form of aggression, and to meet the legitimate aspirations of the inhabitants of East Pakistan, a quick military decision was essential in the East. This could only be obtained by converging thrusts designed for a swift capture of Dacca. So, in the East, the bias was towards an offensive which necessarily had to be sharp, violent and intense. A wary eye had to be kept on the Chinaman as it was on the cards that he might join the fray in collusion with Pakistan. At the same time we could not afford to let our guard down in Nagaland and Mizoram. So, the problem boiled down to "where do we get sufficient troops to meet all the threats?" Raising additional units and formations to the required extent within the available financial resources and time frame was clearly impossible. After all, to decide on an increase in one's armed forces is one thing but to effect the increase in fact, and have new units and formations trained, equipped and welded into battle teams ready for war takes infinitely longer. It was becoming obvious that we did not have the time. Therefore, risks had to be taken in some areas; the quantum of troops in such areas was reduced to increase numbers in others.

It would be naive to pretend that, at this time, there was no contact between us and the Mukti Bahini who were becoming an increasingly painful thorn in the Pakistani Government's side every day. Since Pakistan army patrols often intruded into Indian territory in pursuit of the freedom fighters, regular troops started reinforcing the Border Security Forces already positioned on the border. The Mukti Bahini could either confine its actions to the trans-border areas and so take advantage of the sanctuary that Indian territory provided, or operate in the hinterland and so cause more attrition and damage to the Pakistan Army and administration, while at the same time running additional risks itself. For obvious reasons the latter course, with the advantages it offered, was selected. This option also created, quite unwittingly, an element of deception. The Mukti Bahini, among other actions, also destroyed quite a few bridges in the hinterland. To Pakistan this tended to confirm their assessment that India was not about to mount a full scale offensive but would confine its actions to border areas, capture some territory and create a government in Bangladesh. If this were not so, they reasoned, why would the bridges be destroyed? The upshot was that the Pakistan army dispersed itself in guarding the entire border.

Although it had been decided that the ideal time to commence operations, if no political solutions were found, was some time after October 1971, there was no easing of pressure on Eastern Command to complete preparations at the earliest so that we would not be unprepared if it became necessary to commence operations sooner. The move of Indian Army units and formations to the border led the Pakistan Army to concentrate opposite us, thus denuding the East Pakistan hinterland of troops. The Mukti Bahini revelled in this as it gave them a comparatively free run, and also presented ideal conditions for running their guerrilla operations. The Indian Army had explicit instructions not to enter East Pakistan territory and, except for a few isolated cases where troops may have unwittingly or through excessive zeal disobeyed this order, it was scrupulously followed.

On 9th August 1971 the treaty of peace, friendship and co-operation between India and the USSR was signed. This was a great diplomatic coup as, among other reasons, it effectively neutralised China from any major misadventure. Most countries immediately took up the refrain that we had moved permanently into the Russian camp and were now no more than an appendage of that country. Subsequent events proved this to be fallacious and, in fact, our neutrality remained unchanged. Militarily this step proved a great boon as now all our requirements of military hardware were met far more promptly than before. Prior to this event, we were at a considerable disadvantage in facing Pakistan because it was getting almost unlimited quantities of arms and supplies whereas our import was just a trickle.

As summer turned into autumn, Delhi's social life awakened and the whirl of parties recommenced. I used to be very closely questioned, albeit tactfully, by the Military Attache crowd wishing to glean news about what was going on. I hope I was circumspect enough not to divulge anything, and yet polite enough to appear to be answering the question.

At one such cocktail party the Pakistan Military Adviser, who was already present when I arrived a little late, jokingly enquired whether I was working too hard. To turn the question aside I replied that I wasn't really: it was all routine, and then I added that since his country wasn't doing anything except threatening us, the Chief and I had decided to take some leave. Quite unconsciously, I had created a stir; immediately all ears within hearing distance perked up. How could the Army Chief be proceeding on leave at such a crucial juncture? Yet here was his Military Assistant saying quite emphatically that he was. Some interesting messages must have passed round diplomatic circles that night.

The then Pakistan Military Adviser belonged to the Second Regular Course from our Military Academy. Quite a large number of his Indian batch-mates from the Academy were also posted in Delhi at the time, holding various staff jobs in Army Headquarters. Owing to security restrictions they could not meet each other, although both sides were extremely keen to do so. Finally it was decided that I should host a dinner where both parties would be invited and could reminisce to their hearts' content. Unfortunately, 25th March 1971 intervened and, with the mounting pressure of work, it became impossible to go through with this engagement. Nevertheless, the Pakistan Military Adviser buttonholed me whenever we met to enquire when the promised dinner date would materialise. Finally, one evening when he asked me this question in the presence of many others, I replied that I would let him know in private. He insisted on a reply there and then and had a very red face when I told him that his friends had asked me to convey to him that the dinner date would be on the day he defected! This was a subtle reference to the enormous number of East Pakistanis, serving in various capacities in West Pakistan, who were escaping to India with the intention of enlisting in the service of their own country; a most valuable source of information. He never asked me that question again!

On another occasion the Pakistan High Commissioner buttonholed the Chief to ask why we were being so bellicose and warlike. The Chief asked him to be realistic and enquired whether the High Commissioner really believed all the propaganda his country's publicity media was doling out? He then added, "Mr. High Commissioner, if war comes this time, it will be entirely your doing. I can assure you that it won't be ours. Furthermore, you might take the odd hill here and there but, I guarantee that you will lose East Pakistan. Tell your politicians that."

Intelligence agencies, too, were not spared the Chief's attentions; a spate of questions was shot at them each requiring a specific answer and assessment and generally ending with, "I would appreciate a reply within ten days". After all, intelligence that matters is that which reads correctly the intentions of the enemy and periodic generalisations which intelligence agencies are habitually accustomed to churn out were unacceptable. Of particular interest were the new raisings in Pakistan, import details specifically in regard to tanks and aircraft, the build-up in the Eastern Wing, and dispositions of Pakistan armoured formations. Also of interest was the state of the road connecting Tibet with Gilgit, called the Silk Route. This route was of interest because it provided the only land route between China and

Pakistan via Tibet and Pakistan-occupied Kashmir. Whereas movement on water and, to some extent, even by air, was subject to some surveillance, the land route provided an extremely safe and secure induction facility. The only assessment possible was based on the amount of traffic that flowed along this route.

These intelligence reports were read by the Chief with the utmost care and, as he asked innumerable questions on each report, the authors had to ensure that whatever they put down was analysed logically, factually correct and plausible. He insisted on an assessment on each intelligence report. This assessment, he would explain, might be wrong, but he had to have something to base his plans on. Even RN Kao, the Director of Research and Analysis Wing that dealt with foreign intelligence, was not spared and his reports would be returned with a request for an assessment. Consequently, whenever an intelligence report was discussed, he would insist on everyone giving their assessment. Each speaker would get the most patient hearing, followed by a brief pause, then directions that were simple, to the point and crystal clear.

With the intelligence agencies working flat out to keep pace with the stream of queries flowing out of the Chief's secretariat, building the intelligence picture was helped immeasurably by a regular flow of East Bengali escapees from the Pakistan Armed Forces in both Eastern and Western Wings. No intelligence Chief could have asked for more.

Prior to 25th March 1971, Pakistan had pumped considerable numbers of troops into East Pakistan, time having been gained under the guise of "negotiations". It soon became apparent after this date that there was no let up in the movement of reinforcements. This massive induction was done by sea and air and, in one case, there was even a report that aircraft of the Pakistan International Airways, while engaged in ferrying troops, were surreptitiously flying over Indian territory in some area south of Bombay where our radar coverage did not, at that time, extend. This could never be confirmed, however, but as a precautionary measure, a unit of the Indian Air Force was moved south. Either our airspace was never violated or Pakistan discovered that we knew, but no violation was noticed thereafter. Another act in the guessing game that precedes every war! In any case it was particularly galling to receive reports from our signal elements located in Colombo International airport (part of the troops sent to support Sri Lankan armed forces fighting a local insurrection) that, on occasion, they had to guide Pakistan aircraft carrying reinforcements to the east.

Very soon after 25th March 1971, in response to the Pakistan Army's massing on our western borders, the Indian Army was forced to follow suit. This was after a brief respite following the Chief's unilateral declaration on de-escalation, an account of which has been given previously. Mobilisation created its own problems. At a party in the US Embassy one evening, the US Defence Attache, Col. Porter King asked me the location of I Armoured Division as he had a message to deliver from his Chief to Major General Gurbachan Singh. I advised him to enclose it in an envelope and address it C/o 56 APO. He was insistent, however, on learning the exact location which I refused to tell him, pleading ignorance. After a brief interval, during which we drifted apart, he brought a retired major general to me and asked, "General, where is I Armoured Division?" Promptly came the reply, "Fazilka." So much for security! Just before Porter took up his assignment in Delhi, the Chief had visited the USA and Porter had been his Liaison Officer. For this reason he enjoyed a fairly intimate rapport with the Manekshaws and their staff.

The strategy in the east was for simultaneous thrusts from the west, north and east, all converging on Dacca. Since time was of the essence, the overall aim was to capture the maximum amount of territory in the shortest possible time. The Indian

Navy was required to blockade the sea lanes to the south, and also provide fire support to army formations within range. The Indian Air Force was charged with decimating whatever air element Pakistan had in its Eastern Wing within the shortest possible time. While the army's thrusts from the west and the north were possible, because of excellent road communications, at least up to the border, and the wherewithal required to fight and sustain a war was available, the thrust from the east posed an extremely formidable logistics problem. Silchar, which was considered a likely candidate for the main base to support the offensive operations, was located at the end of a long and tenuous road and rail communication system. Beyond Silchar, further to the west, the road communications were even worse, and the fact that the monsoons were almost upon us did not help matters at all. Apart from Silchar and Agartala there were no air fields available. All these problems were met and overcome with great despatch, however, and the necessary concentration of troops was completed within a remarkably short time.

In 1965, and subsequently, it had been planned to employ the Indian Navy in a purely defensive role. As the new situation presented an excellent opportunity for employing the Navy as it should be, it was decided to move the aircraft carrier, Vikrant, to the eastern shores so that it would be available along with other elements of the fleet both to block East Pakistan when required to do so, and also to provide fire support with guns and the aircraft, aboard Vikrant.

The chief was very conscious of the sensibilities of the Mukti Bahini and had issued very strict orders to ensure that they were always kept 'in the loop' and their requirements met in full.

In the west, the strategy called for maintenance of our territorial integrity. This could be done either by a defensive posture all along the border running from Kashmir in the north to the Runn of Kutch in the west, or it could be achieved by limited offensives in selected places to force Pakistan to react to these. For obvious reasons the latter course was selected. Suggestions by well-wishers both within the country and abroad, some of them pretty bizarre, on how to conduct a successful war were not lacking. These ranged from a pre-emptive strike to capture Lhasa in Tibet to "put the fear of God in Pakistan" to an amphibious assault on Karachi, as "the Sindhis will rise as one man". Another suggested that we could "borrow" (I didn't catch how the gentleman planned to return the loan) a small atomic weapon from the USSR and drop it (probably en route from Moscow) on Islamabad; then a deep thrust through Lahore so that by the time our army fetched up in Islamabad the "atomic fall-out would have disappeared". These suggestions, plus "reliable forecasts" from others, provided much needed humour in an otherwise cheerless atmosphere. My thanks to all those worthy gentlemen and, of course, my apologies that we did not act upon their ideas.

Security of plans naturally received the greatest importance. Contact with foreign nationals, particularly by those who knew of operational plans, had to be discreetly watched. The number of people knowing about these plans had to be kept to a bare minimum, papers on which plans had been written had to be very carefully accounted for and clerks handling such papers had to be verified and then re-verified to ensure that nobody succumbed to the temptations which foreign agents were bound to offer. An amusing incident occurred at about this time when a non-commissioned officer of the Indian Air Force in need of a little money walked across to the Pakistan High Commission, asked to see the Military Adviser and, on being taken to him, suggested that he could offer some valuable information provided the renumeration was adequate. The Military Adviser, a wily gentleman, obtained whatever information he could out of the individual and then, tongue-in-cheek, telephoned the air force authorities and our Director of Military Intelligence to "report" that a non-commissioned officer of the air force was asking him for money and offering to provide some information in exchange. He went on to say that he had advised our man not to be disloyal to his country for a few rupees, had given him fifty rupees to tide him over his immediate financial problems, and had not obtained any information from him. He ended by requesting that we collect this man from their High Commission.

As part of the preparations for war, it was decided to utilise the services of senior officers who were attending certain courses of instruction. Accordingly, the Defence Services Staff College and Senior Officers' Course at Wellington and Mhow respectively were terminated early and student officers and officers who were instructing on these courses were despatched to various formation headquarters on attachment. The National Defence College Course in New Delhi was also terminated prematurely, and the student officers were also attached to selected formations, both to assist permanent incumbents and also to be in reserve if needed.

Another innovation was practised to overcome the shortage of tank crews and officers of the armoured corps which would be accentuated at the outbreak of war when casualties started occurring. A certain reserve of manpower is always kept in war and held at central reinforcement centres to enable men to move forward as required. The new practice was to have these cavalrymen much further forward, so that they could join the same day that a casualty occurred.

While the Chief's attention was thus focussed exclusively on preparations for war, one would have expected him to give lower priority to Army interests in other fields. Not so with this Chief! The Military Secretary to the President, an officer of the rank of major general, was being posted out and the Navy and Air Force had their eye on this appointment which has been traditionally an Army preserve. Obtaining this assignment meant one more vacancy in the rank of major general equivalent and so was not to be sneezed at. The Chief was adamant, however, that the vacancy remain with the Army, and he ensured that it did. Major General RL Chopra was brought in from Bombay where he had been the Area Commander.

The Assam Rifles, that distinguished para-military force raised for our eastern region, had at its head an officer of the rank of major general called "Inspector General" because this force has always been under the Home Ministry in the Indian Government even though, functionally, most Assam Rifles battalions operated under Army command as they served either in border areas or where insurgency was rampant. The Home Ministry decided, probably at the instance of the Police, that when Major General Tuli retired from that post, the job should go to a police officer. Here again the Chief put his foot down; old rules and regulations were produced saying that if that were done, all army officers on deputation with the Assam Rifles would have to be withdrawn as an army officer cannot, under military law, be obliged to obey an order issued by a police officer. The Defence Ministry's help was enlisted and between them they won the case but not without, incidentally, benefiting Major General Tuli, who kept getting one extension after another until the case was finally decided in the Army's favour. Major General MG Hazari was selected to take on this assignment.

Production and Defence Research has never been a very strong point with us. It is not for me to discuss or comment upon this national malady, but it is a fact and the main reasons are lack of competition and accountability. Tank production at our Heavy Vehicles Factory in Avadi was lagging seriously behind schedule and causing innumerable problems in conversion of armoured regiments and in providing adequate spares for the converted ones. At the Chief's instance, an engineer officer, Major

General Kini, was selected to head the Heavy Vehicles Factory. It proved an apt choice as production did pick up. The Director of Ordnance Services, anticipating the outbreak of war and, I suppose not wanting to be left out, produced a helmet for the Chief, sporting the four stars of a general. The Chief wore it the day he received it and on his query, I could truthfully tell him that he looked scary. He never wore the helmet again.

On the political and diplomatic level, efforts at projecting the Indian view continued apace. Politically, of course, no leader could have asked for a better environment. With a massive majority and a severely bruised opposition, Mrs. Gandhi was supreme and could follow the chosen path without the bother of opposition pin-pricks, as the country was impaled on the horns of a grave dilemma. On the diplomatic front, even the venerable Jai Prakash Narayan was enlisted to visit foreign capitals and explain our position. The end result was that although there was sympathy, however, particularly from the world media, no country was willing to remonstrate openly with Pakistan.

DP Dhar, who headed the policy planning cell in the Foreign Ministry, was a very close, personal friend of the Chief and the two met almost every day in brainstorming sessions. Whether or not this was at the instance of the PM, I do not know; these sessions did ensure, however, that the Chief was fully in the picture as regards all political and diplomatic initiatives; in fact, in some cases he was the author.

So the stage was set and we all waited for the day when war would break out. As the Chief used to remark, had we been faced with a sane and rational enemy, it would have been possible to assess with a fair degree of accuracy when war was likely to break out. Faced with what we were, however, it was almost impossible to do so and, therefore, we had to be ready as quickly as possible and maintain that posture subsequently.

8

The War

The days marched on and events inexorably brought us to 3rd December 1971. The original question, "Will there be war?" having long ago become "When will war break out?" Note had, of course, been taken of the Pakistan President's statement which he made (in a fit of drunken rage) that ten days hence he would be fighting a war. The significance of 3rd December 1971 being the first Friday after the Muslim festival of Id and, therefore, an auspicious day as far as Pakistan was concerned to start whatever mischief it wished, had not been forgotten either. By now, however, the armed forces were as balanced, ready and poised for war as it was humanly possible to make them at the time. To this extent, as far as we were concerned, Pakistan could not possibly have selected a more appropriate time to start the war.

Considering the meticulous and detailed preparations that had been made by us in response to the Pakistani crackdown in their eastern wing, the enormous cost to the country of moving the Army and the other two services from their peace-time locations to their battle positions, importing equipment and increasing indigenous production to make up deficiencies and all the talk going on about the imminence of war, we would have been up a gum tree if General Yahya Khan had suddenly announced that he accepted all the demands made by the Eastern Wing. This, as has been mentioned before, was the *casus belli* between the two countries and if it had ceased to exist, there would be no war. To explain to the soldier that he has been moved many hundreds of miles from his barrack, the amenities of peace-time soldiering and his family, to endure the prolonged rigours that near war-time conditions necessitate for no reason at all is, to those explaining, an extremely ticklish problem. Also, the Government would have had no small task to explain to Parliament that the immense expenditure incurred was for no real reason at all. As the Chief used to remark, however, we were faced with irrational men incapable of rational thought and action, and they did exactly what suited us at the time. Winston Churchill's description of Ramsay MacDonald, "He is the world's leading expert on falling down without hurting himself," aptly describes Pakistan's leadership at the time.

By 30th November 1971 all preparations of the three armed services were ready. This fact was reported by the Chief to the Prime Minister and her approval obtained to commence operations on 4th December 1971. There was, incidentally, considerable debate among the three Service Chiefs with regard to H-Hour–the timing of the attack. The Army preferred the attack to start at dusk, after a pre-emptive air strike, so that the hours of darkness could be utilised to thrust deep. The Air Force, on the other hand, preferred the attack to start at first light so that the rest of the day was available for continuous air attacks. The latter was finally selected and orders went out from the Chief personally to the other two service chiefs and all the army commanders. On 3rd December 1971 an officer courier was despatched to the

Defence Minister at Bangalore with a letter from the Chief stating that the Prime Minister had approved launch of operations and since the Defence Minister was out of town, he, in his capacity as Chairman, Chiefs of Staff Committee, had issued the necessary directions. The Defence Ministry was not intimated about the commencement of hostilities.

How did the news of war come down to us? We were all in the Operations Room at about 5.00 pm on 3rd December 1971, being briefed by the Director of Military Operations and his staff, blissfully unaware of happenings outside, but secure in the knowledge that everything was ready, and all arrangements completed. For a change, perhaps because of the prior decision, the Chief had decided to leave office early that day and, immediately after the briefing, he was going home. Suddenly the Defence Secretary, KB Lal, rushed in and blurted out the news that the Western Army Commander had just rung him up to say that three of our airfields in the Western Sector were under attack by Pakistani aircraft. The presence of all of us in the Operations Room, which for some obscure reason did not have a telephone, was why the Western Army Commander, unable to contact anyone of us, rang up the Secretary. Anyway, this was how the news that we were at war came to the Chief. I had imagined that, when the news did come, the occasion would be marked by furious activity with people running around, wild gesticulations and everyone wanting to be heard. What actually happened was exactly the opposite. There was a sudden hush and all eyes turned towards the Chief as if to reiterate that no one else could take the responsibility for the decision now required. This did not take long to be articulated and although I can't recall exactly what he said, it was something to the effect that the day for which we had all worked so hard had come; now, let's get them. Since Pakistan had taken the initiative, my first job was to contact the officer who had carried the letter to

Bangalore for delivery to the Defence Minister, and instruct him to burn the letter and return home.

As in the previous chapter, here also I will not take the reader's time by recounting in detail the course of the war. I shall confine myself, instead, to explaining the routine we followed and narrate some anecdotes about this. Before leaving the Operations Room to return to the office from where detailed executive orders were to be issued, the Chief's first instruction to the DMO was, "Get the Operations Room a telephone." This was done within the hour, and ensured that none of us was ever away from the telephone again.

Immediately after news of the outbreak of war was received, the Chief and I walked back to the office, the pace no brisker than usual, to give the staff the cheery news that the office wasn't to be closed just yet. The Chief rang up each of the Army Commanders and the other two Service Chiefs, passed the news to them and, at the same time, gave them permission to put their operational plans into effect. Neither the Prime Minister who was addressing a mammoth gathering in Calcutta, nor the Defence Minister who was in Bangalore at the time, could be contacted. Consequently, permission to the Army Commanders and the other Service Chiefs had to be given by the Army Chief and it is a measure of the confidence that existed between him and the Prime Minister that there was no hesitation or vacillation—orders were out within ten minutes of our getting the news.

I was to meet my wife at Army House that evening as some ladies had collected there in the afternoon for Canasta. The Chief and I were naturally delayed that evening and the ladies, ignorant of the fact that war had started or that a blackout was enforced outside, carried on with their cards. It was only at about 8.00 pm, when the Chief reached Army House, that the ladies came to know about the war; an indication of how very interesting and engrossing Canasta can be.

That same evening, a good friend, Lieutenant Colonel Guido Narcisso, of the Italian Army serving with the United Nations Observer Group for Kashmir, was to drop by our house and cook us an Italian dinner. He turned up at the house at about 7.00 pm with all the ingredients and the wines, having braved the blackout thinking that it was a practice. He waited for half an hour and then rang up my office to enquire why my wife and I weren't home. I told him the reason and he gasped, "Depi, you are joking?"

On my assuring him that I wasn't, he at last grasped the significance of the blackout and the quiet outside. His next remark was laced with more Italian:

"Then what the hell am I doing sitting here, I must be in my office."

With that he took off and my dinner had to wait a month after the war when we fixed another appointment, and Guido took us through the delightful experience of an exquisite Italian dinner.

Concurrent with all the war preparations that were afoot by this time, the Chiefs of Staff Operations Room had also been prepared for this eventuality. By 3rd December 1971, therefore, an office for the Chief was ready in the new complex. This consisted of furnishing the room, installing the numerous telephones that are required and regular checks to ensure that the room had not been bugged. Following this, I had got the Chief's approval for the layout and now it was merely a question of opening a locked room and moving in to begin work. Life after this fell into a new routine. At about 5.00 am the ADC or I would ring up the Chief of Staff or a senior staff officer at every command headquarters to ascertain the latest developments. I would reach the office at 7.00 am and make a round of the Operations Room and the Joint Operations Centre. All major actions of the three Services with losses and gains of the past 24 hours would be noted down on the Chief's pad. Also noted were the actions planned for the next 24 hours. At 7.30 am the Chief would come in, glance through my handwritten notes, ask a few questions and then pay a quick visit to the Operations Room. He would depart at 7.50 am to brief the Prime Minister at her residence from where he would be back at 8.30 am.

At 9.30 am, the Chiefs of Staff Committee met. Each Service Chief would be accompanied by his director of operations. The procedure used to be that each service operations director would give a resume of activities, insofar as they concerned his service, pertaining to the last 24 hours to include losses and gains, plus moves of army formations and units of the fleet and the air force. The director would also give his assessment for the next 24 hours, and ask for air and naval support for that period. After this briefing, one of the representatives of the Joint Intelligence Committee, an adjunct of the Chiefs of Staff Committee, would give his briefing to indicate the intelligence assessment. Then the Service Chiefs would discuss all that had been said earlier to co-ordinate activities that were to take place within the next 24 to 28 hours, and approve the requirement of air and naval support for that period. I should mention here that when each service reported its gains, particularly in regard to losses inflicted on enemy tanks, aircraft and ships, cognisance was taken only of those reports which were corroborated and, therefore, had no chance of being disproved later. This followed the decision which the Service Chiefs had taken on 4th December 1971 when they met for the first time after the commencement of war.

The Defence Minister would be briefed after the Chiefs of Staff Committee meeting either in his office or, as happened sometimes, in the Chief's office. Ego hassles were conspicuous by their absence.

After a few such meetings an additional point—gallantry awards for acts of bravery performed by members of the three defence services, the Border Security Forces, various police units allotted to the army and, in some cases, civilians—appeared. May I digress here to explain the method followed to make these gallantry awards? When an individual in the field performs an act that is worthy of recognition, and it has to be something really outstanding, as in war everyone is performing valiantly all the time, the commanding officer of that individual writes out a citation explaining the act, and sends it to the concerned service headquarters through the parent formation and other headquarters up the chain. Formation commanders at all levels vet these citations to weed out those that in their opinion are not worthy of recognition with the award of a medal. Finally the citation, if it has passed muster at various levels, reaches the Service Headquarters where each service headquarters has what is called an "Honours and Awards Committee" consisting of three or four principal staff officers and the military secretary, in the case of the Army and equivalents in the Navy and Air Force. This committee meets every day to take stock of all citations sent from headquarters commands and weeds out those recommendations which are not good enough. The approved list is then sent to the Chiefs of Staff Committee from where, after their approval, it goes to the Defence Minister for final approval from the President.

I used to sit in one corner with a mass of telephones when the Chiefs of Staff met so that if some urgent matter warranted, the Chief concerned could be contacted and a decision obtained on the spot. On the third or fourth day, I remember a call coming in from the Western Army Commander, Lieutenant General KP Candeth, to say that the situation in Chhamb, where a Pakistani offensive was underway, was critical and all available air support was required immediately. While the Army Commander held on, the request was conveyed to Air Chief Marshal PC Lal, DFC, his assent obtained and directions issued by him to the Air Officer Commander-in-Chief of Western Air

Command, Air Marshal Minoo Engineer, to divert every available aircraft to Chhamb. Within three minutes, I informed the Western Army Commander. I am sure he must have been most impressed and, of course, delighted.

At the first meeting of the Joint Chiefs, the Chairman had directed that all press reporting must be timely, accurate and truthful. The Chairman also insisted that, within the constraints of security, nothing must be hidden from the media; also, that no incorrect figure or claim was to be given out. Major General MN Batra, an ex-Director of Military Intelligence, and, at that time, one of the Directing Staff in the National Defence College, was given the task of chairing press briefings every evening. He did a remarkably effective job, earning plaudits from press correspondents at home and abroad. It is a fact that our reporting throughout this period was objective, accurate, prompt and truthful.

The Chiefs of Staff Committee meeting would be followed by telephone conversations with the three Army Commanders involved: Eastern, Western and Southern. Sometimes, some corps commander had his share of the grilling too. There would generally be one or two meetings with the bureaucracy after lunch. In the evening at about 7.00 pm, the Defence Minister would go to the Operations Room where the Chief would brief him, and at about 8.00 pm after he had left the office for Army House, I would wend my own weary way home through the blackout which was really effective. At home, with no lights showing, my wife would be seated in front of the TV (a gift from the Chief) watching the news coverage which was truly incredible.

Security of the Chief's person was one of my greatest concerns. This concern was heightened by the fact that Pakistan had available a trained band of paratroopers whose job was to raid headquarters in rear areas. Also, the Chief himself, restless as he is, would barely accept security measures, and could be relied upon to race about all over the place by himself. My problem was further accentuated by the fact that where one deputy to me and two aides were authorised, we actually had only one aide. This was because, very early on, the Chief had accepted my recommendation that a deputy military assistant was wasting an officer; the second aide, Behram Panthaki, had asked to be relieved so that he could be with his Battalion during the war. When I broached the subject of security one day, the threat from Pakistan's elite troops was waved away with an airy, "My Gorkhas and my dogs are more than adequate to look after me."

A day or so later, LN Mishra, then Minister of Foreign Trade and a very close personal friend of the Chief, drove into Army House at about 11.00 pm. The guard, recognising the familiar car, saluted and waved it on without bothering to check who was inside. Arriving in the porch the Minister dismounted and walked into the master bedroom through the open doors, stepping over six peacefully sleeping dogs. The Chief was asleep, so the horrified Minister woke him up and told him how secure he was. I learnt about this the following day; thereafter, an additional Military Policemen Guard was added to the "Gorkhas and dogs".

I should mention, however, while on the subject of dogs, that a visit to Army House by day was sure to be greeted by boisterous canines and, to someone who has not shared the experience, I can assure you that it is not very pleasant to be jumped on by two labradors of formidable size simultaneously. By night these same dogs, like all good guards, slumbered peacefully.

Mr. L.N. Mishra's name evokes memories of many stories. He was, at the time, treasurer of the Congress Party and so the recipient of donations to the Party. One evening he drove into Army House, ascertained that Mrs. Manekshaw was out and dumped a gunny bag under her bed. He then walked into Sam's bedroom and informed him of what he had done. The Chief, naturally, asked what the bag contained and was informed that it was party funds. "Why here?" the Chief asked and was informed that if he took it to his home, his wife might remove some amount. He added in Hindi that Mrs. Manekshaw wouldn't even know about the bag till the next morning when he would come over to collect it.

On another occasion, Mr. Mishra returned from a London trip carrying a fur coat meant for a girlfriend. Before it could be delivered to the girl, however, it was intercepted by his wife, who asked whether it was for her. "It's for Silloo," she was informed and, thereafter, a quick call to Sam ensured that everyone, including Mrs. Manekshaw, was briefed accordingly.

He had a morbid obsession that he was being followed, that his conversations were being taped and someone was going to assassinate him. Whenever he visited the office or Army House, his first question invariably would be "De-bugging *kiya?*" Despite my assurances that the rooms were periodically de-bugged, he would insist on writing anything sensitive he wished to discuss. The chits would then be torn up and handed over to the ADC or me for burning. Our amusement got a rude jolt when he was assassinated at the Patna Railway Station platform a year or so later. It was perhaps this fear that prompted him to hand over to Sam a list of donors indicating amounts received and paid. I am sure a large number of people would love to know where the list is.

I have been asked many times by people from assorted backgrounds and nationalities, whether the war really went as planned. It did, except in a few places which come readily to mind—Chhamb in Kashmir and Longewala in Rajasthan. There, we were momentarily surprised, but recovered fast enough. Except for this the war went exactly as planned. Even the time schedule was adhered to as, well before December 1971, the Chief used to remark that, if war breaks out, "I shall have East Bengal in two weeks."

Morala HW - Chhamb

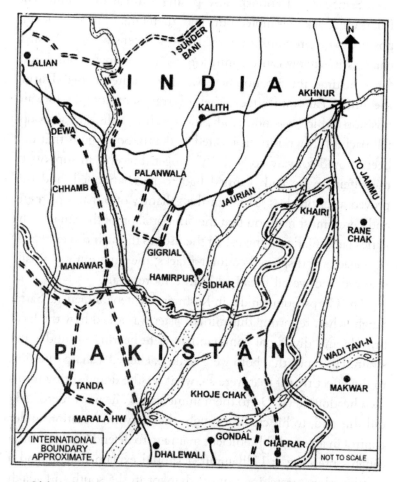

Chhamb in Kashmir was one of the places where things did not go the way we had planned. This was so because we had planned an offensive here to threaten the Marala Headworks in Pakistan: the intention being that Pakistan would react to this threat and, in the process, weaken itself in the area of Sialkot, facilitating our operations in that sector. The area of Chhamb, however, presented an equally attractive objective to Pakistan, as through it, their attacking column could capture Akhnoor, thus severing the road lines of communication running North into both Srinagar and Poonch, also posing a threat to Jammu. The Pakistani attack pre-empted ours and, therefore, from an attacking posture, we were abruptly forced into a defensive one. As such changes inevitably cause confusion, we had to give ground and, for some time, the situation here was very delicately poised. During the initial Pakistani attack, they overran some of our forward positions which was not, really, too much of a disaster as troops fell back to new positions located in depth. Some guns that had been moved forward to "breach" longer, however in support of the offensive we had planned had to be abandoned, and this proved a serious loss. Through the gallantry of our troops there, and here I must mention that the 5th Battalion of the 8th Gorkha Rifles particularly distinguished themselves through two extremely courageous and spirited counter-attacks, the situation was finally restored and we all breathed a little more easily.

The Corps Commander in Kashmir, Lieutenant General Sartaj Singh, when reporting this mini-disaster was asked how the local brigade and divisional commanders were bearing up under the strain. His reply, that both were shaken, elicited a sharp question to the effect that if that were so, what was he doing sitting in his own headquarters. 'Go to them immediately', he was ordered. He did this and, to his credit, brought the awkward situation under control in a remarkably efficient manner. To defend General Sartaj Singh's presence at Udhampur, I should explain that he had a vast kingdom stretching from Pathankot in the south to Ladakh in the north. As the entire border was an extremely active one, his presence at his headquarters was essential and, had he been absent and a crisis had occurred in another sector, the very same Chief would not have hesitated to point out this fact.

Though the Chief had re-assured the officer cadre prior to commencement of operations that, this time, there would be no sackings, at the urging of 15 Corps and Western Command, the

Brigade Commander at Chhamb and the General Officer Commanding 10 Infantry Division were moved out to innocuous appointments. After the war was over, when the war reports on these two officers were received, they were found to be extremely complimentary. The COAS, very upset at this change of heart, inquired why, if the officers had performed that well, their removal had been recommended. Not receiving a satisfactory reply, the Military Secretary was ordered to re-habilitate the two: this was done and to their credit both distinguished themselves and rose to high rank.

The second place involved was Longewala in Rajasthan. Here also, a limited offensive had been planned by us to threaten Pakistan's rail communications running within their territory but parallel to the border. We were pre-empted here also when a Pakistani infantry brigade, supported by an armoured regiment with some artillery, drove into our territory in a very daring thrust to pose a threat to administrative installations that we had raised to support our offensive. Daring is the only complimentary word I can use for this Pakistani thrust because, from a soldier's point of view, the move was a tactical blunder of the highest magnitude. The thrust had very little air cover, and very little terrain reconnaissance had been carried out so most vehicles were bogged down in the sand; it had very little fire support, and finally, to crown it all, it was insufficiently supplied as far as logistics were concerned. The Air Force spotted this enemy move on the very first day after a company of the Punjab Regiment had been contacted by it and held it at bay. After that, it was pigeon shooting as far as the Air Force was concerned, and within two days, this force was more or less decimated. Later an acrimonious debate started over who, between the Army and the Air Force, should claim greater credit. The fact was that both did their jobs well; if the Army had not held up the enemy that night the Air Force would not have got a bunched up, lucrative target.

Longewala

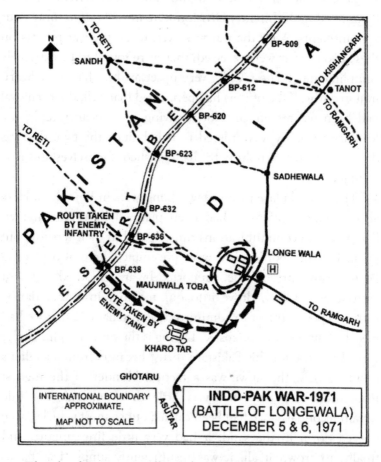

The third was not really a place so much as a person. Much had been expected from 1 Corps operating between Pathankot and Jammu with the task of thrusting towards Sialkot. Pakistani thrusts against Chhamb and Poonch suggested a weaker (comparatively speaking) centre opposite the Corps. 1 Corps advance was painfully slow, however, despite prodding by the Western Army Commander, Lt. Gen. K.P. Candeth, and the Chief. When no progress was evident by 13th or 14th December 1971, the Army Commander sent a confidential note to the

Chief through an officer courier expressing his concern at the slow rate of advance, intimating that if the corps commander failed to comply with the latest warning issued to him, he would be constrained to remove him from command. The corps commander, Lt. Gen. K.K. Singh, was an outstanding staff officer who had served with the Chief as an instructor in the Defence Services Staff College, as Brigadier General Staff in 4 Corps, and lately as Director of Military Operations in Army Headquarters.

The Chief was, naturally, very upset as he had personally selected K.K. to command 1 Corps. Before any harm could be done, however, the ceasefire intervened. Later events proved that the 'scare' was totally unjustified. 1 Corps had captured some 5000 square kilometres of enemy territory; Pakistan's 8 Armoured Brigade was almost decimated; and despite 1 Corps being numerically inferior in armour, the enemy was forced to react. The commanders of Pakistan 1 Corps, 8 Infantry Division and 8 Armoured Brigade were sacked.

The Western Army Commander gave K.K. Singh a glowing report which played a big part in the Corps Commander being awarded the Padma Bhushan for 'great professional ability and coordination of his operations'. He also rose to be Army Commander.

In November 2001, Lt. Gen K.K. Singh gave an interview on the occasion of Basantar Day in Headquarters 1 Corps. I managed to lay my hands on a copy and found that it contained a wealth of professional guidance on how a numerically inferior force can by manoeuvre, outwit a numerically superior force. He advocates, "An armour commander must know when to refuse an armoured battle. In such a situation, when enemy armour is already deployed, have recourse to counter penetration and not counter attack. Manoeuvre again, if necessary quite some distance away and force the enemy armour to move and as it attempts to confront a new situation destroy it as is changes front".

During the planning stage earlier, the Chief had noticed two weaknesses that had not, for some peculiar reason, received the attention they deserved. Poonch in Kashmir was the first. It was apparent from the enemy build-up opposite this sector, that a blow would descend there. Western Army, either through lack of troops or an incorrect assessment (more likely the former), were content to secure it with the troops it had always had. The Chief, however, thought otherwise and ordered another brigade into that area. This not only strengthened the Poonch defences, but also made for a much neater defence – one brigade on either side of the Poonch River. Thus strengthened, Poonch did receive a battering but it weathered the storm and, later, even went over to the offensive and secured some territory.

The second place was Dera Baba Nanak. We had only a brigade here and its task was to cross over and secure the bridge over the river Ravi, one half of which lay in our territory and the other half in Pakistan. A Pakistan counter-offensive was not envisaged but had it come, our brigade, lacking depth, would have found itself unbalanced. Again the Chief had intervened and, while sitting in the Operation Room one day, had mused: "I must give Dera Baba Nanak one more battalion; the problem is where do I get it from?"

Timidly, I suggested that my Battalion, which was sitting on the Indo-Tibet border lamenting their misfortune in missing the war, was available. He liked the idea and within three days the Fourth Eighth Gorkha Rifles found themselves rushed, from the snow-clad peaks I had taken them to in December 1968, to the lush green Punjab plains right into the war, where they acquitted themselves with great credit. Incidentally, at Dera Baba Nanak, it was our turn to pre-empt Pakistan, as we learnt a day or so after our attack went in and secured the bridge, that Pakistan had planned an attack at this very spot to secure our side of the bridge.

It is a truism that a man's worth is really seen in adversity.

We, too, had our setbacks and I would like to describe the Chief's reactions to two developments where, to say the least, events went a little awry. The first was Hussainiwala in the Punjab. The enemy attacked a battalion we had across the river, 15th Battalion, The Punjab Regiment (the famous First Patialas) with a brigade supported by an armoured regiment. The Battalion withstood the initial onslaught well and, though they had given some ground by nightfall, were not unfavourably placed. Early the next morning, however, Western Army asked for permission to withdraw this Battalion as, they said, it had suffered very heavy casualties. I was with the Chief when this request came: without hesitation he turned it down and then addressing me said:

"Don't look so alarmed. First reports are always darker than the actual happening. A bugger gets the wind up and he concocts one hell of a story which, if swallowed by a superior, can be fatal as it is all wrong."

In the event, however, orders to withdraw the Battalion had already been issued by Western Army and so a fait accompli was presented. Within two hours, the actual casualty state came in, and the Chief was proved right: the number of casualties was nowhere near as alarming as first reports had suggested. The Chief was not annoyed over our losing ground without reason, but he was furious at the fact and gave quite a rocket to the corps commander, Naveen Rawlley, that a distinguished battalion with a magnificent fighting record had been prematurely withdrawn—"It will never be able to hold its head up."

The second incident occurred at Chhamb in Kashmir. As narrated previously we were surprised here and for a couple of days the situation was grave. Throughout this period, when news of reverses was coming in and when, if the position had not been stabilised, the situation in Jammu and communications to the north would have been seriously jeopardized, he never showed the strain or even a touch of anxiety. On at least two occasions he was asked if we could withdraw from a position owing to "heavy casualties". He refused and, it transpired later, he was absolutely right as the casualty figures were grossly exaggerated as happens in the fog of war.

It was obvious from the commencement of hostilities that everything hinged on how rapidly operations in the east could be brought to a successful conclusion. All eyes, therefore, were focussed there and the progress of each one of the many thrusts converging on Dacca was the subject of immense interest. 4 Corps, advancing from the general area of Agartala on to Dacca in a south-westerly direction, overcame the hard, outer crust of Pakistani defences and swept forward in what one day will surely be recognized by military historians as a classic pursuit operation—bypassing entrenched enemy and built-up areas, negotiating river obstacles with masterpieces of improvisation, all ranks obsessed with just getting on. The Corps Commander, Lieutenant General, Sagat Singh, was always in the vanguard demanding and ensuring all the time that troops advance just a bit more. As soon as this thrust gathered momentum, it was evident that as far as the Pakistan Army in the east was concerned, the game was up. Now started the propaganda war for which, through the Chief's foresight, preparations had been made well beforehand. Printed leaflets in Urdu, Pushto and English showing emanation from the Chief of Army Staff, India, were airdropped over almost the entire Province suggesting surrender to save senseless waste of life now that the situation had developed wherein further resistance was useless. The text of this leaflet was also broadcast repeatedly by All-India Radio. Exhortations from West Pakistan to the East to continue the fight now that intercession by "the yellow brothers from the North and the 'white ones' from the South" was imminent was the subject of the next lot of leaflets and broadcasts. In these, the Pakistan Army in the east was told to disregard those lies and to surrender, as no brothers, either white or yellow, would be coming to provide succour. All these messages and leaflets concluded with the words that if they surrendered, they had the Chief's assurance that they would be treated like gentleman. This promise was honoured.

Talking of "Yellow brothers" brings me to the subject of the Chinese threat. By virtue of size, if nothing else, the Chinese threat has always been taken very seriously by Indian Army planners. Until 1971, with a hostile East Pakistan separated from Tibet's Chumbi Valley by a narrow corridor that could be severed by a north to south thrust, thus isolating Assam from the rest of the country, this threat was really enormous. With the emergence of Bangladesh the threat remained, but in a diminished form.

Operations by the Chinese against India are governed largely by weather: they have to be conducted when the passes leading into India are free of snow and the Tibetan plateau permits movement of troops and the logistic necessities. We had an early snowfall in the winter of 1971 thus lulling our planners into assuming that if war with Pakistan did break out, closed passes would keep the Chinese away. Intelligence assessments all pointed to the unlikelihood of China joining the fray, but interception of messages passing between East and West Pakistan all spoke of the imminence of Chinese intervention. As it appeared implausible for the West to tell the East a deliberate lie of this magnitude, the Indian Army had to remain on guard against the Chinese too. The apprehension was assuaged, however, when satellite pictures obtained through the Defence Attache of the USSR showed that there was no augmentation of Chinese forces in the Chumbi Valley. Interestingly, the requirement of these pictures was first made to the US and was rejected. A day or so after this rejection, happened to be dining with the Soviet Defence Attache and made mention of our requirement; he promptly agreed and next day we had our pictures.

East Pakistan

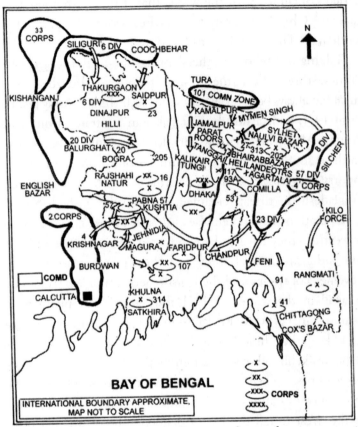

So, throughout the war, another one of my tasks every morning was to obtain data regarding snowfall on all passes leading from Tibet to India. Alas, throughout this period, not once could convey to my worried Chief the happy news that the passes were closed. This used to be his first question every morning when he came to the office.

So much for the reference to the "yellow brothers" whom it was easy to interpret. Reference in the messages to "white brother from the South" used to mystify us and someone even started hare by interpreting it to mean the approach of a Chinese nav force from the South which for security reasons the Pakistanis were calling "white". The mystery was soon cleared, however, when news was received that elements of the American 7th Fleet had passed the Straits of Malacca, steaming in a north-westerly direction. This certainly came as a surprise, because it was impossible either then or now to fathom American motives. After all, it was accepted that the Indian Naval Task Force in the Bay of Bengal was no match for the American fleet, but what could the Americans hope to achieve after they had dealt with the Indian Navy? It was inconceivable that they planned to join the land battle just as they were learning the bitter lesson of such involvement in Vietnam. Perhaps the hope was to intimidate us as part of the policy of the pro-Pakistan tilt.

Be that as it may, when the Chiefs of Staff discussed this influx of American arms into the Indian Ocean, it was decided in all solemnity that when the American Fleet warships contacted Indian Naval Units engaged in the blockade of East Pakistan, the American Task Force Commander would be invited aboard our flagship, offered a drink and then politely asked to steam south. This was how seriously an American intervention, or the threat of it, was taken.

On 11th December 1971, Major General Rao Farman Ali, Pakistan's Military Governor in the Eastern Wing, telephoned an appeal to the Pakistani representative at the United Nations to seek an immediate ceasefire, on the declaration of which Pakistan's entire Defence Forces and civilian employees in East Pakistan would be withdrawn under United Nations auspices. Before the appeal could be passed to the Secretary General, however, it was vetoed by General Yahya Khan. Nevertheless, damage had been done as the appeal indicated that the war was going badly for Pakistan in the east.

It was around 4.00 pm on 15th December 1971 when Porter King, the genial Defence Attache at the United States Embassy in

New Delhi, called to ask for an immediate meeting with the Chief. Since the Chief was free, he arrived within fifteen minutes. The message Porter carried was from Lieutenant General Niazi, commander Pakistani forces in East Pakistan, seeking a ceasefire. About the same time, the UNDP representative in Delhi, Dr. McDermot, also called with a similar message received through his channels. The Chief called up the Prime Minister and, after apprising her of the message and obtaining her approval, confirmed to Porter that the ceasefire offer was acceptable, provided it was unconditional. Furthermore, Indian armed forces would cease firing at a stipulated time late that evening. A similar message was relayed to Jagjit Arora, the Eastern Army Commander, and the other two services, the Indian Navy and the Indian Air Force.

Within two hours Eastern Army called to say that General Niazi had accepted the terms, but sought a slight extension to allow his headquarters to inform all subordinate headquarters and units. This was approved and, later that night, the guns fell silent on the eastern front and, at 4.30 pm the following day, 16th December 1971, the surrender ceremony was held at the Maidan in Dacca. Not only had a magnificent military victory been won but, on the political plane, the map of South Asia was altered with the emergence of a new nation: Bangladesh. Victory has many parents and here, too, quite a few staked their name to fame. The person mainly responsible was, however, without question, Sam Manekshaw. Congratulations poured in and the Chief, true to style, turned away from the maps of the East to pore over maps of the North and West. Considerable pressure was exerted on the Chief, not a little by me, to fly to Dacca and receive the surrender; he refused, stating that it was Jagjit Arora's show and he must bask in the limelight.

As each converging thrust on Dacca fulfilled its mission, we had started to thin out and move troops to the Western front. Consequently, by the time hostilities ceased in the East, a fairly substantial reserve had been built up behind the Western front, poised for offensive operations. After the surrender ceremony in Dacca was over, however, the Prime Minister met the Chief and conveyed to him the Government's decision to offer Pakistan a unilateral ceasefire. I have no doubt that the Chief, as a soldier, must have resented this decision because we were now in a strong enough position to undertake offensive operations and we also knew that Pakistan was running short of tanks and ammunition of certain categories. The Army had also endured enough tension ever since Independence in 1947, and would have preferred, now that war had started, to settle matters for good. The Government's decision, however, was in keeping with our avowed policy of not coveting Pakistan territory; operations in the West, therefore, had lost all relevance unless, of course, Pakistan wished to continue the war. As an Indian, therefore, the Chief realised that this was the correct decision to take. Among the few in whom the Chief had confided about this latest decision, the fond hope persisted that Pakistan would refuse to accept our offer, and decide to fight in order to avoid the humiliation that an acceptance was bound to bring. Alas, this proved to be wishful thinking.

Accordingly, the following day India declared a unilateral ceasefire in the West which Pakistan accepted and the war was over. In the process the Indian Army had suffered 3,153 killed and 8192 wounded, the geography of the sub-continent was altered by the emergence of Bangladesh and 93,000 prisoners of war were captured. In the bag, we were delighted to discover after Dacca fell, were two prominent underground leaders from Nagaland, too. They were Thinuselie Angami, the self-styled Commander-in-Chief of the underground Naga hostilities, and Nedelie Angami, a self-styled brigadier. Both had been provided very comfortable billets and there was a liberal supply of wine and women to help them forget, I suppose, the trials and tribulations that they had endured while being chased around by the security forces. And no doubt it prepared them for the time when they hoped to go back and continue their depredations in Nagaland.

The war in the east was likened by many to a swift, efficient surgical incision and this, I think, aptly describes the whole affair. In the west, by the very nature of the strategy for operations, it had been a hard slogging match with minor pin-pricks in a few places without committing Army Headquarters reserve formations. In the bargain we inflicted fairly heavy losses on Pakistani armour and aircraft, and also secured large areas of Pakistani territory. We lost some territory, too, but the gains exceeded the losses.

The number of formations that we discovered in the east was greater than we thought. Moving such numbers of troops, and the wherewithal required to fight a prolonged war, over the vast distance from Karachi around Cape Comorin to Dacca was a magnificent administrative feat earning plaudits from every Indian Army soldier who knew about it. The strategic prudence, however, of moving troops to an area which even a layman knew had limited defensive potential rather than retaining them in the west where, perhaps, these same troops could have been used more profitably was questionable.

I cannot conclude this chapter without narrating an account of a "clash" that occurred between the Chief with his fetish for detail and that brilliant leader and outstanding staff officer, Major General Inderjit Singh Gill, PVSM, MC, the Director of Military Operations. It occurred in the last few days and the subject was the whereabouts of an infantry brigade moving from the east to the west. The DMO, an extremely harassed man at the best of times, even more so now, answered that the Brigade had left Delhi in different trains at 3.00 pm that afternoon. "Where is it now, Inder?" enquired the Chief, who obviously wanted to know the railway stations the trains were passing at that instant. Back came the reply from the unruffled DMO, who looked the Chief straight in the eye, understanding exactly what was required and unflinchingly replied, "I told you, they are in a train." The Chief left the office early that evening. Inder Gill later rose to be Western Army Commander.

It was a great victory; before we move on it is worth examining what factors contributed to it. First of all, it was the great rapport that existed at all levels: between the politicians and the services, among the three services, and finally, in each service itself. The Cabinet had given the Chiefs of Staffs Committee explicit directions on what it required from them and, having made this clear, had left the execution to the professionals, giving them all the assistance they asked for. Second: politically, the country united as one and pulled together. Some cynic might attribute this to the overwhelming majority Mrs. Gandhi enjoyed, but an objective appraisal would reveal that, given the right cause, our people do unite. Three: diplomatically, this was a remarkable coup of sorts as it went through despite the infamous US tilt. The most amazing part was that, despite apprehensions, the Islamic Bloc remained neutral at least ostensibly and physical aid in the form of aircraft and manpower promised to Pakistan, was not provided. Ironically, the one Islamic country we had expected support from, Afghanistan, did not oblige. The support sought was to move troops to the Durand Line to force Pakistan to tie down some formations. The fourth factor was the meticulous planning that preceded the war. Some details have already been narrated previously but it would take a whole book to cover all aspects. Suffice it to say that it is incredibly hard and painstaking work with no shortcuts. There was no hurrying, there were no "ifs" and "buts" and though, in every war, some reaction is unavoidable to counter what the enemy is doing, in this case it was reduced to the inescapable minimum. As the surgeon keeps what he requires during the course of an operation nearby so that he can pick up any instrument easily with the minimum of movement, so, too, our preparations had ensured that every formation, every dump and all the necessities of war were so positioned that there was no need for anyone to search for whatever was required. This massive preparation with all its attendant concomitants was helped immeasurably by a very highly competent set of Directors at Army Headquarters with whom the Chief dealt directly rather than through the PSOs. Last, but not the least, was the superb bravery and professional competence displayed by all officers and their men. I realised during the months that preceded the war the importance of motivation, and that this is only possible if every man is convinced that what he is doing is right. In this case it had been made abundantly clear to the troops, the sailors and the airmen that the war was not of our seeking: yet they also knew that we would have to fight if the intolerable strain on our economy caused by the massive influx of refugees from East Pakistan were not removed. The soldier also knew that everything needed to outfit him, equip him and position him in the most advantageous manner had been completed, and now the result rested on his battle performance. In such circumstances who will not perform as valiantly as they did? While on this subject, I must make particular mention of the courage and devotion to duty displayed by the officer class, particularly the younger ones. The ratio of killed and wounded between officers and soldiers was abnormally high on the officers' side. This indicates that nowhere was an officer found lacking while leading his men. Incidentally, 1971 was the first major victory the Indian Army had won over a first-class foreign enemy after several years—the previous victory was by Chandragupta Maurya over the Macedonian General, Selecus, in 303 BC.

There was no dearth of professional improvisation. For the first time helicopters were employed offensively in the capture of Sylhet and crossing the River Meghna; again, we saw an airdrop at Tangail; perhaps the first time Paratroopes were employed offensively; we saw our first amphibious assault at Cox's Bazaar the Indian Navy went on the offensive for the first time, attacking Karachi and inflicting enormous damage; and for the first time psywar was successfully conducted forcing the Pakistan armed forces in the East to surrender.

The Hamood-ur Rahman Commission appointed by the Pakistan Government to examine the conduct of the 1971 war submitted its report, which was never made public because of its scathing indictments. Pakistan's claims that the war in the East would be fought in the West never took off owing to the monumental incompetence of the high command. Pakistan lost half its navy, a quarter of its air force and a third of its army. It also lost over 14,000 sq km of its territory in the west. India attacked Karachi harbour during 4/5 December 1971 and inflicted considerable damage, sinking two ships and immobilising one. Huge fires lit up the Karachi sky and continued for days.

Messages of congratulations flowed in, and each one had to be answered. There was even one from Kim Yadav whom I have mentioned earlier:

"You have won the war: all by yourself, without me—a remarkable achievement. My congratulations."

Before concluding this chapter, I feel I must refer to the controversy in regard to the timing of the war. What would have happened if hostilities had commenced in April–May, 1971, must remain in the realms of speculation. The proof of the pudding, however, is in the eating; so the decision to defer commencement of operations was correct. It took a very brave man indeed to stand up to Mrs. Indira Gandhi and get her to see his point of view despite the enormous political pressure she was subjected to. Fortunately, for the country, such a man was there: we were equally fortunate in having a Prime Minister who took the advice of the professional and, unlike latter-day politicians, subordinated political exegencies to national interests.

9

Aftermath

Those of us who had believed that with the end of the war there would be some relief from work were in for a rude shock. These fond hopes were quickly dispelled as we found that if anything, the tempo had increased.

The end of the war saw one set of problems happily resolved and the birth of fresh ones. Now, the most important task was to provide relief and rehabilitation to those who had lost life and limb, war widows and families of soldiers who had died. The response from the country to the various appeals for help was very heartwarming. It will stand to the everlasting credit of our people that, big or small, everyone contributed his mite voluntarily and generously.

I remember letters containing donations that brought tears to one's eyes: a mother who had lost her son saying that she had saved Rs 7,000 for her son's marriage; now that he was no more, she felt sure that he would like this amount to go towards the welfare of the men he had been privileged to command. A child wrote to say that for one month she had saved all her pocket money, which she now wished to contribute towards the Jawans' Welfare. And so on—a never-ending stream of letters enclosing cash, cheques, drafts and parcels containing every conceivable item that could be put to some use.

Maximum credit for this fund raising must go to Mrs. Manekshaw. She worked very long hours, driving herself with enormous patience and vigour, providing sorely needed assistance to the hardworking hospital staff in caring for patients, organising fetes, premieres, sales and the like; visiting cities as far apart as Calcutta, Madras and Bombay to plead for help and obtaining a very generous response. By the time she relinquished the Chairmanship of the Army Wives Welfare Organisation in January 1973, she had collected approximately two-and-a-half crore rupees in cash and about five crores worth of presents—a fantastic feat (remember, this was 1972).

Whenever a premiere was organised, the producer, director and most of the cast would also be in Delhi for the occasion. As all these ladies and gentlemen are extremely busy people, their stay in Delhi had to be reduced to the barest minimum. Therefore, the only possible social engagement would be a cocktail party at Army House. At the premiere of *"Amar Prem"*, Rajesh Khanna and Sharmila Tagore were there; in the entourage was a young Gujarati girl with a very short haircut, wearing a white kurta and something in between a trouser and a pyjama, also in white. Clad thus she was inviting mistakes as far as sex went and, sure enough, after a while the Chief went up to her as she stood by the open window, patted her on the back and remarked, "Young man, you will catch a chill standing there." The girl's eyes bulged but she could only mutter something like "thank you" as she walked away. Dutifully, before the faux pas could be repeated, I whispered to the Chief as he stood alone that it was a girl, not a young man. To corroborate, I asked him to observe her chest very closely and the truth dawned on him. I think he gave me full points for observation that evening.

It came to light that donations to army welfare funds were entitled to an income tax rebate only up to a certain amount; above it the rules did not permit deduction. To overcome this legal impasse the Chief wrote a letter to the Finance Minister, Mr. Y. B. Chavan, explaining that this was preventing larger donations and appealing to him to permit deduction on all amounts. In his reply Mr. Chavan regretted his inability to alter the rules. Having a soft spot for the army, however, as he was once a very successful defence minister before moving on to other portfolios, he suggested a way out. This was that all donations should be made to the Prime Minister's Relief Fund as donations to this are not liable to income tax. In the covering letter the donor could mention that the amount was to be utilised for army welfare work. Thereafter, donations above the stipulated amount used to be made out in favour of the Prime Minister's Relief Fund and, on learning this we used to have the money credited to our welfare funds.

Individual idiosyncracies were not absent when certain people made very handsome donations. In one case an industrialist offered to pay the cost of one battle tank, provided, and this was his stipulation, that he could present the cheque to the Prime Minister in Rashtrapati Bhavan in the presence of the President and the three Service Chiefs. Considering that the amount involved was something in the region of Rs. 15 lakhs, this was a small favour to grant and everyone concerned readily agreed.

Owing to the personal interest of the Prime Minister and the Defence Minister, various welfare measures were rushed through legislation: under these, relief on a scale hitherto unheard of was provided. The Chief used to say, "My wife and I go round with a begging bowl to collect money, so that none of my wounded soldiers or any of my war widows ever has to beg." By this collective action, immense good was done and I don't think any other country in the world ever had such lavish relief measures as were instituted in our country.

States and individual industrialists vied with each other in offering jobs to war-wounded and war widows. In the process, though it was not possible to give back to a war-wounded the limb he had lost or to a war widow, her husband, monetarily it was ensured that they would be better off than they would have been if there had been no loss. Whatever else they sought was, within reason, provided with utmost despatch.

It was in pursuance of this drive to raise funds that we found ourselves in Bombay one day, where the Chief had been invited to preside over the Filmfare Awards. The entrance to the theatre where the ceremony was held was blocked by a sea of humanity and it was only when we got out of the car that we realised that the gathering was to see the Chief and not the screen stars. In fact, throughout the function, it was the latter coming in a very coy fashion to talk to him or obtain his autograph.

David, that great character actor of the Indian screen, very ably compered the ceremony which consisted of the usual speeches, variety entertainment and, of course, the awards presentation ceremony itself. The Chief was introduced as the "architect of our great victory", "while Pakistan is sacking its soldiers we are honouring ours". In his reply which kept the audience in stitches, the Chief said, "I was not aware that I would be seeing so much beauty and so much talent: if I had known this I, too, would have put on my war paint. It is, perhaps, because I lack this that the knocking sounds you hear are my knees."

He thanked the film industry for all they had done, "for my soldiers by providing them so much happiness and joy in forward areas by going to those inhospitable areas and putting up shows.' In conclusion, he went on to say: "Next time the Income Tax chaps raid your houses and catch you, remember then that the

sympathies of all soldiers are with you." The last in reference to
the numerous raids being conducted in Bollywood those days.

Following this address, the award ceremony took place. During
the course of this, Mr. I.S. Johar, the well known humourist,
suddenly produced an award that he had received the previous year
and, coming on to the stage, took charge of the microphone and
announced that this year there had been, for some reason, no
award made to the best comedian. In view of this he had been
forced to bring out the award that he had won last year which he
was delighted to present to someone who had brought so much
mirth and happiness to all the guests that evening. He presented
the award to the Chief amidst much laughter and amusement.

During the war, when we were calling upon the Pakistan army
to surrender, the Chief had pledged that, if they surrendered
unconditionally, he would guarantee their security. Accordingly,
immediately after the surrender ceremony, all people of West
Pakistan origin in Bangladesh had been rounded up and were
protected by the army. Some witch hunts had, of course, started
in Bangladesh, but as they involved Bengali collaborators, the
army did not interfere in that particular activity as it was outside
our scope.

The next problem, therefore, after taking charge of the
prisoners of war was to move them out of Bangladesh almost
overnight as their presence in that country was both fraught with
danger and an irritant to Bengali sensibilities. We had, of course,
catered for the fact that prisoners of war would be captured and
require housing, but not for the vast numbers that actually
turned up. Consequently, prisoner of war camps had to be
improvised to house these "guests". As our troops were all in
the positions they had occupied during the war, it was decided
to make use of peace-time cantonments for this purpose.
Accordingly, the prisoners were moved to selected cantonments
which had to have security fencing and special lighting

arrangements rigged up overnight; guards had to be found as the borders were still active and available troops were all committed. Again the pressure mounted and, with a superhuman effort from the railways and all other agencies that were concerned, the prisoners were transported to the camps they were to occupy for the next twenty-one long, weary months.

Pakistan propaganda notwithstanding, actually the prisoners were extremely well treated. They had the same rations as our troops, and the same clothing; all possible amenities were provided, and, to cap it all, when disengagement took place and our formations returned to their cantonments, they camped outside in tents while the prisoners of war continued to occupy their barracks. It took a lot of explaining to our troops to provide a satisfactory answer as to why they, victorious from the war, were housed in tents without even a modicum of comfort, while the losers were occupying comfortable billets with fans, running water, and coolers.

A word here about escape attempts. Every soldier who is taken prisoner in war is duty bound to use every opportunity to try and escape. It was not surprising, therefore, that there were many escape attempts, some of which proved successful and others abortive. In the course of the latter, some prisoners were shot and killed. This, too, is not surprising as all his life the soldier is taught to shoot to kill; to expect him, when confronted with a prisoner in his charge running away, to change suddenly and shoot to maim, is impossible.

In January 1973, at a press interview he gave to foreign press correspondents at the Ashoka Hotel in New Delhi, the Chief was asked why the sentries could not shoot to maim and the question received more or less the same answer. Another question, "Why have such a large number of prisoners been killed?" elicited an irascible answer:

"You from the United States?" On the questioner giving an affirmative answer, he continued: "More prisoners die in your penitentiaries in one year than have died in all my improvised camps. Secondly, so far as a prisoner of war is duty bound to try and escape, so, too, is the sentry equally duty bound to prevent it. The sentry sees a prisoner running away, he picks up his rifle, aims at the biggest target he can see, the man's back, and fires. He has only one simple intention, which is to hand over the same number of prisoners to his relief as he took over and not be accused by his superior of permitting a prisoner to escape during his tour of duty."

Welfare of prisoners continued to get a great deal of attention. The Principal Staff Officers Conferences were the usual venue where questions like "Summer is coming; has each prisoner of war been issued a mosquito net?" or "Winter is coming, has each prisoner of war been issued all items of warm clothing?" Muslim festivals were not forgotten and, at each one, every camp would be given a message of felicitation from the Chief for its inmates. Having done all this, he used to feel terribly hurt when Pakistan propaganda, obviously politically motivated, used to accuse us of ill-treating prisoners.

Very high priority, and something which of course commenced almost as soon as the war ended, was re-grouping and re-equipping of our units and formations. Because of timely stocking, expenditure was replenished almost within the first two weeks or so. Considering that this involved making up deficiencies that exist as a result of usage, wear and tear, enemy action and include manpower and other items as diverse as all the different types of ammunition, firearms, food, even water, vehicles of all sorts, radio equipment, clothing and so on, one can imagine the magnitude of this formidable task and the meticulous planning that was required to ensure that this entire action took place within the shortest possible time.

Concurrent with re-grouping and re-equipping was the matter of reorganisation and reviewing of operational plans. It had been evident for some time that for one army commander to exercise effective control over operations extending from Fazilka at the western edge of Punjab to Ladakh in Kashmir, with Pakistan on one side and the Chinese on the other, was an almost impossible feat. Accordingly, a case was made to split Western Command and reorganise it into a smaller Western Command and a new Northern Command. Likewise, the task of 15 Corps which extended from Pathankot to Ladakh was eased by raising and positioning another corps headquarter in Kashmir (16). The task of 11 Corps, responsible until then for the entire Punjab border, was also eased by dividing its area of operational responsibility with another corps headquarters (10). All this was part of the obsession to have everything neat and tidy.

Reorganisation meant movement of troops, and one such move created a minor problem. The US Defence Attache had obtained permission to move by road to Srinagar from Delhi on a particular date. After permission was accorded, Western Command decided to move some light tanks to Srinagar by road on the same date, so requested that the road be closed to traffic to facilitate the move. When Porter King saw the cancellation, he was livid; he called me up for an urgent appointment with the Chief. On meeting the Chief, he stated that the cancellation was an insult and that he had asked his Chief to relieve him. After he left, the Chief called me in and asked me to see Porter and advise him to cool down. I went over that evening and despite his persistent questioning about the reason why his trip was cancelled and my refusal to enlighten him (quoting ignorance), he agreed to forget the affront. When I was leaving, however, he asked me to drop by after a few days "for a drink or a meal". I did this to be shown an aerial photograph of a tank on a transporter. A subtle hint to suggest how efficient US information gathering was!

The construction of defences all along the border in Punjab at enormous expense had also made it equally evident that a war of manoeuvre in this sector was practically impossible and the only area that permitted mobility was Rajasthan. To defend this area where it was anticipated that future operations could take place, a new corps (2) was moved in to conduct operations. Additional armoured brigade headquarters were raised, and loose armoured regiments were allotted to them to form more armoured brigades to increase the weight of the punch.

Operational plans were reviewed in the light of extra formations that had been released from the east and were now available for employment in the west. At one such review, while on the subject of Pakistan's war preparedness and her capability, at that time, to wage war, the Chief remarked that, with almost the entire senior echelon of the Pakistan Armed Forces having been sacked or removed from office, Pakistan's capability was limited and would remain so until the younger lot, who had been catapulted into senior rank, could find their feet. He then turned round and addressing all of us asked:

"Suppose I were to sack all the corps and army commanders today, what would be the effect on the morale of the Indian Army?" In the hush that followed that was really not a question but a statement of fact, I could not help murmuring:

"I do not know what the effect would be on the others, but my morale would certainly be very high."

It was in February 1972, I think, that the Government received and approved a request from the Soviet government for the Chief to visit the USSR to speak to their Military hierarchy about the conduct of the war. For some reason a great deal of secrecy was maintained over this visit. I presume Dr. Kissinger's secretive and recent visit to Peking was fresh in everyone's mind, so why not a touch of James Bond here, too? Anyway, preparations for the visit continued in the utmost secrecy and very few people were informed. The whole cover, however, was blown sky high when the French Military Attache rang me up one day to request on behalf of his Army that the Chief spend a day in Paris en route to London-Moscow. On my asking as to how he knew that the Chief was proposing a visit, he told me that he had the news from his Visa Section which had been given the Chief's passport by our Foreign Liaison Section for making the necessary endorsement. They had read the other endorsements, and the cat was out of the bag.

Soldiers love medals and the Indian Army is no exception. But we in our country have been rather miserly in granting medals for some reason. This was remedied, and five medals were instituted during the tenure of Sam Manekshaw. Among these five was what we in the Services call the Wound Medal awarded to personnel who are wounded by enemy action. Characteristically, the Chief stipulated that this particular medal would be awarded with retrospective effect, but from 15th August 1947, thus debarring himself as his wound was received in World War II.

On 30th March 1972 he took the salute at the Passing Out Parade of the IMA once again. A copy of his address is at Appendix V.

The Chief was due to complete 58 years on 4th April 1972: existing orders stipulated that an officer of the rank of General could serve up to 58 years of age or do a three-year term in office whichever came first. In this case, although the three years were to expire in June, the age restriction came into effect beforehand.

There had been rumours, of course, that General Manekshaw would continue in office with a grant of extension. There was nothing on paper, however, and it was all in the realm of speculation. I, for one, could never imagine that the Government would let him go, for two reasons. One: disengagement had still not taken place and the borders continued to be active, and two: age notwithstanding, it was inconceivable that a man of his talents would be allowed to retire just after he had been instrumental in winning such a decisive victory.

I broached the subject one day and he replied, albeit jokingly, that although he hadn't been given any indication it was quite on the cards that he would just be asked one fine morning why he had not taken his leave pending retirement when he knew that he had to retire on 4th April 1972. Until he was asked he would continue until the evening of 3rd April 1973, "We will continue to work flat out."

In mid-March 1972, he was summoned to the first of many meetings with the Prime Minister. During these, she attempted to get him to agree to "carry on" after 4th April. He refused for the simple reason that "my officers are all retired on the date of superannuation; how can I face them by agreeing to carry on in service?" He would not budge from this stand despite much pressure, and one can imagine the magnitude of this when one realises the tremendous respect he has always borne for the Prime Minister. All his friends and family, I suspect, were also trying their best to persuade him to agree, but he stuck to his resolve.

On the evening of 31st March 1972, he had his last meeting with the Prime Minister. He returned home at about 10.00 pm and my wife and I were there waiting to hear the outcome. A smile, which did not quite conceal the hurt in his eyes and he told me:

"Well, it's all over! I retire with effect from 3rd April 1972. As the 2nd is a Sunday, tomorrow will be my last day in office. Dispose off all the staff by the 2nd, so that on the morning of 3rd April there will not be a single soldier here. We will take some days to pack up and vacate the house."

So, on 1st April, there were plenty of gloomy faces in the Secretariat as we went about our chores. At about 11.00 am, a handwritten envelope marked "Personal" and addressed to the Chief was handed to me. It was from the Prime Minister's Secretariat. I took it in, handed it over to him and waited while he read it. When he got up, it confirmed my suspicion that he had been summoned yet again. I walked down the corridor with him and, thinking I would have a last try, asked him to give in. "If the Prime Minister wishes you to continue," I added, "surely there must be a reason? Furthermore, you've made your position clear and so, if you agree to carry on, no one can point a finger at you."

He stopped, glared at me and roared: "Even you have joined them; you want me to give in. How will I be able to see my face in the mirror every morning? No, there is no question of my agreeing."

Resignedly, I returned to my office thinking it was worth a try, and never mind if it had failed.

The Chief returned at about 11.30 am and I followed him into his office. He looked at me with his usual smile and said:

"Ok, sweetheart, there is no change. I retire the day after tomorrow. Instead of today being my last day in office, I shall come in tomorrow even though it is a Sunday." With that he picked up his cap and cane and walked away, his step just as jaunty as ever, his carriage erect and a smile for everyone.

There was an Investiture in Rashtrapati Bhavan that evening: I was at home and, quite by chance, tuned in to hear the 3.00 pm news to hear if the retirement was being announced. You can imagine my delight when, instead of announcing the retirement, the announcer stated that it had been decreed that General Manekshaw "will continue in office at the President's pleasure, until further orders".

There was no way to contact him until 5.00 pm when the Investiture ended and so I waited at Army House. He got out of the car, smiled broadly when he saw me and asked if I had heard the news. When I told him that I had, the smile became broader. "Why didn't you tell me?" I asked. To which came the retort: "What day is it today?"

Glumly, I realised what he meant; it was April Fool's Day.

Political discussions with Pakistan started as soon as the war concluded. The Chief was invited to all meetings held in the

Ministries of External Affairs and Defence to formulate our case. One of the recommendations made by Army Headquarters was that the line known as the Ceasefire Line in Kashmir, drawn in 1949 after cessation of hostilities then, must be made more permanent and tangible; disputes must be settled on a bilateral basis in future with the United Nations Truce Observers recalled, and the line henceforth called the Line of Actual Control. From this we sought another advantage—a strategic one. Prior to this the existing quantum of forces in Kashmir could not be disturbed under the old agreement; if they were, the United Nations' Observers lodged a protest. Consequently, we were at a grave disadvantage as Pakistan, with its cantonments located conveniently close to the border could concentrate troops quickly at almost negligible cost, whereas for us to counter meant moving troops over vast distances; even moving a gun into Kashmir invited a ceasefire violation. A remedy for this was now sought.

While all this was being finalised, a formation commander in Kashmir created a tactical blunder by trying to occupy an area of no military significance without reference to his superiors. He compounded the blunder by not creating an adequate reserve and so, when Pakistan reacted, we lost two posts in the area of Kaiyan on our side of the ceasefire line. When further inquiries were made, it was revealed that the officer had taken that step because he had omitted to inform his higher headquarters of the fact that, despite claiming to have occupied some territory across the ceasefire line, he had actually not done so but had permitted the enemy to establish a small pocket in our territory. In the process of trying to rectify this omission on the quiet, he found himself losing a little more territory. I mention this incident merely to emphasise that reporting in war must be completely truthful as a lie here can have fatal consequences. Also, with this loss, Pakistan started crowing that when properly led, its soldiers were far superior to those in the Indian Army. As the result was there for all to see in this case, the incident did play a big part in raising Pakistani morale, badly shattered after December 1971.

In March 1972 the Simla Agreement was signed and, in this, one of the clauses accepted our viewpoint. In anticipation of this agreement, plans had already been made and based on these. Lieutenant General PS Bhagat, VC, the newly appointed Northern Army Commander, was nominated to represent the Indian Army with a team of officers at the joint talks that were held in turn across Wagah in Pakistan and at Suchetgarh in our territory to demarcate the Line of Control and decide on territorial gains and losses.

The Chief kept a very close watch on these talks, and it used to be amusing to hear when the party came back, that both Lieutenant General Bhagat and Lieutenant General Hamid Khan, who represented Pakistan, used to make identical excuses, "excuse me while I go round the corner", whenever they wished to refer a delicate point to their respective Chiefs. How they established contact from the washroom, I have no idea.

After a great deal of give and take, the chances of detente between India and Paksitan hinged on whether a small enclave which Pakistan had occupied, called Thakochak, should be returned to us or stay with Pakistan. The legal experts on both sides put up cases justifying the stand taken by their respective representatives, and so ticklish was the issue that both sides appeared to be correct. The Indian stand was that, as we had vacated a vast territory we had occupied in Sialkot and Sind, there was no obvious reason why Pakistan should retain the enclave it had occupied. The Pakistan stand was that one of the clauses of the Simla Agreement stipulated that all gains along the international border and cease fire line would be given up. Thakochak lay across what we call the International Border (south of Jammu). This was not accepted by Pakistan as they consider Kashmir to be theirs so there was no question of an international border. In their view, therefore, Thakochak lay neither across the cease fire line nor the international border.

Finally, the Cabinet decided that the two Army Chiefs should meet to sort out this problem. Very soon after this decision was taken, one morning I was startled to be told that there was a call from my opposite number in Pakistan, requesting that the Chief attend the telephone as General Tikka Khan wished to speak to him. I might clarify here that, after cessation of hostilities in December 1971, it had been decided by the two governments to reactivate a telephone line, that had long lain dormant, to connect the two operations rooms at Rawalpindi and New Delhi. It was on this line that we now talked. The Chief, unfortunately, was not in his office at that time and so I had to make an excuse and say that as soon as the Chief was located, I would ask him to speak to the Pakistani Chief. The meeting which the Chief was attending prolonged, however, and as he had not returned by 2.00 pm, I rang up Rawalpindi then to tell the Secretary (in the Pakistan Army, whom we call Military Assistant is known as Private Secretary to the Chief, in short PSC) that, as the Chief had still not returned, he would have to talk to General Tikka Khan the following morning or later that evening. Being Friday, I was sure his Chief would want to go for his prayers. The Chiefs spoke to each other later that evening and decided where to meet. We had asked for the meeting to be in Rawalpindi, but were told later by General Tikka Khan that he had deliberately kept it at Lahore as the public there was much more understanding and cosmopolitan than that of Rawalpindi. They feared trouble if Rawalpindi were kept as a venue.

A day or so later the Chief, the Director of Military Operations, one General Staff Officer Grade I from the Military Operations Directorate, one ADC, an attendant, a party of press correspondents and I left in an Indian Air Force aircraft for Lahore. We were received by General Tikka Khan, Lieutenant General

Hamid Khan, the Corps Commander who had represented Pakistan during their talks with Lieutenant General PS Bhagat, their DMO, the Pakistan Army Chief's Secretary, his ADC (who we learnt later also happened to be his son) and a horde of their press correspondents. After introductions, we were directed to cars that were parked on the tarmac and drove off to the peacetime location of their Corps Headquarters, which is about three kilometres from the airport.

I travelled with the Chief. The car, incidentally, was a beautiful black Cadillac and, during the course of conversation, I learnt that General Tikka Khan had flown from Rawalpindi that morning in his own aircraft of Pakistan Army Aviation, something lacking in our Army as the Army Aviation was to come much later.

On arrival at Corps Headquarters, a sumptuous tea was served; the service was superb and the waiters immaculate. Tea over, the two Chiefs and the DsMO adjourned to the conference room, where discussions started. I will not go into the lengthy discussions that took place, but suffice it to say that the talks were inconclusive.

Lunch was served in what is the Station Artillery Mess: in the Pakistan Army they have gone in for a system of having station officers' messes for reasons of economy. The Chief, as is his wont, went round the Mess to see the trophies and silver on display, of which there was an impressive array. Suddenly he stopped in front of a particular trophy and asked what a trophy of 54 Sikhs (his old Battalion) was doing in the Artillery Mess. Someone sheepishly admitted that it was in the Mess for the special occasion. At the bar I asked the immaculately clad barman if I could see some of the liquor produced in Pakistan. Unfortunately, he didn't have any readily available, but he did remark that Murree produced excellent beer (a claim which I can corroborate) and gin. Elaborating, he added that previously the officers used to drink Booths and Gordons Gin but now they drank Murree Gin *"Kion kih English Gin to sab Dacca men reh gai"* (Because the English gin was all left behind in Dacca). Barely able to conceal my laughter, I hurried out and I hope they were not too hard on the poor barman who had, I thought, made a rather witty remark.

We returned to Delhi where the stalemate was reported to the PM. The politicians and bureaucrats then got together again to solve the impasse, but to no avail, and finally the Chief was requested to visit his opposite number once again and sort this problem out once and for all. In her instructions to the Chief, the PM directed that, if need be, we should give up claims to Thakochak. Thereupon the Chief, naturally, asked that if this was the decision why did she not send her Foreign Minister. The reply was interesting: the country would accept such a decision coming from the Chief, not from a politician. The Chief's reaction was predictable: "She is making a monkey out of me, but it's for the country." The underlying (and unstated) urgency to resolve this minor irritant was to get on with implementation of the Simla Accord and thus provide Mr. ZA Bhutto the "space" he needed to establish his position and bring his country around to accepting the Line of Control as the International Border. Alas, Zia-ul-Haq had different plans.

We were all packed and ready to go to Tehran at the invitation of the Imperial Iranian Armed Forces Chief. For a change, I was accompanying the Chief on a foreign tour and so, naturally, I was not a little excited at the prospect. The Government's decision that the Iranian visit be postponed, however, and the Chief go to Pakistan upset all these dreams and so, on the appointed day it was at Lahore we landed instead of Tehran. Mrs. Manekshaw used to insist that as far as travelling abroad was concerned, I had a jinx on me. Obviously, she was right.

After a repeat of the earlier airport ceremony, we went to the same Corps Headquarters and talks started once again.

Finally, it boiled down to the following arguments:

One: the matter must be resolved as, if it was not, the whole world would laugh at us because two chiefs had not been able to solve their differences over a few kilometres of territory. If they could not sort out even this minor matter, how could we be expected to resolve bigger issues?

Two: since Thakochak had assumed such importance through the news media of both countries, it was imperative that, as a quid pro quo, we hand some area which was equally well known and in the limelight over to Pakistan.

There were some theatrics. For example, the Chief got up at one stage announcing that he saw no reason for continuing the discussion and he could not understand why he had even been called to Lahore if Pakistan had nothing concrete to offer. There was a brief break for lunch which we had, again, in the Artillery Brigade Officers' Mess. After lunch which was, if anything, even more sumptuous than on the previous occasion, we waited for coffee on the lawns and talk veered to the construction of officers' accommodation, a subject that coincidentally appeared to be dear to both Chiefs. The Chief was advocating the construction of multi-storeyed accommodation to conserve space, and General Tikka Khan favoured the bungalow type of accommodation where every house is single-storeyed and has its own compound, when suddenly the Chief said:

"You know, the reason I favour multi-storeyed accommodation is because we just don't have any land. If you have gone in for single-storeyed accommodation, it means you have plenty of land: if you do, why don't you give Thakochak back to me?" Tikka Khan was nodding his head in agreement while compliments were being showered upon him but suddenly stopped when the impact of the last sentence dawned upon him.

There was a moment's stunned silence and then everyone dissolved into laughter.

Eventually the dispute was amicably settled with Thakochak coming to us, and a small Indian enclave in the Kayian area (north of Srinagar), surrounded on three sides by Pakistan to go to that country. A press announcement approved by the two Chiefs was issued, and we started for the airport.

Whenever the Chief travelled out of Delhi, I carried a few presents which, if he so desired, he could give away. During the Lahore visit, I was carrying a couple of Indian watches made by Hindustan Machine Tools. I suggested the Chief give one to the driver, but the latter just wouldn't accept it despite all the persuasion by the Chief. Finally, General Tikka Khan was asked to intercede, and it was only when he did that the driver accepted the gift. As we settled in the aircraft for the return flight to Delhi and the engines roared to life, the Director of Military Operations, Major General Inderjit Singh Gill, a normally taciturn man not much given to sentimentality, echoed everybody's thought when he said, "I had heard that you were an absolute wizard at this sort of thing; today I was able to see that you really are."

I do not wish to enter into the ramifications of the business of Thakochak: getting it back was, indeed, no mean achievement. A soldier's actions are not supposed to be publicised, perhaps rightly so; consequently, the magnitude of the event received little publicity. In any case, the following day all of us who knew the inside story were disgusted to read a news item by the columnist, Kuldip Nayyar, stating that the Chief was to retire early in January 1973. So much for bouquets for a difficult job well done!

During the Chief's tenure as Eastern Army Commander, prior to 1969, he had finally secured permission to construct a new Military Hospital in Calcutta. Work on this began during 1970, and construction was completed in 1972. The then Eastern Army Commander, Lieutenant General JS Arora, persuaded Sam to perform the opening ceremony of the new building which everyone knew owed its origin and existence to the Chief. He agreed and whilst speaking at the opening ceremony, remarked:

"There has been a race between my retirement and completion

of this building. The former almost won, then the President was pleased to order me to continue in service, so I stand here today and perform this most pleasant task. Having done this, I now await the President's pleasure and, when I receive notice, I can retire a happy man."

Immediately after the ceremony concluded, when the guests began a guided tour of the new building, I started a furious race to meet each and every news correspondent that was covering the ceremony with a request to delete the "last one". Not one let me down!

I will now take the reader back to early 1972 for a few moments. On a date prior to 26th January 1972, the Prime Minister had ordered that the Army Chief be promoted to the rank of Field Marshal and appointed Chief of Defence Staff, and that the announcement be made on the morning of Republic Day, 26th January 1972. For some unfathomable reason, this was not done. Thereupon the Prime Minister directed that the announcement be made on the morning of 28th January 1972 as the Chief and the other two Service Chiefs were being awarded the Padma Vibhushan that afternoon. This, too, fell through and nothing more was heard by us. Over the years the bureaucracy has evolved a perfect system to stall what, to them, is an unwholesome direction. A very simple expedient is resorted to: a point concerning one service will be referred to the other two services and views sought. If one or both service headquarters send a negative reply, the project is consigned to the dustbin as being "unacceptable to the other service headquarters". I have no doubt that this proposal, too, met this fate as though the Navy was agreable to Sam's promotion as Chief of Defence Staff, the Air Force was vehemently against it. Citing as a very unconvincing reason that this would amount to belittling the Air Force achievements. Anyway, around mid-December 1972, the matter was raked up again.

This time, whether it was the Prime Minister's insistence or the fact that the appointment of Chief of Defence Staff was not proposed in the "packet", saw old objections mysteriously disappear and, on 28th December, while the Chief was visiting Kerala in response to a Rotarian invitation and I was in Delhi, preparing for a pleasant afternoon of reading in the sun, a call came from the Joint Secretary (G) in the Defence Ministry who asked me to drop by his office. When I did so, I was given the news that the Government had approved the promotion and that it would take effect from 1st January 1973. Did I know how the investiture should be organised? Did I know what badges of rank were to be worn? Did I know anything about the baton that Field Marshals were supposed to carry?

Putting forth my most confident manner, I answered all queries in the affirmative, and then took my leave hurriedly to engage in a hasty bit of research including a quick overseas call to our Assistant Military Adviser in London, Vinod Badhwar. I then proceeded to order the badges of rank and, as a temporary expedient, a baton worked in silver. Even the stationery was ordered for delivery on the evening of 31st December. To maintain secrecy, while ordering the baton and badges of rank, I explained that these were for presentation by the Chief to Field Marshal Surendra Bahadur Shaha of Nepal, a very close friend of the Chief and one who had beaten the latter to the rank by about fifteen days. The Stationer, Devinder Khanna of New Delhi Stationery Mart, Connaught Place had to be told the truth of course, but he did not let me down.

While talking to Vinod Badhwar, I had asked him to let me have the specifications and design of a British Field Marshal's baton. As an afterthought I had added that if he could "pick one up somewhere", he might send it over. When he called back the next day I was startled to hear that batons in London were made to order and each cost £1000 and then with, I suppose, tongue-in-cheek he enquired whether I still wanted one. I declined hastily, and then repeated that I did not want one in case the vagaries of the overseas communication system had given him the impression that I did.

The formal announcement was made on 31st December 1972: it made the Secretariat Staff's day and we had a glorious New Year's Eve. The next day, the Chief came to the office sporting the Field Marshal's badges of rank, again in black, and five stars were now displayed on his car. Congratulations poured in and, as usual, each message had to be answered: a never-ending nightmare for the very hard-pressed Personal Assistants, but they bore the strain remarkably well. There were letters and telegrams from people from all walks of life; a very touching one from the UK Field Marshal Sir Claude Auchinlek, an ex-Commander-in-Chief: "From one Field Marshal to another, may I say how delighted I am." The joy of the Chief's promotion was for me, at least, tinged with a little sorrow, because I knew that it had been decided that he would relinquish office (not retire, as Field Marshals remain on the active list) on 15th January 1973.

The matter of announcing this was solved by him in his own inimitable manner. On 3rd January 1973, while addressing an investiture parade at Lucknow after he had pinned Sena and Vishisht Seva Medals on some eighty officers and men who, among others, had distinguished themselves during the war in December 1971, he broke away from the text I had prepared, and in so doing, hurt me not a little, stating:

"I've worked very hard and now I am tired. So, I have asked the Prime Minister to let me go. I shall relinquish office on 15th January 1973."

Needless to say, Lucknowites were most distressed over this news and, consequently, dinner that evening in the Command Officers Mess was a very subbued affair. Lieutenant General H.K. Sibal, MVC, the Army Commander, in proposing a toast to the

Chief, praised both his leadership and his other qualities. In replying, the Chief thanked the host for his kind words and his hospitality and then said:

"A man in the Army is what his seniors have made him. If I have attained this position, it is because I have had excellent teachers: there is one here this evening, to whom I owe a debt I can never repay—Major General Hira Lal Atal."

General Atal, a retired General Officer settled in Lucknow, had been sipping his liqueur while the speeches were going on and this last remark brought him up short. Tears came in his eyes and he could hardly speak, so moved was he, as he went up and embraced the Chief.

In the first week of January 1973, the Government decided that Lieutenant General G.G. Bewoor, PVSM, the Southern Army commander, would be the next Army Chief in succession to the Field Marshal who would relinquish office on 15th January 1973. I might add here that the Chief's choice, which he could only convey to the Prime Minister verbally, was Lieutenant General P.S. Bhagat, VC. Mrs. Gandhi was, however, under tremendous pressure from Mr. Y.B. Chavan to grant General Bewoor an extension beyond his retirement date and appoint him as COAS. During one discussion on the subject between the Chief and the Prime Minister, she mentioned that one reason why Bewoor was preferred over Bhagat was that the latter was pro-Sikh. On the Chief's asking how this conclusion was reached, she remarked that there were numerous photographs of Bhagat with Sikh troops. The Chief's explanation that Bhagat, being a Colonel of the Sikh Light Infantry, naturally appeared in these photographs, evidently was not accepted.

I think it was on the 2nd or 3rd January that a note was handed over to me. It came from the Ministry and sought the Chief's approval to the announcement it was intending to make that evening over the radio and to the press, announcing the name of the new chief. I showed this note to the Chief who asked me to take it back to the Joint Secretary (G) who had initiated it, with a request that the announcement be made the following evening as the Chief himself wished to ring up General Bewoor the next morning to break the news and congratulate him. I walked across and saw the official concerned and conveyed the request to him. Why, he wanted to know, was it necessary for the Chief to telephone General Bewoor when this should really be done by the Government. When I asked him whether the Field Marshal was not equally a part of the same Government, I got the reply that Government meant the Defence Secretary. On my pointing out that if the Chief was a soldier so the secretary was a bureaucrat and the government really meant the elected representative of the people who in this case should be the Defence Minister, I was given a baleful glare and the cryptic answer that we should not quibble over such matters. What mattered was that the announcement was made the next day after the Chief spoke to Bewoor.

The last few days were spent in perusing old files, extracting some letters I thought the Chief would like to retain and destroying the remainder. Each member of staff was asked where he would like to be posted; instructions were issued accordingly. When my turn came, I was asked my choice and, as I was in the promotion zone, I suggested that I had better go and command a brigade in a field area as I had done four years in Delhi. "Nonsense", he said, "your task here has been no bed of roses and you can go wherever you wish." In the event, I did not go where I wanted, but was sent where the Service wished me to go.

10

Making Way for New Beginnings

Once it was decided that the Field Marshal would relinquish office on 15th January 1973, various other problems started to rear their heads. First of all was the actual time of relinquishment as the Chief of the Air Staff, Air Chief Marshal PC Lal, was also scheduled to retire on 15th January 1973. The Government desired that the Army Chief relinquish office first, so that his successor could take over as Chairman, Chiefs of Staff Committee by virtue of seniority in office. For the brief interval, in between, the Chief of Naval Staff, Admiral Nanda, would hold the appointment till he retired. This was resolved by timing the successions so that the new Army Chief took over in the morning and the new Air Chief was appointed that afternoon.

Next was the matter of pay and privileges, such as house, staff, guard, flag and car. In the British system, a field marshal is technically put on half pay on relinquishing office; actually he is given one of the many appointments British ingenuity has devised. By virtue of the appointment the incumbent enjoys all the perks of office. This was unacceptable here, however, as half pay would mean Rs. 2250, which was more than a retired President or a retired Chief Justice received at the time. Next, if the amount the government finally decided on was called "pay" then neither was commutation of pension possible nor technically at least, could the Provident Fund finally be withdrawn and the account closed. The amount could not be called a "pension", because a field marshal never retires. This impasse was resolved by naming it the monthly pension of a General, Rs. 1200, plus an honorarium of Rs. 400 special to the rank of Field Marshal.

A case was presented to the Government by Army Headquarters suggesting that the Field Marshal be authorised a small secretariat, a ceremonial guard at his residence to pay appropriate compliments to the residential flag, a staff car, and a house in Delhi. This was turned down; pettiness at its ugliest.

The Field Marshal was granted the six months' leave he was entitled to and permitted, during the period of this leave, to occupy a government house. No house offered was fit for occupation, however, and so those few which were offered were turned down. After a few days in Army House, the Manekshaws moved to the Military Engineering Services Inspection Bungalow in Delhi Cantonment. Here they were to stay until 15th July 1973 when, on completion of the six months' leave, they left for Coonoor in the Nilgiris where their own house was under construction. Coincidentally, this date also coincided with the ugly controversy that broke at the time. More of this later.

During February 1973, when news of their moving to the Inspection Bungalow was intimated to the Prime Minister, she wished to know why the Army House had been vacated when alternative accommodation was not available. It was explained that Army House is traditionally the residence of the Army Chief and it would hardly be correct to deny him this. A little later the Minister for Housing wrote to the Field Marshal regretting the delay in allotment of a house and explaining that with the appointment of seven new ministers and ministers of state at the centre, the lack of suitable houses had become even more acute.

Prior to this, the Prime Minister, in a bid to circumvent the earlier impasse created by the news of his being appointed Chief of Defence Staff, had suggested to the Field Marshal that he accept a new job under creation, namely, Member Defence in the Planning Commission with Minister of State status. He had accepted the offer and it was for this reason that he remained in Delhi after relinquishing office: had it not been so, he would have moved down to Coonoor immediately after he relinquished office as his advice had always been:

"After retirement, get away from the scene of action, as your remaining there can mean embarrassment to both parties."

He was hardly the man to disregard his own advice and so, if he stayed in Delhi, there must obviously have been some pressing reasons. How the job offer was withdrawn or was declined will be explained a little later.

Though he had relinquished office on 15th January 1973, the volume of correspondence continued at its old rate. The public had read somewhere that a Field Marshal never retires, so it was generally assumed that he was continuing as Chief of Army Staff, too. Consequently, requests for postings, complaints, and articulation of various types of problems continued to arrive in a never-ending stream. He insisted that every letter be answered even if the reply stated that the letter was being passed to the Chief of the Army Staff. I was on four months' leave from 1st February 1973 onwards, so mornings used to mean a visit to my old office to collect the mail and sort it out, get letters ready for signature by the Field Marshal, and then a trip to the Inspection Bungalow to show him all these and get his approval for sundry other points. I am cynical enough to have expected someone in the secretariat staff to have pleaded "rush of work" or some such excuse to avoid what I was giving them at this time as the ex-

Military Assistant was taxing them a great deal over their own full-time jobs. To their credit, however, not once did anyone even venture an excuse, thereby confirming my admiration for those very fine staff members.

I might explain here the circumstances under which I was granted four months' leave as the annual authorisation is two months. In 1971, owing to the imminence of war, personnel who could not take leave were permitted to carry it forward to 1972. Consequently, I started the four months' leave on 31 December 1972, recalled myself to be on duty on 1 January 1973, and restarted my leave with effect from some date after 15 January. My leave bonanza did not end here: later in the year, while commanding a brigade (and working on this manuscript), I was offered two more months due for 1973!

On 26th January 1973 came the announcement that I was awarded the Vishisht Seva Medal for my little part in the 1971 campaign and afterwards. The Chief had meant to keep this secret and not let me know. The cat was let out of the bag in early January, however, when the names had been passed through me for discussion by the Chief with the Ministry of Defence. I respected the secret. Incidentally, during this period my unofficial designation, which even the telephone directory somehow carried, was the high-sounding title—Military Assistant to the Field Marshal. Very soon after the award was announced, I was asked by the wife of the Australian Military Adviser at a party what the letters VSM stood for. She was delighted to hear my reply that they stood for "Very Sweet Man".

After relinquishing office, the Field Marshal was driven around in an ancient black Dodge from the pool that provides transport for Army Headquarters and visitors to it, named, in Army parlance, Army Headquarters Transport Company. The driver was still the faithful Naik Kani Ram who must have remembered nostalgically the automobiles of more recent vintage that he had driven previously

At a party in DSOI,Delhi.On Sam's left is Mrs. Korla, wife of Maj Gen S.K. Korla,DSO, MC. In the background ADM Nanda

The author being introduced to His Majesty the King of Nepal

Three Commanding Officers of 4th Battalion, the 8th Gorkha Rifles

Sam and Silloo with Officers and families of 4/8 GR in Shillong

Sam as GOC-in-C Eastern Command presenting the
Command Football Championship Trophy to the author who
was then Commanding 4/8 GR in Shillong

Sam on visit to Basanter through Minefields (1 Corp-Sialkot Sector)

H.E. the Ambassador of Thailand who formed the
Whisky Brandy Club, showing the evening offers.

Sam & the author with Jem Padam Singh, MC, under whom
Hav Lacchman Gurung won the VC in May 1945 at Taungdow in Burma

COAS, Pakistan, General Tikka Khan
welcoming Sam at Lahore Airport

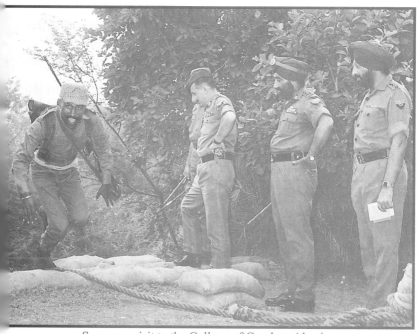

Sam on a visit to the College of Combat. Also in
the picture is Maj General Onkar Singh Kalkat, the Commandant

COAS visits Ferozpur and Fazilka Sector. Behind him,GOC
11 CORPs, Lt Gen NC Rawlley MC

Distributing prizes at the conclusion of
the Gorkha Brigade Boxing Championship

COAS visits the Rajasthan Sector. To the right is the GOC-in-C
Southern Command, Lt Gen GG Bewoor

COAS visits Amritsar Sector on 19.2.72. On the extreme
right is Major (Late Maj Gen) SD Sood the ADC

COAS visits Amritsar Sector on 19.2.72

COAS visits Amritsar Sector on 19.2.72

India Pak Army Chief meeting at Lahore

India Pak Army Chief meeting at Lahore

War memorial inauguration, IMA, Dehra Dun.

The COAS visits the author's Battalion 4/8 GR in the area of
Badrinath (UP-Tibet Border)

COAS visits Amritsar Sector on 19.2.72 with Sikh Troops - it was
'SATSIRIAKAL' 'PIND KERA HAI'(Where is your
Village?) 'SINGHNI KITHE HAI' (Where is the family?)

The COAS visits 15 CORPS in J&K with 5/8 GR

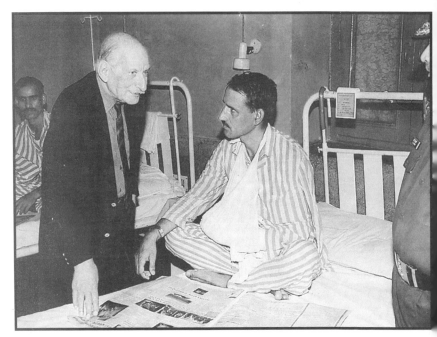

Visiting the base hospital, Delhi Cantonment, to console casualties of the Kargil Battle

Mrs. Manekshaw with wives of Officers of 5/8 GR Yol Cantt Mrs. Depinder Sing
2nd from left, standing on her left is Maja, on her right is Sherry

Consoling a Kargil Battle casualty at the Army Hospital

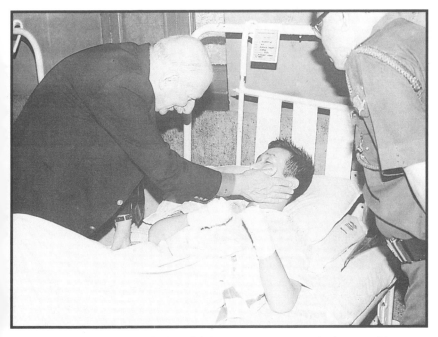

Visiting the base hospital, Delhi Cantonment, to console the casualties
from the Kargil Battle

The Field Marshal inaugurating the
Golden Jubilee Celebrations of his Alma Mater,
The Indian Military Academy, Dehra Dun
March 1982

The Field Marshal (then COAS) taking the Salute at
the Passing out Parade, March 1972

Field Marshal in conversation with Lt (now Brig) RK Arora and his parents at the Commandants House, IMA in March 1972. Maj Gen AA Rudra is also in the picture.

Pride of Flags

Padma Buhshan by Dr. Zakir Hussain - OUR NATIONAL HERO

Mementoes from Civil and Military Organisations and Awards

Mementoes from the Border Security Force

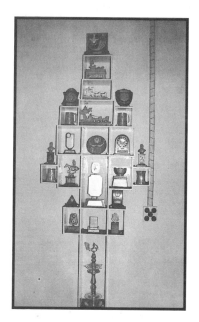

Mementoes from various Clubs

Presents by his Regiment - 8 GR

Entrance to the Manekshaw Museum located in Happy Valley, Shillong

Visitors book: at the entrance

Mementoes presented by Lacchman Gurung, VC, 4/8 GR

whenever he tinkered with the old and sorely battered engine of his present charge. The Field Marshal had been requested to flag off the Delhi Vintage Car Rally in 1973. He had agreed to this, and had also agreed with my suggestion to grant five minutes to a very persistent young gentleman who wanted to record an interview for Delhi Television. The interview was fixed for the afternoon just before Mrs. Manekshaw distributed the prizes and the interviewer had all his questions written down to avoid fumbling and off-the-cuff improvisations.

The first question was:

"Field Marshal, you must be interested in vintage cars which explains your presence here: but tell me, are you thinking of acquiring a vintage car?"

He wasn't quite prepared for the answer which was:

"Oh yes, indeed, I am most interested in vintage cars. As far as acquiring one is concerned I don't have to go very far, as the Defence Ministry have been kind enough to give me a vintage car for my use which I am running these days."

That finished the interview, however, because the interviewer just couldn't stop laughing.

In March 1973 the Field Marshal and Mrs. Manekshaw were invited by the British Chief of General Staff to visit the UK. He asked for permission for two officers of his choice to accompany him. This was not agreed to by the Government who suggested that two officers from the staff of our High Commission in the UK should accompany him instead. When the British Military Adviser in New Delhi, Major General L. Scott Bowden, asked where the Field Marshal would like to go during the visit, there was only one demand; could he visit the battalion he was commissioned into, 2nd Battalion, the Royal Scots. This was arranged and, as he told me later, he was delighted to see them. The historic letter referred to in Chapter I, was a consequence of this visit.

While on such visits, the Chief is expected to host a reception or dinner in the country visited. The reception the Field Marshal hosted was a grand affair and among the guests were all officers, serving and retired, who had some association with the 8th Gorkha Rifles and 54 Sikh.

In late January 1973 he gave an interview to a representative of *Dateline Delhi*, a New Delhi weekly. As this was to create a tremendous furore later in the year, I shall dwell on the matter in a little more detail to explain what happened, not to put forward excuses as they are not necessary. The uproar was triggered off by some comments attributed to the Field Marshal that appeared as a news item in practically every daily in the country in the month of April 1973. The reader is requested to note two significant facts in this regard. One: nearly every daily carried this report, and two: it appeared in April, just before Parliament debated the Defence Budget. The obvious conclusion is that the report was masterminded by someone inimical to the Field Marshal; otherwise how can one explain reference to this remark in every newspaper and agency report. The news item contained the following alleged remarks:

One: "London is my favourite city as I feel at home there."

Two: "Jinnah had asked me to join the Pakistan Army in 1947. If I had, you would have had a defeated India."

During the Defence Debate in Parliament, some Members of Parliament raised this issue, and remarks that appeared in the book "Fighting General" by Tom Pocock were quoted showing that the subject of the book, General Sir Walter Walker of the British Army, and the Field Marshal had met while the former was passing through Delhi when each had expressed similar views about politicians and the amount of interference they should be allowed in defence matters. Having read thus far, the reader may judge whether the Field Marshal could ever be accused of doubting the supremacy of the elected representatives. He could not tolerate interference in routine matters, however, as discipline would certainly have suffered had he allowed it, and an Army without discipline is merely a rabble.

Coming back to the interview with *Dateline Delhi*, the first question was:

"Field Marshal, which is your favourite city?" The exchange went on something like this:

FM: "In India or abroad?"

Q: "The whole world."

FM: "My favourite city abroad is London, as I feel at home there. I know the language and the people, and they know me."

How much difference the ommission of one word makes!

Now, to the second remark. This was certainly made as it appeared in print, but the context? It was said in jest, and if anyone expected an interview with Sam Manekshaw to be a dull, mundane affair, he or she was in for a surprise. His ready wit finds expression in practically every sentence he utters.

When he was accused of trying to corner all the glory for the victory and to imply that he alone was singlehandedly responsible for the events of 1971, did anyone point out the charming, congratulatory letters he wrote to the other two Services Chiefs after the ceasefire in December 1971, extolling the achievements of the Air Force and the Navy? Did anyone recall his oft-repeated statements about how much his task was aided by the help, co-operation and guidance he received from every quarter, particularly the Prime Minister and the Defence Ministry? No, no one remembered that, unfortunately, so it was obvious that the aim was to crucify him.

The next question that arises is, why? The answer to this must wait until further facts are available, when I am certain that the truth will surface. However, one can speculate on the basis of circumstantial straws. First: the Defence Minister, Babu Jagjivan Ram, had often hinted to the Chief, who enjoyed enormous popularity at the time, that the latter "join" him. The Chief had understood the motive which was to align with the minister against the Prime Minister, but he chose to deflect his answer by appearing to misinterpret the suggestion. He would reply on the lines that as Chief he was already joined to his Minister. The latter resented this rebuff. Second: the Prime Minister, all her many virtues notwithstanding, was basically a very insecure person. Any perceived rival was axed. So when the controversy orchestrated by the Defence Ministry broke, she, who could have silenced the critics with one interjection or statement, chose to keep quiet, thus removing from the scene an imagined alternate centre of power.

While this unsavoury controversy was raging, the Field Marshal was, as mentioned earlier, on an official visit to the United Kingdom as the guest of an old friend, the British Chief of General Staff, General Sir Michael Carver. I know that he was under considerable pressure from his innumerable friends and well-wishers at this time to issue a press statement to correct what had been published beforehand. I also know that his quality of hitting back when he felt that injustice was being perpetrated must also have been severely strained. But true gentleman that he is, he refused to do anything, secure in the knowledge that his political masters, if no one else, would correct the mistaken impression that was being created. Alas, he was to be proved wrong; no one spoke in his defence.

I left Delhi on posting to command a brigade in May 1973: consequently, I was not there when he returned from the visit to the United Kingdom. But I did take a few days off in June to go and see him. Apart from a touch of bitterness, which had crept in (and who can blame him for that?), he appeared as full of bounce as ever. He confided that it was not the criticism which had hurt him but the fact that no one had spoken in his defence and, "if they cannot defend me, a Field Marshal, what security does a junior officer have?" He did write a letter to the Prime Minister telling her how hurt he was over her inexplicable silence.

What effect this controversy had on the job the government planned to give him, I know not. I can only assume that it did have an adverse effect because nothing more was heard of the original offer. Some offers to head a Public Sector Undertaking were made, but he rejected them as, "I don't want to spend my time asking my subordinates where to sign."

The Manekshaws left Delhi on 15th July 1973 for Coonoor where they stayed with their friends, the Cawas Patels, while the finishing touches were given to their own house. In a letter written from Coonoor, he mentioned that pressure reminiscent of the Bangladesh days is maintained here on everyone to get the house and grounds ready soon "so that we can move in".

All gifts and presents he had received over the years, some of his old uniforms, mementoes, and his papers were all passed on to the 58 Gorkha Training Centre, home of the Regiment he loved and for which he has done so much. The Regimental Centre now houses all these in a room called the "Sam Bahadur Room" where visitors to Dehradun (later on, Shillong) can see the maestro's last touch of graciousness towards his Regiment.

11

The Nilgiris

While commanding the Defence Services Staff College in Wellington in the Nilgiris, the Manekshaws had bought a portion of a hilly spur above the road outside Coonoor. Here they built their house calling it Stavka, in memory of his visit to the Soviet Union. Normally, a house gets furnished to suit the design and construction; here the house was designed to accomodate all the bric-a-brac Mrs. Manekshaw had accumulated so painstakingly over the years. A call on Stavka was sure to end in a tour with the Field Marshal explaining the layout and the antecedents of various pieces. It generally ended with a door being quietly opened onto a group of Gorkha ladies and children, spouses and offspring of the staff, watching some TV programme, a daily evening ritual. In 1999 a small cottage was constructed on the premises; a gift to one of the oldest members of the staff. "How much did the cottage cost?" I asked him. "More than the main house did," he answered.

By the time the Manekshaws were settled in their new home in Coonoor, there was a re-shuffle of union ministers: Mr. Bansi

Lal, an old friend from Haryana where he had been a very successful Chief Minister, was appointed Defence Minister. Among his first orders were the directions to provide a small staff to the Field Marshal and proper reception, transport and accommodation arrangements whenever he visited any defence station. These elementary facilities and courtesies had been denied earlier, apparently at the behest of Mr. Jagjivan Ram. To digress in lighter vein, at one of their meetings, after he moved to Delhi, Mr. Bansi Lal asked Sam to explain the difference between a gun and a howitzer. This was explained and Sam asked why Mr. Bansi Lal, as Defence Minister, did not ask the Army Chief. Mr. Bansi Lal's reply was typical of the rustic Jat: "If I ask the Chief, he will think I am ignorant."

The private sector, ever in a hurry, were not ones to ignore a man of his stature. Consequently, offers of directorship and chairmanships came in a flood. He accepted whatever he could not refuse. Even then the number was formidable, resulting in his confiding to me that he could manage only five to eight days every month in his home; the rest were spent in hotels attending board meetings or, as he did with the East India Hotels, serving on Selection Boards to screen candidates for jobs with the Oberoi Hotel Chain.

Never one to forget old friends, he invited me to join a couple of boards which he was chairing and it used to be a pleasure to meet him frequently and see him conducting business with the same erudition, clarity of thought, and lucidity of expression all mixed with wit and humour, as in the days in uniform. On each such board meeting, he would ensure that he and I had one meal together where the menu invariably consisted of fried rice and prawns followed by a dessert of dates and ice-cream, all preceded by one, never more than two, whisky and sodas.

In 1977, Mr. Morarji Desai, then Prime Minister, asked Sam to head the Sports Authority of India. Nothing of note occurred during this tenure. Later, sometime in 1996, Mr. Narsimha Rao, asked him to join the board of the Indian Red Cross. At the first meeting he attended, when the Health Minister, who chaired the Board, made his concluding remarks and got up to leave, he was asked when the next meeting would be held.

Minister: "In September."

Sam: "September has thirty days, which day?"

The Minister gave a certain date; the meeting did not take place and, thereafter, it was an interminable wait for a meeting to be held regularly.

He was a Director with Escorts when Mr. Swaraj Paul made his famous takeover bid. Alarmed, the Government stepped in and changed the complete board leading to the famous remark: "This is the first time in history when a Naik has displaced a Field Marshal." The pun: Mr. Naik was the man who replaced him. "Naik" is also corporal in the Indian Army.

What did I learn from this man? The first lesson was that it is a lonely perch on the top branch as doubts assail major decisions. These get exacerbated as so-called well-wishers start their, "we could have done it this way". However, he acquitted himself with equanimity, poise, confidence and dignity. With the extraordinary vision he had developed, he would have made a brilliant Chief of Defence Staff. Even more than the professional angle, very healthy precedents would have been set in as far as relations are concerned between the Chief of Defence Staff and the Prime Minister on the one hand and between the former and the three service Chiefs. It is the country's misfortune that this was not to be.

The second lesson was that of loyalty; loyalty to subordinates, peers and superiors. In 1971, after the Pakistani crackdown in the erstwhile East Pakistan, orders had been issued that an old favourite, Major General Vir Vohra would be the Director of Military Operations. At the time, however, he was on a course of instruction in the UK at the Royal College of Defence Studies (equivalent to our National Defence College). Major General I.S. Gill who was Director of Military Training came to officiate as Director of Military Operations when Major General K.K. Singh proceeded on promotion to Command 1 Corps. So we had a peculiar situation where, on the eve of war, we had an officiating Director of Military Operations, the most vital of directorates in the planning and conduct of operations. I mentioned this anomaly to him just before the outbreak of war and he told me that he had promised Vir Vohra this particular appointment. On my pointing out that loyalty and promises must be subordinated to professional requirements, however, he ordered the Military Secretary to confirm Inder Gill as Director Military Operations.

The next quality that stood out was character. Witness the manner in which he stood up to the Prime Minister and the Council of Ministers to stress the need to delay commencement of operations against East Pakistan when the politicians were, for equally valid reasons, almost all for immediate military intervention. Flowing from this, it is interesting to speculate what course of events would have taken if the Prime Minister had chosen to disregard his advice. Knowing him, I am certain that he would have resigned.

Years later I was to learn another lesson in character. It was asked of me and the Brigade I was commanding to disarm the Sikkim Guards in 1975 when Sikkim was merged with the Union. The Chogyal was a personal friend of Sam's and also an Honorary Major General in my Regiment. During my stay in Sikkim he had been most kind to us, always extending warm and generous hospitality. Therefore, when the task of disarming the Guards came to me, it was performed with a sadness of heart. After the event, I stayed away from the Palace as I felt that I would not be able to face the Chogyal. A few days later a niece of the Chogyal came to see me and enquired why I had not been to see him. I made the usual excuses of having been out of town and so on and was on my way out immediately after the meeting. She heard me out and then stated that the Chogyal, in sending her, had mentioned that I would make the same excuses. She continued she had a message from her uncle, however, which went something like this. He understood that I was given a task and, as a soldier, I had to carry it out. If I had refused, somebody else would have been found to do it. Therefore, he understood my compulsions and bore no grudge; he invited me to see him. I did and we both embraced, and had a good cry on each other's shoulder.

Sam was an intensely practical, down-to-earth man and the following incident will serve to illustrate this. The Army has many stringent rules in regard to contact with foreign nationals. Some of these are quite absurd but no one is willing to effect change. One day saw the Director of Military Intelligence, Major General D.K. Chandorkar, meeting the Chief with a complaint that, despite existing orders, many junior officers were meeting foreign nationals. There was urgency in the complaint as the December 1971 war with Pakistan was around the corner. I happened to be in the Chief's office at the time and saw what happened next. The first direction from the Chief to the DMI was "sit down". The Chief went on, "Let us take a specific incident: My ADC gets invited by the US Defence Attache for a meal. The Attache will ply him with drink and it is on the cards that the youngster will get drunk. The Attache will attempt to extract whatever information he can and then bid the Aide goodbye. What will the Attache do next?" he questioned. The DMI, quite bemused with the direction his simple complaint had taken, muttered that he did not know. "I will tell you" said the Chief. "He will spend the rest of the night, pulling out his hair trying to decipher what the Aide had told him." The solution lay, the Chief always stressed, in maintaining security of information on a need-to-know basis. These officers would have sufficient experience to be able to withstand any allurements that may be offered.

I mentioned earlier that some of the security orders were absurd. I will amplify. While I was MA, the Chief had given me carte-blanche to meet and interact with any of the foreign diplomats serving in Delhi. Consequently, many friendships were forged. After 15th January 1973 when Sam relinquished office, I handed over my job to the new incumbent and then started to enjoy my accumulated annual leave. During this, contact with foreign friends continued. After about a month I got a letter from the Military Intelligence Directorate stating that my car had been noticed parked outside so and so diplomat's house. My attention was drawn to para X (or whatever) of the Rules: I was to desist from such contact. I replied briefly that while I was MA, I was privy to all the secrets and there was no bar on my meeting foreign nationals. Now, when I was no longer privy to classified information, how had I suddenly become a threat? I concluded by stating that during the previous four years I had developed friendships and these could not be severed while I was still in Delhi; after I left Delhi these contacts would automatically dry up. I heard nothing more on the subject.

He was considerate to a fault. Once Major General Z.C. Bakshi (Zoru to his friends), a very highly decorated soldier and one of our better leaders, was commanding the Nagaland division. For compassionate reasons he wanted a posting to Jammu. The division here had recently been taken over by Major General K.V. Krishna Rao, who later rose to be Army Chief. Convinced about the genuineness of Zoru's request, no summary postings were issued; instead, the Chief telephoned Krishna Rao, explained the problem and asked if it would be all right to swap stations with Zoru. Who can refuse to comply or grudge the change when the problem is tackled with such grace? It was such acts which won him friends and earned him their loyalty. When Field Marshal Carriappa was promoted, the Government through some perverse sense of discourtesy, announced it as an Honorary appointment. Sam was the first to point out this discourtesy to the Government and the word "Honorary" was quickly withdrawn.

He was incredibly receptive to ideas that had merit: once while accompanying him to attend an Ex-servicemen's rally, I mentioned that soldiers from non-technical arms needed to be provided vocational training prior to retirement to better equip them for the post-retirement period. He agreed and in his speech to the rally announced that vocational training was being started. On return from the rally, the point was conveyed to staff at Army Headquarters with directions to expedite commencement of vocational training. This is how vocational training started in the Army.

I learnt that, since everyone is paid, every man has to perform 100% in his job. "Passengers" have no place in the service and if any exist, they must be got rid of at the earliest to make place for someone who works. A commander must delegate to avoid getting enmeshed in detail to the detriment of his primary function of guiding, thinking ahead and retaining a clear head. Delegation also provides another essential element of leadership—bringing up of subordinates to assume higher responsibility with competence. He must strike a reasonable balance between, sitting in his office and visiting field formations and units. Subordinates must know that the commander is there to guide and help, not to terrorise. Above all, I learnt of the virtue of humility and how, as one rises in rank, concern and tolerance for others around increases correspondingly.

Witty, articulate and knowledgeable as he has always been, he was a popular speaker, deluged with requests to deliver talks on diverse subjects. The Defence Services Staff College, his neighbour, and the College of Combat at Mhow were "regulars" who asked him over at least once a year. Excerpts of a talk he delivered at the staff college in 1998 on the subject of leadership are given in

Appendix II. In the question and answer session that follows the talk, he opens up with details of the enquiry that was ordered against him in 1962.

The Philosopher Isaiah Berlin once remarked that one should never underestimate the role of shame and humiliation in human affairs. Another great trait Sam displayed was that of turning away from revenge to justice and dignity. The court of enquiry ordered against him in 1962 and the delay in his promotion could have made him vengeful; in fact not one officer who testified against him was victimised or harassed. When someone who has been shamed and humiliated refuses to inflict his pain and anguish on others, we witness moral greatness and the creation of an aura that endures. Power, in a normal human being, can generate passion; in his case, passion was the agent that provided the power.

Monty Palit in his book, *War in the High Himalayas: The Indian Army in Crisis, 1962*, makes some caustic remarks concerning Sam Manekshaw's advice to defer operations against East Pakistan in 1971 and Indira Gandhi's acceptance of this advice. He states that this decision inflicted untold misery upon the people of East Pakistan and was an undeserved indictment of the officers and men (implying an inability to readjust, at short notice from the election duties formations were then supervising to operations against a first class enemy); and even a severe self-indictment on the part of Sam Manekshaw as he had been, by that time, Chief for two years.

To begin with, if the 1962 conflict threw up any lesson, it was that all preparations must be complete before operations are launched. The 1962 debacle was a direct consequence of this precept being violated. It is surprising, to say the least, that Monty Palit of all people (he was Director Military Operations at the time) should come up with this criticism. Secondly, a Chief has to view the situation not only from the narrow prism of military affairs, but has also to concern himself with the political ramifications. In April 1971, the world was still convinced that the crackdown was an internal affair for Pakistan. This perception had to be altered by proving that, in fact, India was the victim and unless correction was applied diplomatically, there would be no other alternative for India but to resolve it militarily. This process needed time so that the Indian position could be explained in all the capitals of the world. Then there was the Chinese angle. Intervention in April 1971 would have been an open invitation to China to overtly assist Pakistan and justify its action on the pretext that India had committed aggression against a smaller neighbour. Fourthly, due to a near total absence of infrastructure in Tripura, it would not have been possible to launch major operations from that direction, leaving only the Northern and Western axes; a strategically unacceptable course of action. Then there was also the weather consideration and the need to get Pakistan to disperse its forces in East Pakistan to facilitate the major offensive. Intervention in April 1971, therefore, may have won us the battle, but we would have lost the political and diplomatic war and the goodwill of the world.

I have attempted to describe some of the attributes of this great man that endeared him to the rank and file, and earned him worldwide fame and respect. There must assuredly be many more, and the point to note is: no one view can hope to comprehend so large a man.

Colour Presentation at Nasirabad on 09-12-1970

COAS visit to 14 GTC Sobatu

At social functions, he seldom stayed in one place, preferring instead to mingle and converse with the maximum number of guests.

COAS's visit to PARA Brigade & PARA unit in Agra

COAS addressing Indian POWs on their repatriation
from Pakistan on 26-12-1972

Command Hospital Foundation laying ceremony by COAS on 10-11-1970

COAS visits Poonch

COAS at Gyantse Day celebrations

COAS welcomes Indian POWs at a Reception Camp in New Delhi on 03-12-1972

COAS visits Div Area on 19-02-1972

Reception for the Press by COAS

COAS's visit to Pathankot to meet and interact with the troops

COAS's visit to 14 GTC Sobatu

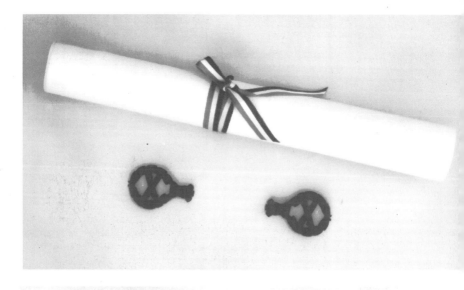

The President of India

To General Sam Hormusji Framji
Jamshedji Manekshaw, M.C. Greeting.

I do by these Presents Constitute and
Appoint you to the Rank of Field Marshal
in the Indian Army from the 1st day of
January Nineteen Hundred and Seventythree

And I do hereby give and grant you full
power and Authority to have, hold and enjoy
your said Rank accordingly, together with all
and singular the privileges thereunto belonging
And I do hereby command all the Officers and
men of the Indian Army whom it may concern
to acknowledge you as a Field Marshal as aforesaid

Given at New Delhi this 1st day of
January Nineteen Hundred and Seventythree

President of India

Principal Secretary to the Govt. of India
Registered No. F.M. 1 Ministry of Defence

भारत का राष्ट्रपति

जनरल सैम हॉर्मुसजी फ्रामजी अमशेदजी
मानेकशा, स्म. सी. को स्वस्तिवचन।

मैं इन उपहारों द्वारा आपको भारतीय थल सेना में
फील्ड मार्शल के रैंक में १९७३ के जनवरी मास के पहले
दिवस से प्रतिष्ठित और नियुक्त करता हूँ।

रुबम् तदनुसार मैं आपको अपने उक्त रैंक को उसके
संलग्न समस्त और विशेष अधिकारों सहित ग्रहण, भारण
और उपभोग करने की पूर्ण शक्ति और प्राधिकार रुतम द्वारा
प्रदान और स्वीकृत करता हूँ। तथा मैं भारतीय थल सेना
के समस्त पदधारियों और व्यक्तियों को जिनका भी वास्ता
हो, आदेश देता हूँ कि वे आपको उपर्युक्त रूप में फील्ड मार्शल
स्वीकार करें।

सन १९७३ के जनवरी मास के आज पहले ठिकान
को नई दिल्ली में प्रदत्त।

भारत का राष्ट्रपति

रक्षा मंत्रालय में भारत सरकार का
प्रमुख सचिव
पंजीयन संख्या रफ स्म-१

Scroll, Badges and Order of Field Marshal ordered by President of India on 02-01-1973

Field Marshal Sam Manekshaw calls on Prime Minister Indira Gandhi after the 1971 war.

The colonel of the regiment, 8 GR, laying a wreath at the grave of Field Marshal Sam Manekshaw.

Field Marshal Sam Manekshaw was awarded the title *Friend of Bangladesh* at a special ceremony in Dhaka on 27th March, 2012. The author received the award from the President of Bangladesh on his behalf.

The author and his wife with the Foreign Minister of Bangladesh at the award ceremony to honour Field Marshal Manekshaw.

12

Valhalla

The end, premature to all the well-wishers, was painful in more ways than one. It started when the idyll of Coonoor was shattered by the passing away of Mrs. Manekshaw on 17th June 2008. She was the one who created a home from the house they lived in whenever and wherever they moved; she was always the perfect foil—calm and collected to his restlessness; a great lady in every sense of the term, devoted not only to the family but to all friends, acquaintances and more importantly, even to the household help.

Though corporate duties kept Sam away from home almost 20-25 days every month, her passing away was an enormous blow. Man that he was, he never showed it by any emotional outpour, but to people close to him and those that knew him well, the loss was palpable. The family rallied to look after him, providing more love and affection to soften the loss.

Strong as a man may be physically and mentally, the heart cannot be denied its way of dictating life. Sam, with all his attributes of physical fitness and mental robustness, started to gradually wither. One manifestation was in two attacks of severe pneumonia which left him very weak. He was hospitalised in the

Military Hospital in Wellington and once even evacuated to the Research and Referral Hospital in New Delhi. It was here that he had the famous exchange with the Prime Minister Mr Manmohan Singh, who had dropped in to see him. After the opening pleasantries, came the first question enquiring about the PM's age. On the latter telling him what it was, came the typical response, "You are still a *bachha* (child)." When it was Sam's turn and the question was regarding how many children the Prime Minister had. To the answer, "two daughters" came the comment, "Good for you. If you had a son, he would have been clamouring to take over your job!"

In 2007 the Government suddenly woke up to the grave injustice that had been perpetrated on Sam Manekshaw in the matter of pay and allowances. To make up, the Defence Secretary was sent to Wellington to present a cheque of arrears, amounting to over rupees one crore. Receiving it in his hospital bed, Sam had to have the last word by expressing the hope that the cheque would be honoured! It was. Despite the financial retribution, another gross injustice continued; the Field Marshal was still number 12 in the Warrant of Precedence clubbed with the chiefs of staff of the three services, when he should have been placed above the cabinet secretary.

Around this time, Lt. Gen JFR Jacob came out with one more book about his experiences in war and peace. Such books, written by military leaders, are to be welcomed as coming generations can read and learn from experiences contained therein. I have not read the book but a few newspapers and at least one periodical have published reviews and I have perused these. Some of the views expressed by the author are patently unfair and need correction. As Military Assistant to the Chief of Army Staff during the period 1969–1973, I was junior in rank to General Jacob but had a seat where the screen was wider. Later, I was to serve under General Jacob; I found him to be kind, considerate, fair and courteous, always displaying impeccable integrity and character. Therefore, it is all the more mystifying to find him leveling unfair and unwarranted criticism.

Sam is accused of lacking strategic sense; not designating Dacca as the main objective; and being obsessively concerned that China would intervene in the war. Additionally, Lt Gen JS Aurora, who commanded Eastern Army during the 1971 war and to whom General Jacob was Chief of Staff in the rank of Major General, is accused of sycophancy; also that Sam Manekshaw did not like the Army Commander.

What is strategy? The Webster's Dictionary defines strategy "as the science and art of employing the political, economic, psychological and military forces of a nation or group of nations to afford the maximum support to adopted policies in peace and war". In layman's language, strategy means the creation of a favourable environment so that the achievement of the national aim is facilitated. On 25th March 1971, when Pakistan cracked down on its eastern wing, the Prime Minister, Mrs Indira Gandhi, was briefed by the COAS late in the evening in the Army Headquarters Operations Room. The meeting ended with the Chief stating that delay was necessary and there was nothing he could do at the moment. The PM smiled, thanked him and left. Therefore, the claim that around this time, the COAS ordered the Chief of Staff of Eastern Command, bypassing the Army Commander, to commence offensive action is preposterous. What must have happened is that some cautionary orders would have been issued from Army Headquarters and memories of these may have created a mistaken impression in General Jacob's mind writing many years after the event. In any case, if an order was issued, how could it have been refused by any soldier let alone a staff officer? In the next few days, the BSF was directed to examine the possibility of creating pinpricks along the Indo-East Pakistan border to divert the attention of the Pakistan Army from the genocide they were engaged in. Therefore, the assertion that Mr Rustomji, Director, BSF, at the time was planning to "invade" East Pakistan is equally absurd.

I have already given details of the meeting of the cabinet and how despite every minister recommending early intervention, the lone voice of the COAS advocated delay. The reasons he gave to support his view bear repetition and were as follows:

(a)   The Army was widely dispersed at the time, overseeing elections in Assam and Bengal. Units and formations would need time to move back to parent cantonments, marry up with heavy equipment, re-equip and reorganize before they were ready for war.

(b)   The modernisation process of the armed forces was way behind schedule (sounds familiar!).

(c)   The northern passes were fast opening up and the chances of Chinese intervention was very real.

(d)   The monsoons were due shortly, flooding the rivers and countryside in East Pakistan making offensive operations time consuming and more difficult.

(e)   World public opinion needed to be moulded to see India as a victim rather than the matter being seen as an internal affair of Pakistan.

(f)   Existing infrastructure would permit the opening of only one axis of attack from West Bengal. Time was needed to develop infrastructure for opening more axes from Tripura and Meghalaya.

The PM, far-sighted and visionary as she was, saw merit in the recommendations of the COAS; closed the meeting and, a day or so later, gave the COAS permission to start operations at a time of his choosing. This was an extraordinary display of strategic sense on the part of Sam Manekshaw, not to mention an incredible show of character, and a rare display of statesmanship on the part of the PM. Sam Manekshaw stood firm and had his way to create the right circumstances that eventually resulted in a great victory.

Criticism is also directed over Dacca not being designated as the main objective. When operational plans were being finalised, it was quite clear that speed would be of the essence as world public opinion notwithstanding, the US and China would mount pressure in the Security Council to stop operations. Therefore, the aim was to capture maximum territory in the shortest possible time. Designating Dacca as the main objective would have negated the prime requirement of speed, not to mention that it would give Eastern Command two contradictory aims, i.e, capture Dacca and occupy maximum territory in the shortest possible time. When operations commenced on 3rd December 1971, the advances were so swift with Pakistan Army defences bypassed, that it became apparent that the apprehension about Dacca being defended in strength was no longer valid. In light of this, around 9th December 1971, Dacca was designated as the objective. This change of plan as a result of developing situations showed flexibility, another essential quality of a military leader.

The next item on the criticism agenda concerns, what General Jacob terms, Sam's obsession with China intervening. While General Jacob saw the war through the narrow prism of one sector, the COAS, with many more inputs, was seeing a much wider screen. Also, radio intercepts between East and West Pakistan, with the former clamouring for assistance from the "Yellow" and "White" brothers and the West's reassurances that they were "coming" created the justifiable concern. So, rather than terming this as an "obsession" it has to be viewed as prudence, more so as the white brothers did actually venture into the Indian Ocean. In any case, during the first week of December satellite pictures provided by the USSR confirmed that there were no abnormal Chinese moves. Hence, the release of two brigades from the Indo-Tibet border sought by Eastern Command was really no secret from the COAS as claimed by the author.

Next, we come to the amazing criticism leveled against the Army Commander, Lt Gen JS Aurora. To begin with, Gen Aurora was no pushover as a small incident that occurred will confirm. The COAS wanted to speak to the Army Commander one day. He was not available and so also were the other senior officers, the Chief of Staff and Brigadier General Staff. When they finally did get to talk, the COAS mentioned the absence of all three to which the reply was, "Now you are going to teach me how to run my Army". How do I know this? I know, because I was listening to the conversation as, those days, the MA's telephone did not get disconnected when the COAS was on the line and the MA was expected to remain on listening watch. After the ceasefire, the PM wanted the COAS to take the surrender. He graciously declined stating that it was General Aurora's victory and he would take the surrender. Does this show dislike?

Remaining with Gen Aurora an incident is referred to where, as host, he poured a drink for the COAS and Mr. DP Dhar, a close friend of Sam, and, at the time, Chairman of the Policy Planning Division in the External Affairs Ministry. Is it degrading for a host to do this? It is very much part of hospitality, especially Indian hospitality, for a host to offer a drink to a guest. General Aurora was a great military leader and he discharged the heavy responsibilities that were entrusted to him with great competence and elan.

During Sam's hospitalisation, by a happy coincidence, the Colonel of the Regiment, 8 GR, Lt. Gen. SK Singh, VSM, was posted in Headquarters Southern Command and then in Delhi to oversee arrangements and assistance. This was a big help.

After some time, recovering in the Army Hospital in Delhi, Sam started demanding that he be sent back to Wellington. This was agreed to but it was considered expedient to accommodate him in the Military Hospital in Wellington so that better medical care and attention could be provided. Numerous well-wishers dropped in and to the constantly asked question "how are you" would be the stock answer accompanied with a smile, "I am better" and on 29th June 2008, he quietly slipped away to Valhalla where Viking warriors of yore went after death in battle.

Controversy did not desert him even in death. At the funeral ceremony the next day, attendance was woefully thin; neither the services nor the Government were adequately represented. The absence of "brass" was attituted to the explanation that there was "confusion in the warrant of precedence"! The Government also failed to put out an appropriate obituary honouring an icon who had won India's most decisive victories. In a belated attempt to make up, the Government opened a Condolence Book and kept it at the Martyr's Memorial at India Gate in New Delhi. The Book had to be kept for two extra days due to the huge public response.

Some months later, Western Command, then under Lt. General Tej Sapru, Colonel 4 GR and President Gorkha Brigade, arranged a memorial service to honour the Field Marshal in the NCC Campus in Delhi Cantonment. I was also invited to attend and speak, joining a galaxy of far more eloquent speakers and distinguished leaders than me. I narrated a few incidents from his life to highlight the many qualities of head and heart he possessed in such abundance. Since the disrespect shown to him at his funeral still rankled, I brought it up too. "If by some supernatural miracle I could meet the Field Marshal today and ask him his views on the thin attendance at his funeral, his reply without doubt would be, 'If the f——s didn't attend my funeral, I won't attend theirs'." I concluded by alluding to the closing scene in the film, *Gladiator*, where the Queen, pointing at the dying Gladiator, orders her guards, "Honour him, he was a soldier of Rome." I ended by pleading to the Defence Minister, who was also present, to honour this great soldier of India by the award of the Bharat Ratna.

Around 20th March 2012, Maja Daruwala, Sam's younger daughter called me from New York to ask if I would represent the

Field Marshal at an Investiture Ceremony in Dacca where the Government of Bangladesh was honouring those who had assisted the liberation struggle in 1971. I told her that I would be honoured and proud to do so. Thereupon, she informed the Bangladesh High Commission in Delhi. The latter took me in hand with an efficiency and warmth that was breathtaking.

My wife and I arrived in Dacca on 23rd March 2012 to find ourselves amidst a galaxy of invitees from all over the world. The hospitality was warm and generous; the schedule worked out by our hosts was back-breaking but interesting; and the kindness and friendship we encountered wherever we went and whoever we met, was heart-warming. Every guest was made to feel at home and no effort was spared to make our stay happy, comfortable and enjoyable. Photographs of the Awards Ceremony and the social events that preceded and followed are included in the book.

The Colonel of the Regiment, Lt. Gen SK Singh had by now moved to Delhi as Vice Chief of the Army staff. He was instrumental in organising a ceremony for the family on 3rd April 2012, the 98th birth anniversary of the Field Marshal. Perhaps to make up for past lapses, the attendance on this occasion was good with the Defence Minister and the Army Chief present. Sam and Silloo were laid to rest alongside each other and gravestones were affixed on the graves. Some photographs taken on the occasion are included within.

Finally, did he add to the vocabulary that is soldiering? If greatness is judged by a silhouette a person has popularised, a sensibility he has nurtured and an aesthetic that is unmistakably his own, we can conclude that he did, indeed, add to the vocabulary and add substantially. It was a pleasure and an education working with him and I will always continue to admire his professionalism and intellectual brilliance, and treasure his greatest gift to me: his friendship.

Appendix I

Field Marshal Sam Manekshaw as Chief Guest in the Centenary Year (1969) at Sherwood College, Nainital

Your Grace, the Metropolitan of India, My Lord Bishop of Lucknow, Mr. Principal, ladies and young gentlemen of Sherwood:

Yesterday evening when my A.D.C. told me that I would have to speak here, I was horrified. I thought the Principal had asked me to come and join the celebrations; I did not realise he wanted me to sing for my supper! Believe me, as I stand here, I am terrified. Those near me can almost hear my knees knocking and my teeth chattering. For eight years in Sherwood, I was at the receiving end.

It is customary on these occasions for the guest speaker to give a learned discourse or advice to young gentlemen. It is not my fault that, although I received my early education in Sherwood, I am not learned. Sir, I am fit neither to give you a learned discourse nor advice, I really want to tell you what Sherwood has done for me.

Sherwood has taken me to my present position. First and foremost, I learned to live alone and independently. I learned to fight—from the time I got up in the morning till the time I went to bed. When I went down to wash, I could not find my towel, and while I was looking for my towel, somebody pinched my soap. This, my young gentlemen, happened for eight years. I am rather disappointed as I look at you carefully (I shall put on my glasses) to see so few scared faces. In my time, the guest speaker saw nothing but black eyes. I fought, and it stood me in good stead during the war in Burma, where we came up against the Japanese.

What else did I learn from Sherwood? During the war in Burma, I went without food for many days. I was hungry. I withstood this and said to myself, "After all, I went through eight years of hunger in Sherwood." I was hungry in the morning; I was hungry in the afternoon, hungry when I went to bed at night. Does a similar situation prevail now? I learnt in school to hate my enemies. How?...Thanks to St. Joseph's next door and when we played them on the Flats. From the corner of my eye I see His Grace, the metropolitan, and the Bishop frowning. "You should love your neighbour," is what they say. So we should, though I can almost hear the boys say, "except St. Joseph's".

Sir, it is a great privilege and a great honour to be able to come back to Sherwood after thirty years, to come back as a chief guest, to come back to address you boys who will grow up to be fine gentlemen. I thank you very much for having given me this privilege. May I hope that some day, some of you will join the armed forces to rise to high positions.

Appendix II

Field Marshal Sam Manekshaw's Lecture at Defence Services Staff College, Wellington on *Leadership and Discipline*; 11th November, 1998

Commandant, ladies and gentlemen, I am fully conscious of the privilege, which is mine, to have been invited here to address the college. A while ago I was invited to a seminar where the subject was youth, and people said that the youth of this country was not pulling its weight, that society generally was not satisfied with how the young were functioning. When I was asked what I thought about it, I said that the youngsters of this country are disappointed, disturbed and confused. They cannot understand why all these untoward things are happening in this country. They want to know who is to blame. Not them. If they want to study at night and there is no power, they want to know who is to blame. Not them. If they want to have a bath and there is no water, they want to know who is to blame. Not them. They want to go to college and university and they are told there are not any vacancies; they want to know who is to blame. Not them. They say—here is a country which was considered the brightest jewel in the British crown. What has happened to this bright jewel?

No longer are there excuses with the old political masters saying that the reason why we are in this state is because we were under colonial rule for 250 years. They turn around and say that the British left us almost fifty years ago. What have you done? They point to Singapore, they point to Malaysia, they point to Indonesia, they point to Hong Kong. They say they were also under colonial rule and look at the progress those countries have made.

They point to Germany and to Japan who fought a war for four and half years—whose youth was decimated, and industry was destroyed. They were occupied, and they had to pay reparations; Look at the progress those countries have made. The youngsters want an answer. So, ladies and gentlemen, I thought I should give you the answer.

The problem with us is lack of leadership.

Commandant, ladies and gentlemen, do not misunderstand me when I say a lack of leadership. I do not mean just political leadership. Of course, there is a lack of political leadership, but also a lack of leadership in every walk of life, whether it is political, administrative, in our education institutions, or whether it is in our sports organisations. Wherever you look, there is a lack of leadership. I do not know whether leaders are born or made. There is a school of thought that thinks that leaders are born. Ladies and Gentlemen, we have a population of 960 million people and we procreate at the rate of seventeen million—equalling the total population of Australia—each year, and yet there is a dearth of leadership so, those of you who still contribute to the fact that leaders are born, may I suggest you throw away all your family planning, throw away the pill, throw away every inhibiting factor and make it free for all. Then perhaps some day a leader may be born.

So, if leaders are not born, can leaders be made? My answer is yes. Give me a man or a woman with common sense and decency, and I can make a leader out of him or her. That is the subject which I am going to discuss with you this morning.

What are the attributes of leadership? The first, the primary, indeed the cardinal attribute of leadership is professional knowledge and professional competence. Now you will agree with me that you cannot be born with professional knowledge and professional competence even if you are the child of the Prime Minister, or the son of an industrialist or the progeny of a Field Marshal. Professional knowledge and professional competence have to be acquired by hard work and by constant study. In this fast-moving technologically developing world, you can never acquire sufficient professional knowledge.

You have to keep at it, and at it, and at it. Can those of our political masters who are responsible for the security and defence of this country cross their hearts and say they have ever read a book on military history, on strategy, on weapons developments? Can they distinguish a mortar from a motor, a gun from a howitzer, a guerrilla from a gorilla, though a vast majority of them resemble the latter.

Ladies and Gentlemen, professional knowledge and professional competence are a sine qua non of leadership. Unless you know what you are talking about, unless you understand your profession, you can never be a leader. Now some of you must be wondering why the Field Marshal is saying this. Every time you go round somewhere, you see one of our leaders walking around, roads being blocked, transport being provided for them, security being provided for them. Those, Ladies and Gentlemen, are not leaders. They are just men and women going about disguised as leaders— and they ought to be ashamed of themselves!

What is the next thing you need for leadership? It is the ability to make up your mind to make a decision and accept full responsibility for that decision. Have you ever wondered why people do not make a decision? The answer is quite simple. It is because they lack professional knowledge and professional competence, or they are worried that their decision may be wrong and they will have to carry the can. Ladies and Gentlemen, according to the law of averages, if you take ten decisions, five ought to be right. If you have professional knowledge and professional competence, nine will be right and the one that might not be correct will probably be put right by a subordinate officer or colleague. But if you do not take a decision you are doing something wrong. An act of omission is much worse than an act of commission. An act of commission can be put right. An act of omission cannot. Take the example of the time when the Babri Masjid was about to be destroyed. If the Prime Minister, at that stage, had taken a decision to stop it, a whole community—180 million people—would not have been harmed. But, because he did not take a decision, you have at least 180 million people in this country alone who do not like us.

When I was the Army Chief, I would go along to a formation, ask the fellow what you have done about this and I normally got an answer, "Sir, I have been thinking... I have yet not made up my mind," and I coined a Manekshawism. If the girls will excuse my language, it was "if you must be a bloody fool, be one quickly". So remember that you are the ones who are going to be the future senior staff officers, the future commanders. Make a decision and having made it, accept full responsibility for it. Do not pass it on to a colleague or subordinate.

So, what comes next for leadership? Absolute honesty, fairness and justice—we are dealing with people. Those of us who have had the good fortune of commanding hundreds and thousands of men know this. No man likes to be punished, and yet a man will accept punishment stoically if he knows that the punishment meted out to him will be identical to the punishment meted out to another person who has some godfather somewhere. This is very, very important. No man likes to be superceded, and yet men will accept supercession if they know that they are being superceded, under the rules, by somebody who is better than they are but not just somebody who happens to be related to the Commandant of the staff college or to a Cabinet Minister or by the Field Marshal's wife's current boyfriend. This is extremely important, ladies and gentlemen.

We in India have tremendous pressures—pressures from the government, pressures from superior officers, pressures from families, pressures from wives, uncles, aunts, nieces, nephews and girlfriends, and we lack the courage to withstand those pressures. That takes me to the next attribute of leadership—moral and physical courage.

Ladies and gentlemen, I do not know which of these is more important. When I am talking to young officers and young soldiers, I should place emphasis on physical courage. But since I am talking to this gathering, I will lay emphasis on moral courage. What is moral courage? Moral courage is the ability to distinguish right from wrong and having done so, say so when asked, irrespective of what your superiors might think or what your colleagues or your subordinates might want. A "yes man" is a dangerous man. He may rise very high, he might even become the Managing Director of a company.

He may do anything but he can never make a leader because he will be used by his superiors, disliked by his colleagues and despised by his subordinates. So shallow—the "yes man".

I am going to illustrate from my own life an example of moral courage. In 1971, when Pakistan clamped down on its province, East Pakistan, hundreds and thousands of refugees started pouring into India. The Prime Minister, Mrs. Gandhi had a cabinet meeting at ten o'clock in the morning. The following attended: the Foreign Minister, Sardar Swaran Singh, the Defence Minister, Mr. Jagjivan

Ram, the Agriculture Minister, Mr. Fakruddin Ali Ahmed, the Finance Minister, Mr. Yashwant Rao Chavan, and I was also ordered to be present.

Ladies and gentlemen, there is a very thin line between becoming a Field Marshal and being dismissed. A very angry Prime Minister read out messages from Chief Ministers of West Bengal, Assam and Tripura. All of them saying that hundreds and thousands of refugees had poured into their states and they did not know what to do.

So the Prime Minister turned round to me and said, "I want you to do something."

I said, "What do you want me to do?"

She said, "I want you to enter East Pakistan."

I said, "Do you know that that means war?"

She said, "I do not mind if it is war."

I, in my usual stupid way, said: "Prime Minister, have you read the Bible?" and the Foreign Minister, Sardar Swaran Singh (a Punjabi Sikh) in his Punjabi accent said, "What has Bible got to do with this?", and I said, "The first book, the first chapter, the first paragraph, the first sentence, God said, 'let there be light' and there was light. You turn this round and say 'let there be war' and there will be war. What do you think? Are you ready for a war? Let me tell you: it's the 28th April, the Himalayan passes are opening now, and if the Chinese give us an ultimatum, I will have to fight on two fronts."

Again, Sardar Swaran Singh turned round and in his Punjabi English said, "Will China give ultimatum?"

I said, "You are the Foreign Minister. You tell me."

Then I turned to the Prime Minister and said, "Prime Minister, last year you wanted elections in West Bengal and you did not want the communists to win, so you asked me to deploy my soldiers in penny pockets in every village, in every little township in West Bengal. I have two divisions thus deployed in sections and platoons without their heavy weapons. It will take me at least a month to get them back to their units and to their formations. Further, I have a division in the Assam area, another division in Andhra Pradesh and the Armoured division in the Jhansi-Babina area. It will take me at least a month to get them back and put them in their correct positions. I will require every road, every railway train, every truck, every wagon to move them. We are harvesting in the Punjab, and we are harvesting in Haryana; we are also harvesting in Uttar Pradesh. And you will not be able to move your harvest."

I turned to the Agriculture Minister, Mr. Fakruddin Ali Ahmed, "If there is a famine in the country afterwards, it will be you to blame, not me." Then I said, "My Armoured Division has only got thirteen tanks which are functioning."

The Finance Minister, Mr. Chavan, a friend of mine, said, "Sam, why only thirteen?"

"Because you are the Finance Minister. I have been asking for money for the last year and a half, and you keep saying there is no money. That is why." Then I turned to the Prime Minister and said, "Prime Minister, it is the end of April. By the time I am ready to operate, the monsoon will have broken in that East Pakistan area. When it rains, it does not just rain it pours. Rivers become like oceans. If you stand on one bank, you cannot see the other and the whole countryside is flooded. My movements will be confined to roads, the Air Force will not be able to support me and, if you wish me to enter East Pakistan, I guarantee you a hundred per cent defeat."

"You are the government," I said turning to the Prime Minister, "now will you give me your orders?"

Ladies and Gentleman, I have seldom seen a woman so angry, and I am including my wife in that. She was red in the face and I said, "Let us see what happens." She turned round and said, "The cabinet will meet this evening at four o'clock."

Everybody walked out. I being the juniormost man was the last to leave. As I was leaving, she said, "Chief, please will you stay behind?" I looked at her. I said, "Prime Minister, before you open your mouth, would you like me to send in my resignation on grounds of health: mental or physical?"

"No. Sit down, Sam. Was everything you told me the truth?"

"Yes. It is my job to tell you the truth. It is my job to fight and win, not to lose."

She smiled at me and said, "All right, Sam. You know what I want. When will you be ready?"

"I cannot tell you now, Prime Minister," I said, "but let me guarantee you this that, if you leave me alone, allow me to plan, make my arrangements, and fix a date, I guarantee you a hundred per cent victory."

So, Ladies and gentleman, as I told you, there is a very thin line between becoming a Field Marshal and being dismissed. Just an example of moral courage. Now, those of you who remember what happened in 1962, when the Chinese occupied the Thag-la ridge and Mr. Nehru, the Prime Minister, sent for the Army Chief, in the month of December and said, "I want you to throw the Chinese out." That Army Chief did not have the moral courage to stand up to him and say, "I am not ready, my troops are not acclimatised, I haven't the ammunition, or indeed anything." But he accepted the Prime Minister's instructions, with the result that the Army was beaten and the country humiliated.

Remember, moral courage. You, the future senior staff officers and commanders will be faced with many problems. People will want all sorts of things. You have got to have the moral courage to stand up and tell them the facts. Again, as I told you before, a "yes man" is a despicable man.

This takes me to the next attribute: physical courage. Fear, like hunger and sex, is a natural phenomenon. Any man who says he is not frightened is a liar or a Gorkha. It is one thing to be frightened. It is quite another to show fear. If you once show fear in front of your men, you will never be able to command. It is when your teeth are chattering, your knees are knocking and you are about to make your own geography, that is when the true leader comes out!

I am sorry but I am going to illustrate this with another example from my own life. I am not a brave man. In fact, I am a terribly frightened man. My wife and I do not share the same bedroom. "Why?" you will ask. Because she says I snore. Although I have told her, "No, I don't. No other woman has ever complained."

I am not a brave man. If I am frightened, I am frightened of wild animals, I am frightened of ghosts and spirits and so on. If my wife tells me a ghost story after dinner, I cannot sleep in my room, and I have to go to her room. I have often wondered why she tells me these ghost stories periodically.

In World War II, my battalion, which is now in Pakistan, was fighting the Japanese. We had a great many casualties. I was commanding Charlie company, which was a Sikh company. The Frontier Force Regiment in those days had Pathan companies, Punjabi musalmaan companies and Sikh companies. I was commanding the Sikh company, young Major Manekshaw. As we were having too many casualties, we had pulled back to reorganise, re-group, make up our casualties, our promotions.

The Commanding Officer had a promotion conference. He turned to me and said, "Sam, we have to make lots of promotions. In your Sikh company, you have had a lot of casualties. Surat Singh is a senior man. Should we promote him to the rank of naik?" Now, Surat Singh was the biggest badmaash in my company. He had been promoted twice or three times and each time he had to be marched up in front of the Colonel for his stripes to be taken off. So I said, "No use, Sir, promoting Surat Singh. You promote him today and the day after tomorrow I will have to march him in front of you to take his stripes off." So, Surat Singh was passed over. The promotion conference over, I had lunch in the mess and I came back to my company lines. Now, those of you who have served with Sikhs will know that they are a very cheerful lot—always laughing and joking and doing something. When I arrived at my company lines that day, it was quite different, everybody was quiet. When my second-in-command, Subedar Balwant Singh, met me I asked him, "What has happened, Subedar Sahib?" He said, "Sahib, something terrible has happened. Surat Singh felt slighted and has told everybody that he is going to shoot you today."

Surat Singh was a light machine gunner, and was armed with a pistol. His pistol had been taken away, and Surat Singh had been put under close arrest. I said, "All right, Sahib. Put up a table, a soap box. March Surat Singh in front of me." So he was marched up. The charge was read out—threatening to shoot his commanding officer whilst on active service in the theatre of war'. That carries the death penalty. The witnesses gave their evidence. I asked for Surat Singh's pistol which was handed to me. I loaded it, rose from my soap box, walked up to Surat Singh, handed the pistol to him then turned round and told him, "You said you will shoot me." I spoke to him in Punjabi naturally. I told him, "Have you got the guts to shoot me? Here, shoot me. "He looked at me stupidly and said, *"Nahin, Sahib, galtee ho gayaa."* I gave him a tight slap and said, "Go out. Case dismissed."

I went around the company lines, the whole company watching what was happening. I walked around, chatted to the people, went to the Mess in the evening to have a drink, and have my dinner, but when I came back again Subedar Balwant Singh said, "Nahin, Sahib, you have made a great mistake. Surat Singh will shoot you tonight."

I said, *"Bulao Surat Singh ko."*

He came along. I said, *"Surat Singh, aaj raat ko mere tambu par tu pahera dega, aur kal subah 6 baje, mere liye ek mug chai aur ek mug shaving water lana."* Then I walked into my little tent.

Ladies and gentleman, I did not sleep the whole night. Next morning, at six o'clock, Surat Singh brought me a mug of tea and a mug of shaving water. Thereafter, throughout the war, Surat Singh followed me around like a puppy. If I had shown fear in front of my men, I should never have been able to command. I was frightened, terribly frightened, but I dared not show fear in front of them. Those of you who are going to command soldiers, remember that. You must never show fear. So much for physical courage, but, please believe me, I am still a very frightened man. I am not a brave man.

What comes next? The next attribute of leadership is loyalty. Ladies and Gentlemen, you all expect loyalty. Do we give loyalty? Do we give loyalty to our subordinates, to our colleagues? Loyalty is a three-way thing. You expect loyalty, you must therefore, give loyalty to your colleagues and to your subordinates. Men and women in large numbers can be very difficult, they can cause many problems and a leader must deal with them immediately and firmly. Do not allow any nonsense, but remember that men and women have many problems. They get easily despondent, they have problems of debt, they have problems of infidelity—wives have run away or somebody is having an affair with somebody. They get easily crestfallen, and a leader must have the gift of the gab with a sense of humour to shake them out of their despondence. Our leaders, unfortunately, our "so-called" leaders, definitely have the gift of the gab, but they have no sense of humour. So, remember that.

Finally, for leadership; men and women like their leader to be a man, with all the manly qualities or virtues. The man who says "I do not smoke, I do not drink, I do not (No, I will not say it)" does not make a leader. Let me illustrate this from examples from the past. You will agree that Julius Caesar was a great leader—he had his Calphurnia, he had his Antonia, he also had an affair with Cleopatra and, when Caesar used to come to Rome, the Senators locked up their wives. And you will agree that he was a great leader. He was known in Rome as every woman's husband and he was a great leader. Take Napoleon, he had his Josephine, he had his Marie Waiewska, he had his Antoinette and Georgettes and Paulettes. And you will agree he was a great leader. Take the Duke of Wellington—do you know that the night before the battle of Waterloo, there were more Countesses, Marchionesses and other women in his ante-chamber than staff officers and Commanders. And you will agree he was a great leader. Do you know, ladies and gentleman, a thought has just struck me. All these leaders—Caesar, Napoleon and the Duke of Wellington— they had one facial feature in common, all had long noses.

So much, ladies and gentleman, for leadership, but no amount of leadership will do this country much good. Yes, it will improve things, but what this country needs is discipline. We are the most ill-disciplined people in the world. You see what is happening— you go down the road, and you see people relieving themselves by the roadside. You go into town, and people are walking up and down the highway, while vehicles are discharging all sorts of muck. Every time you pick up a newspaper, you read of a scam or you read of some other silly thing. As we are the most ill-disciplined people in the world, we must do something about discipline.

What is discipline? Please, when I talk of discipline, do not think of military discipline. That is quite different. Discipline can be defined as conduct and behaviour for living decently with one another in society. Who lays down the code of conduct for that? Not the Prime Minister, not the Cabinet, nor superior officers. It is enshrined in our holy books; it is in the Bible, the Torah, and in the Vedas. It is in the teachings of Nanak and Mohammed. It has come down to us from time immemorial, from father to son, from mother to child. Nowhere is it laid down, except in the Armed Forces, that lack of punctuality is conduct prejudicial to discipline and decent living.

I will again tell you a little story about that. Some years ago, my wife and I were invited to a convocation at a university. I was asked to be there at four o'clock. I got into the staff car with my wife, having chased her from about eleven o'clock in the morning with: "Don't forget, darling, you have got to be on time. Get properly dressed. You have to leave at such and such time'. Eventually, I got her into the car. I told the driver, "*Thoda aayisthe, thoda jaldi,*" but we got to the university and the convocation address place at exactly four o'clock. We were received by the Vice Chancellor and his Lady. We were taken into the convocation hall, and the Vice Chancellor asked me to get on the platform, asking my wife to do so, too. She gracefully declined and said she much rather sit down below as she seldom had an opportunity of looking up to her husband. Anyway, on the platform, the Vice Chancellor sang my praises. As usual, there were 2000 boys and girls who had come for the convocation, there were deans of university, and professors and lecturers. Then he asked me to go to the lectern and address the gathering. I rose to do so and he said (*sotto voce*), "Field Marshal, a fortnight ago we invited a VIP from Delhi for the self same function. He was allowed to stand on the lectern for exactly twenty seconds. I wish you luck." I said to myself, had the Vice Chancellor mentioned this in his letter of invitation, I wonder if I should have accepted.

Anyway, I reached the lectern, and I addressed the gathering for my allotted time of forty minutes. I was heard in pin-drop silence and, at the end of my talk, was given a terrific ovation. The Vice Chancellor and his lady, the dean, the professors and lecturers, the boys and girls, and even my own wife, standing up and giving me an ovation. After the convocation was over, we walked into the gardens to have refreshments. And I, having an eye for pretty girls, walked up to a pert little thing wearing a pair of tight-fitting jeans and a body-hugging blouse, and I started a conversation with her. I said, "My dear, why were you so kind to me, I not being an orator nor having the looks of Amitabh Bachhan, when only the other day you treated a VIP from Delhi so shamefully." This pert little thing had no inhibitions. She turned round and said, and I quote, "Oh, that dreadful man! We asked him to come at four o'clock He came much later and that too accompanied with a boy and a girl, probably his grand children. He was received by the Vice Chancellor and his lady and taken to the platform. He was garlanded by the Student Union President, and he demanded garlands for those brats too. So, the Union President diverged with the garland that was meant for the Vice Chancellor and gave it to the brats. Then the Vice Chancellor started singing the worthy's praises. Whilst he was doing so, this man hitched up his *dhoti*, exposing his dirty thighs, and scratched away. Then the Vice Chancellor said, "This man has done so much for the country, he has even been to jail." And I nearly shouted out, "He should be there now." Anyway, when the Vice Chancellor asked him to come to the lectern and address the convocation, he got up, walked to the lectern and addressed us thus, "Boys and girls, I am a very busy man. I have not had time to prepare my speech but, I will now read out the speech my secretary has written." We did not let him stand there. Without exception, the whole lot of us stood and booed him off the stage."

Now you see, ladies and gentleman, what I mean by discipline. Had this man as his position warranted come on time at four o'clock, fully prepared and properly turned out, can you imagine the good it would have done to these 2000 young girls and boys? Instead of that, his act of indiscipline engendered further indiscipline. I thanked my lucky stars, having been in the Army for so many years, that I arrived there on time, that I had come properly dressed, that I didn't wear a dhoti to show my lovely legs, that I didn't exhibit an itch or eczema, to hurt the susceptibilities of my audience by indulging in the scratching of the unmentionables.

Now, ladies and gentleman, you understand what I mean by discipline. We are the most ill-disciplined people in the world. So far, all of you have been very, very disciplined. Will you bear with me for another two minutes? Having talked about leadership, having talked about discipline, I want to mention something about character. We Indians also lack character. Do not misunderstand me. When I talk of character I don't mean just being honest, truthful, and religious, I mean something more. Knowing yourself, knowing your own faults, knowing your own weaknesses and what little character that we have, our friends, our fans, the "yes-men" around us and the sycophants, help us reduce that character as well. Let me illustrate this by an example:

Some years ago, Hollywood decided to put up the picture of the great violinist and composer, Paganini. The part of Paganini was given to a young actor who was conversant, somewhat, with the violin. He was drilled and tutored to such an extent that when the little piece, the Cadenza, was filmed, it was perfect. When the film was shown, the papers raved about it, and the critics raved about it. And this man's fans, "yes-men", sycophants, kept on telling him that he was as good a violinist as Heifetz or Menuhin. And do you know that it took eight months in a psychiatric home to rid him of his delusion?

Do you know, Commandant, that the very same thing happened to me? After the 1971 conflict with Pakistan, which ended in thirteen days and I took 93000 prisoners, my fans, the "yes-men" around me, the sycophants, kept on comparing me to Rommel, to Field Marshal Alexander, to Field Marshal Auchinleck and, just as I was beginning to believe it, the Prime Minister created me a Field Marshal and sent me packing to the Nilgiris.

A hard-headed, no-nonsense wife deprived a psychiatric home (what we in India call a lunatic asylum) of one more inmate.

I thank you very much indeed. Thank you.

~

Question: In 1962 war, what was your appointment? Were you in a position to do something about the situation?

FM: In the 1962 war, I was in disgrace. I was a Commandant of this Institution.

Mr. Krishna Menon, the Defence Minister, disliked me intensely. General Kaul, who was Chief of General Staff at the time, and the budding man for the next higher appointment, disliked me intensely. So, I was in disgrace at the Staff College. There were charges against me—I will enumerate some of them— all engineered by Mr. Krishna Menon.

I do not know if you remember that in 1961 or 1960, General Thimayya was the Army Chief. He had fallen out with Mr. Krishna Menon and had sent him his resignation. The Prime Minister, Mr. Nehru, persuaded General Thimayya to withdraw his resignation. The members of Parliament also disliked Mr. Krishna Menon, and they went hammer and tongs for the Prime Minister in Parliament.

The Prime Minister made the following statement, "I cannot understand why General Thimayya is saying that the Defence Ministry interferes with the working of the Army. Take the case of General Manekshaw. The Selection Board has approved his promotion to Lieutenant General over the heads of 23 other officers. The Government has accepted that."

I was the Commandant of the Staff College. I had been approved for promotion to Lieutenant General. Instead of making me the Lieutenant General, Mr. Krishna Menon levied charges against me. There were ten charges. I will enumerate only one or two of them—that I am more loyal to the Queen of England than to the President of India, that I am more British than Indian.

That I have been alleged to have said that I will have no instructor in the Staff college whose wife looks like an ayah. These were the sort of charges against me.

For eighteen months my promotion was held back. An enquiry was made. Three Lieutenant Generals, including an Army Commander, sat at that enquiry. I was exonerated on every charge. The file went up to the Prime Minister who sent it up to the Cabinet Secretary, who wrote on the file, "if anything happens to General Manekshaw, this case will go will down as the Dreyfus case". So the file came back to the Prime Minister. He wrote on it, "Orders may now issue," meaning I will now become a Lieutenant General. Instead of that, ladies and gentleman, I received a letter from the Adjutant General saying the Defence Minister, Mr. Krishna Menon, has sent his severe displeasure to General Manekshaw, to be recorded. I had it in the office where the Commandant now sits. I sent that letter back to the Adjutant General saying what Mr. Krishna Menon could do with his displeasure, very vulgarly stated. It is still in my dossier.

Then the Chinese came to my help. Krishna Menon was sacked, Kaul was sacked and Nehru sent for me. He said, "General, I have a vigorous enemy. I find out that you are a vigorous General. Will you go and take over?"

I said, "I have been waiting eighteen months for this opportunity," and I went and took over.

So your question was 1962, and what part did I play, none whatsoever, none whatsoever.

I was here for eighteen months, persecuted, inquisitions against me but we survived... I rather like the Chinese.

Question: The Army has changed and progressed. Do you find any difference in the mental make-up of the young officers compared to your times?

FM: Over the years, things have changed ... there is a lot of difference, dear. In my time, my father used to support me until I became a Lieutenant Colonel. I used to get an allowance to be able to live. Today, the young officer has not only to keep himself but has to send money home.

In my time, we did not have all these courses. The only course I ever did (of course, we had the four rounds of courses that every officer had to do), but we had mules there so I had to do a course in training mountain mules. Today the young officer hardly stays in his regiment. He is sent from one place to another to do this course and that course, and he does not get a chance of knowing his men. We knew our men. Also there wasn't so much work in those days. We got up in the mornings, did Physical Training for half an hour, came back, dressed, had breakfast, then went to our company lines and spent all our time avoiding the Commanding Officer.

Those Commanding Officers were nasty chaps. They did not give a damn for anybody. I will give an example of the Commanding Officer. I was made quartermaster of my battalion. The Commanding Officer sent for the Adjutant and myself. He said, "I want to take the battalion out tomorrow morning for an exercise." We did not have motor cars, we had to indent for mules so I as quartermaster indented for a company of mules: He said we were going to leave for the exercise at 6.30, so I ordered the company of mules to arrive at six. At eleven o'clock at night, the Commanding Officer changed his mind. He said, "I will not go at 6.30, we will go at nine o'clock." There was nothing I could do. I got on my bicycle, went off to the lines, where the mules had arrived. I told them to unsaddle, and go into the shade when who should arrive on a horse but the General, a Cavalry Officer with his daughter!

I touched my hat. He said, "What are those animals doing here, young man?" I said that we were going out on an exercise.

"When are you going?"

"Nine o'clock."

He tore strips off me—"going at nine o'clock and you have the animals waiting here at six o'clock". He was riding with his daughter on a horse. What could I say to a general officer, I had two pips on my shoulder. Suddenly, who should be coming on a bicycle, but the Commanding Officer! He touched his hat, said, "Morning, General."

Turning to me, he said, "What is the matter, Sam?"

I said, "Sir, the General is angry with me because we are going out at nine o'clock and the mules are here at six."

He turned round to face the General, and said, "I will thank you General to know who commands this regiment. Me, and not this young man. I will not have you ticking him off in front of your daughter."

He turned back to me and said, "Have you had your breakfast, Sam?"

"No."

"Go along. Have your breakfast."

I was delighted to go off. But when we came back from the exercise, at about eight o'clock in the evening, in my letter rack, was a letter from the General's wife, inviting me to tea the next day. Now I did not want to have tea with the General's wife! But that's the sort of thing that happens.

When I became the Field Marshal, I was the guest of Her Majesty in England. I had given a reception at India House where the Commanding Officer with his wife were also invited. He came in, shook hands with my wife, shook hands with me, and walked off. Everybody was drinking. After about half an hour, when everybody had arrived, I walked up to him with a glass of whisky in my hand, and he turned round to me, "May I call you Sam?"

"Please do, Sir. You used to call me 'bloody fool' before. I thought that was my Christian name!"

The difference between the officer now and then—my first confidential report written by him. Before you went in to sign your confidential report, you had to go in front of the Adjutant, beautifully turned out. We did not have any medals in those days. We had to have a sword to go into the CD's office then. I walked in there, saluted the Adjutant, he looked me up and down and said, "You are going to see the Colonel now? Look at you! Your bloody strap is filthy dirty, look at your belt, it is disgusting. Go on, go and get dressed." I walked out, waited for five minutes and came back.

He looked me up and down, "Much better."

Then he said, "You are going in there. Do you have a fountain pen?"

I said, "Yes."

"The CO will read your report. You will initial on the left hand corner. Is that understood?"

"Yes."

I walked in there, saluted the Colonel, "Mr. Manekshaw reporting, Sir."

He looked me up and down, thrust the report on me—one line—"This officer, I beg his pardon, this man, may someday become an officer."

I initialled it and walked out.

Khaled Sheikh, another officer from my regiment, who became the Foreign Minister of Pakistan and a Governor there, came out. "Khaled, what report have you got?" I said. He said, "One line— this officer tends to be irresponsible." I said, "That's a bad report, Khaled." He said, "Uh! Last year the bugger said I was irresponsible."

But we did not mind. Today, if the Commanding Officer writes and says this officer is irresponsible, the officer wants to appeal to the President of India saying he is more responsible than the Commanding Officer.

That was the difference, dear. We simply did not give a cuss.

Anything else?

Thank you Gentleman, thank you for your kindness. Thank you for your patience and your discipline. I am delighted to see you all here.

Appendix III

Address to Passing Out Gentlemen Cadets by General SHFJ Manekshaw, MC, Chief of the Army Staff on 14th June 1969 at the Indian Military Academy, Dehradun

Gentlemen,
I am delighted to be here this morning to take the salute at your Passing Out Parade. I have seen your turnout, I have noticed your drill, I have watched your marching. I commend you on it. In fact, your standard is comparable to the one I saw here 40 years ago when I was a Gentleman Cadet. You have my congratulations.

At moments like this, it is customary for the Reviewing Officer to utter words of great wisdom, to propound thoughts, to make forecasts of world events and to dish out masses and lashings of advice. That, Gentlemen, is not my fault. You are leaving here this morning as officers, as leaders. You will be going from here to your units which are deployed on the border. They are facing an enemy whom they have but recently fought and vanquished. You are going to be given command of troops in an operational area. You are indeed fortunate.

Your tasks will be to administer to their needs and to lead them in battle. What sort of men will you be leading? You will be leading veterans, men who have fought, men who have won, men who are used to good leadership. Make sure you give it to them. In the years to come, some of you will fall by the wayside. It is inevitable. Others will keep their heads just above water and there will be a few of you, like me, who will get to the top ranks of the military hierarchy. Given your fair share of luck, equal opportunity, it will depend on you whether you fall by the wayside, keep your head above water or rise to giddy heights.

There is no comfort for you when you leave here. The luxury and the cosiness that you have experienced at Kharakvasla and at the Indian Military Academy, ceases to exist from this morning. Today you become soldiers. You have in front of you a life of hardship, a life of great adventure. Make the most of it.

May the winds of fortune blow kindly on you wherever you go. May you have your fair share of luck. You have great opportunities and a lifetime of adventure. I envy you.

Thank you, Gentlemen.

Appendix IV

General
SHFJ Manekshaw, MC
Chief of the Army Staff
is pleased to appoint
Messrs New Delhi Stationery Mart
as his
Printers and Stationers
By Order of the
Chief of the Army Staff

Army Headquarters
New Delhi
The 30 December 1970

Lieutenant Colonel
Military Assistant to the
Chief of the Army Staff

Appendix V

Address by General SHFJ Manekshaw, MC, Chief of the Army Staff to the Passing out Gentlemen Cadets, 30th March, 1972

Gentlemen,

I have been wondering for some time what I should say to you on this parade. After much thought, I have decided that some of the remarks I made here a couple of years ago could bear repetition.

As I stand here this morning, I recall with nostalgia the time when I was a Gentleman Cadet at this Institution some 37 years ago. Since I passed out from here as a mere Gentleman Cadet, many things have changed. Wars have been fought, technical developments have taken place, missiles and nuclear warheads have changed the very complexion of warfare, so that our survival has become a problem. But for us soldiers one thing has remained unchanged, one thing for us soldiers has remained fixed and unchanging. Our task today is the same as it has always been. And what is our task? Our task is to fight to win wars, to defeat the enemy. If you lose, the nation is destroyed. In order to enable you to carry out your mission, we at this Institution have helped in building your character. We have built your physical strength, your moral courage and your mental calibre. We have taught you to be resourceful, deliberate, unyielding, determined and, above all, to be completely honest. In short, we have taught you to become leaders.

Now when you pass out from here in a few hours' time, what sort of men are you going to lead? Gentlemen, you are going to command men who are courageous, gallant, chivalrous, disciplined and honest, whose fathers and whose grandfathers have sacrificed their lives, shed their blood so that you should survive. No finer body of men will you get anywhere. You will have the proud privilege to command them, and lead them in battle. Gentlemen, you are indeed fortunate.

As I look around, I see many parents, relations, friends and sweethearts. They are looking at you passing out from here this morning with a great deal of pride. They are proud of you as indeed I am, too. Make sure that your future actions don't betray either them or me.

And, finally, may the winds of fortune blow fair on you wherever you go. And may you have your proper and fair share of happiness and luck. I thank you.

Index

1 Corps, 166, 218

4 Corps, 10, 167, 169, 262

11 Corps, 188

15 Corps, 137, 165, 188

8 Gorkha Rifles, 8, 9, 28, 97, 98, 112, 263

48 Gorkha Rifles, 168

58 Gorkha Training Centre, 17, 97

61 Cavalry, 96

ADC, 23, 26, 107, 108, 111, 118, 157, 164, 195, 196 ,

Adjutant General, 36, 37, 59, 80, 121, 251

Afghanistan, 176

Agartala, 109, 124, 147, 169; Conspiracy Case, 124

Air Chief, 131, 159, 205

Air Force Station, 26, 107

Air Force, 26, 27, 76, 101, 107, 108, 120, 146, 147, 148, 154, 166, 173, 195, 201, 211, 241

Airmen's Board, 44

Akbar, 89

Akhnoor, 164

Al Ahram, Egyptian Newspaper, 132

All, Maj. Gen., Rao Farman, 156

Allouetee, 107

Alma Mater, Sherwood College, 2

Amar Prem, 182

Ambassador, 119

American 7th Fleet, 172

American War College, 74

Amritsar, Hindu Sabha College, 1, 2, 73

Angami, Mowu, 14

Angami, Nedelie, 175

Angami, Thenuselie, 175

April 3, birth of Sam Manekshaw, 1; 1939, marriage with Silloo Bode, 5

Area Headquarters Officers' Mess, 4

Armed Forces Medical Inspection Room, 99

Army Act, 64

Army Chief, 2, 13, 21, 28, 33, 36, 92, 120, 129, 131, 143, 156, 196, 200, 205, 206, 216, 220, 232, 242, 250

Army Commander, 11, 12, 13, 15, 19, 22, 26, 55, 71, 81, 94, 136, 137, 139, 155, 159, 160, 173, 176, 194, 199, 203, 229, 230

Army Headquarters, 7, 9, 10, 26, 27, 33, 63, 70, 98, 102, 125, 136, 167, 175, 193, 206, 208, 227

Army Hospital, 43, 230

Army House, 6, 29, 30, 50, 51, 75, 156, 161, 162, 163, 182, 206

Army, 2, 5, 6, 7, 8, 10, 11, 12, 13, 14, 15, 19, 21, 22, 23, 24, 26, 27

Army Wives Welfare Organisation, 182

Arora, Lt. Gen. Jagjit Singh, 140

Arunachal Pradesh, 132

Ashoka Hotel, 74, 186

Assam, 12, 75, 128, 150, 170, 228, 240, 241

Assistant Military Secretary, 22

Atal, Maj. Gen. Hira Lal, 203

Atkins, 64

Australia, 7, 236

Avadi, 150

Avro, 107

Auchinlek, Field Marshal Sir Claude, 202

Awami League, 124

Badhwar, Vinod, 201

Bakshi, Maj. Gen. Z.C. (Zoru), 220

Balli, 25, 53, 120

Bangalore, 27, 155, 156

Bangladesh, 48, 118, 142, 170, 173, 175, 185, 213, 231, 232

Bareilly, 23

Batra, Maj. Gen. M.N., 161

Battalion, 3, 4, 5, 8, 9, 12, 17, 19, 20, 21, 22, 25, 41, 55, 88, 97, 111, 121, 161, 167, 168, 169, 198, 209, 243, 252 ; 2nd, 3, 4, 21, 48, 209; 4th, 3, 17, 48; 5th, 165; 6th, 112; 8th Gorkha, 5

Bay of Bengal, 123

Bengal, 12, 228, 240

Bewoor, Lt. Gen. G.G., 203, 204

Bhagat, Lt. Gen. PS., 194, 196

Bhaiya Rajwade, Maj. Gen., 30

Bhutan, 132

Bhutto, Z.A., 7, 197

Black Watch, 23

Bombay, 1, 5, 106, 117, 125, 146, 150, 182, 200; Elphinstone College, 5; School of Arts, 5

Border Command, 76

Border Security Force Headquarters, 42

Border Security Force (BSF), 42, 133, 227, 228

Bowden, Maj. Gen. L. Scott, 209

Brigade football, 21

Brigade of Guards, 28

Bristol Cream, 80

British Army Officers, 22

British Army, 4

British Chief of General Staff, 209

British Government, 123

British Indian Army, 3

British Infantry Battalion, 3

British Military Adviser, 209

Bubanj, Lt. Gen., 75

Burma (now Myanmar), Burma, 5, 21, 75, 234

Cadillac, 26, 196

Caesar, 56, 245, 246

Calcutta, 11, 14, 15, 18, 20, 21, 24, 26, 29, 51, 60, 156, 182, 199

Campbell, Maj. Gen. W.T., 4

Canasta, 156

Candeth, Lt. Gen. K.P., 137, 159

Cape Comorin, 106, 175

Cariappa, Gen. K.M., 28, 44, 129; Field Marshal, 37, 129

Carver, Gen. Sir Michael (now Field Marshal), 4

Ceasefire Line, 193

Cawas Patels, 213

Central Government, 62

Central Public Works Department, 28

Chairman of the Joint Chiefs of Staff, 76

Chandorkar, Maj. Gen D.K., 219

chapatis, 120

Chatterji, Admiral, 130

Chaudhari, Gen. J.N., 37

Chavan, Y.B., 183

Chhamb, 159, 160, 164, 165, 166, 169

Chibber, 93

Chief, 5, 6, 7, 11, 14, 18, 23, 24, 25, 26, 27, 29, 30, 33, 34, 35, 37, 38

Chief Designate, 9, 10

Chief engineer, 29

Chief of Air Staff, 131

Chief of Army Staff, 24, 27, 117

Chief of Defence Staff, 76, 200, 201, 217, 262

Chief of Naval Staff, 74, 130, 205

Chiefs of Staff Committee, 130, 131, 132, 155, 158, 161, 205

China, 14, 75, 84, 114, 142, 145, 170, 223, 227, 229, 240

Chinaman, 141

Chinese, 9, 11, 13, 75, 79, 126, 128, 132, 170, 171, 172, 223, 228, 229, 240, 242, 251

Chittagong, 123

Chogyal, 218, 219

Chopra, Maj. Gen. R.L., 150

Chumbi Valley, 79, 128, 170

Churchill, Winston, 154

Civilian Staff Officer, 108

Clement Town, 11

COAS, 28, 33, 165, 203, 227, 228, 229, 230

College of Combat, 90, 221

Colombo, 146

Commander-in-Chief, 14, 159

Command Headquarters, 21

Commandant, 8, 77, 235, 236, 239, 249, 250, 251

Commanding Officer, 3, 12, 44, 112, 243, 252, 253, 254

company, 166, 239, 243, 244, 252

Congress Party, 103, 162; split, 87

Congress, 97

Coonoor, 206, 207, 213, 215, 225, 261

Corps Commander, 15, 165, 169, 196

Corps of Engineers, 98

Court of Inquiry, 9

Crookes lenses, 3

DSO, 73

Dacca, 141, 146, 169, 173, 174, 175, 197, 227, 228, 229, 231

David, 184
December 1963, Sam took over as Army Commander, 27
Defence Minister, 11, 60, 66, 93, 116, 125, 155, 156, 158, 161, 183, 216, 231, 232, 239, 250, 251
Defence Ministry, 38, 66, 73, 93, 150, 155, 201, 209, 211
defence service, 131
Defence Services Officers Institute, 75
Defence Services Staff College, 9, 23, 27, 77, 90, 149, 215, 221
Dehradun, 3, 17, 25, 54, 97, 213, 262
Delhi/New Delhi, 1, 5, 8, 9, 10, 11, 12, 23, 24, 34, 36, 39, 40, 43, 47, 56, 65, 76, 79, 80
Depi, 22, 157
Dera Baba Nanak, 167, 168
Desai, Morarji, 216
Dhar, D.P., 151, 230
Dhar, P.N., 130
Dhaula Kuan, 27, 72
Dias, A.L., 18
Diniyar, 22
Directing Staff, 35, 161
Director General of Medical Services, 59
Director of Medical Services, 99
Director of Military Intelligence, 148, 161, 219
Director of Military Operations (DMO), 7, 58, 132, 137, 155, 167, 195, 199, 218
Director of Military Training, 38
Director of Ordnance Services, 40

Director Weapons and Equipment (DWE), 25
Diwan, Capt. G.M., 6
D'jam Gen, 74
DOS, 40
Duegan, Mr., 89
Dum Dum Airport, 14
Duncan Eykyn, 4
Durand Championship, 21; Line, 176
Dussehra, 55

Earl of Orhnay, 1st, 4
East Bengal (now Bangladesh), 48, 164
East Pakistan, 11, 59, 123, 124, 125, 126, 128, 132, 139, 140, 141, 144, 145, 147, 170, 171, 172, 177, 217, 218, 222, 223, 228, 239
Eastern Air Command, 131
Eastern Army, 11, 16, 27, 83, 136, 140, 173, 227; Commander, 55, 139, 140, 173, 199
Eastern Command, 12, 19, 21, 41, 139, 142, 227, 229
Edinburgh, 4
Electrical and Mechanical Engineers, 98
Elphinstone College, Bombay, 5
Embassy, 73, 146, 173
engineer, 29, 113, 150
Engineer in Chief, 59
Engineer, Air Marshal Minoo, 160
England, 2, 8, 250, 253, 261
Escorts, 217
Ex-servicemen's Rally, 35, 71
External Affairs, 45, 193, 230

Extract Digit (ED), 39

Family Welfare Centre, 20
Fazilka, 146, 188
February 4, 1934, Sam received commission, 3; February 22th, 1926, Sam was wounded, 5
Ferguson, Bernard, 23
Ferozepur, 46
Field Marshal, first, 4, 261
Fighting General, 210
Football Championship, 21
Foreign Ministry, 151
Fort William, Calcutta, 21, 24
Fourth Estate, 51
France, 101, 102

Gandhi, Mahatma, 48
Gandhi, Indira, 125, 179, 222, 262
Gangtok, 106
Garhwal Rifles, 111
Gayatri Devi, Rajmata, 113
General Officer, Commanding (GOC), 13, 20, 87, 165
General Staff Officer Grade, 195
Gentleman Cadet, 255, 258
George, Hamilton, 4
Gilgit, 144
Gill, Maj. Gen. I.S., 46
Gorkha Brigade, 21, 54, 231
Gorkha Hat, 98
Gorkha Rifles, xii, 8, 9, 22, 28, 48, 97, 98, 112, 165, 168, 210, 263
Gorkha Training Centre, 213
Governor, 18, 172, 254
GR, 46, 230, 231

Gun runner (FF), 41, 91, 92
Gupta, Private Secretary, 52
Gurbachan Singh, 87, 146
Gurung, Hav Lachhman, 48
Guwahati, 109
Gymnasia, 89

Haksar, P.N., 130
Hamid Khan, Lt. Gen., 194
Hamlet, 13
Harish Sarin, 61, 93
Haryana, 216, 241
Hazari, Maj. Gen. M.G., 150
Heavy Vehicle Factory, 150
Heikel, Mr., 132
High Commission, 73, 148, 149, 209, 232
Higher Command Course, 90
Himalayas, 9, 106, 222
Hindi, 46, 47, 162
Hindu Sabha College, Amritsar, 2
Home Ministry, 150
Home Secretary, 109
Horatio Nelson, 28
Hussainiwala, 168
Inder Vohra, Brig., 66
India, 1, 6, 7, 35, 39, 78, 85, 95, 106, 119, 123, 124, 127, 128, 129, 142, 144, 170, 172, 174, 194, 210

Indian Army, 146, 194
Indian Military Academy (IMA), Dehra Dun, 3, 31, 259
Indian Naval Task Force, 172
Indian Ocean, 172, 229
Indo-Tibet border, 167

Infantry Division, 27, 30, 165
Infantry School, 90
Inspector General, 150
Intelligence Bureau, 109
International border, 83, 195
Investiture Parade, 55
Iranian Joint Services, 74
Islamabad, 148
Islamic Bloc, 176
Italian Army, 157

J.J. School of Arts, Bombay, 5
Jacob, Lt. Gen. J.F.R., 226
Jagjivan Ram, 125, 216, 261
Jagtiani, Diljit, 20
Jagtiani, Maj. Kumar, 20
Jain, 52
Jai Prakash Narayan, 151
Jaipur, 113; Royals, 113
James Bond, 189
Jammu, 74, 164, 166, 169, 194, 220
Jammu and Kashmir, 74
Jamuna, River, 44
Jangi Lat, 6, 43
January, 1973, Sam Manekshaw
    relinquished office, 220
Jat, 44, 216
Jawaharlal Nehru University, 77
Jawan's Welfare, 182
Jinnah, 210
Johar, I.S., 185
Joshimath, 22, 25, 55
June 6, 1969, Gen.
    Kumaramangalam retires;
    Manekshaw takes over, 26
Jungle Warfare School, 11
Junglee, 50
Junior Commissioned Officer
    Clerks, 52

Kaiyan, 193
Kalkat, pvsm Maj. Gen., Onkar
    Singh, 13, 140
Kamraj Plan, 129
Kanchanjanga, 106
Kangra Valley, 94
Kani Ram, 208
Kashmir, 7, 11, 137, 138, 145, 147,
    157, 164, 165, 167, 169, 193,
    194
Kao, R.N., 145
Kaul, Lt. Gen. B.M., 9
Kaul, T.N., 130
Kennedy, Jack, 56
Kerala, 201
Khan Gen. Tikka, 195, 196, 198,
    199
Khan, Gen. Yahya, 124, 154, 173
Khan, Lt. Gen. Hamid, 194
Khandka (sword), 119
Khanna, Devinder, 201
Kharakvasla, 259
Khukri, 4, 119
King George II, 4
King of Nepal, His Majesty, 119
Kini, Maj. Gen., 150
Kipling, 64
Kissinger, 189
Kit Maintenance Allowance, 49
Kohlapur, 73
Krishna Menon, V.K., 9
Kumaramanglam, Gen. P.P., 23,
    24, 26, 27, 55

Ladakh, 10, 132, 165, 188
Lahore, 1, 5, 39, 148, 195, 197,
    198, 199

Lal, Bansi, 216
Lal, K.B., 93, 155
Lal, Pratap, 131
Lal, Air Chief Mar. P.C., 205
Leh, 106
Lhasa, 148
Li, Admiral, 97
Liaison Officer, 118, 146
Lieutenant Colonel, 26, 36, 87, 117, 251
Lieutenant General, 8, 9, 194, 196, 250
Limey, 8
Line of Actual Control, 193
London, 51, 95, 162, 190, 201, 202, 210, 211
Longewala, 163, 164, 166
Lucknow, 202, 203, 233

MacDonald, Ramsay, 154
Madhya Pradesh, 63, 90
Madras, 182
Maharashtra, 73
Maidan, 173
Maja, 19, 231
Major, 41, 52, 96, 98, 113, 139, 140, 142, 146, 149, 150, 178, 217, 223
Major General, 41, 140, 146, 149, 150
Manekshaw, Doctor, 1, 2
Manekshaw, Sam, Gen., 262
Marala Headworks, 164
Master General of Ordnance, 33, 59
Matron, 95, 110
Matron-in-Chief, 95
Maurya, Chandra Gupta, 178

McDermot, Dr., 173
Member of Parliament, 43, 44
Menezes, 46
Meyers, Lt. Col. (now Brjg.) Peter, 22
Mhow, 90, 149, 221
MI, 107
Military Assistant (MA), 23, 33, 105, 117, 143, 195, 208, 226
Military Attache, 39, 102, 116, 143, 190
Military Cross, 6
Military Engineering Service, 19, 22, 26, 28
Military Law, 62
Military Nursing Service Officers, 95
Military Operations Directorate, 7, 8
Military Police, 44
Military Secretary, 159
Ministry of Defence, 47, 52, 88, 116, 208, 261
Ministry of External Affairs, 116
Mint, 81
Mishra, L.N., 162
Mistry, Dini, 22
Mizo Hills, 11, 12, 13
Mizo, 11, 12, 13, 41, 139
Mizoram, 13, 41, 124, 132, 141
Mogul Gardens, 16
Moscow, 148, 190
Mountain Division, 12, 13
Mrs. Manekshaw, 16, 18, 19, 24, 26, 27, 50, 56, 58, 73, 74, 95, 107, 108, 114, 115, 118, 125, 162, 163, 182, 197, 209, 215, 225; Silloo Bode, 21

Mukti Bahini, 137, 140, 141, 142
Murree Gin, 197

Nadirshahi orders, 7
Naga Hills, 13
Nagaland, 11, 12, 13, 14, 124, 132,
    139, 141, 175, 220
Nainital, 1, 26
Nair, 52
Nanda, Admiral, 130
Narayan, Jai Prakash, 129
Narcisso, Lt. Col. Guido, 157
National Defence College, 76, 77,
    149, 161, 218
Nathu La, 13, 75, 112
Naval Assistant, 73
Naval Secretary, 73
Naval Staff, 130, 205
Navy, 58, 73, 76, 101, 120, 130,
    147, 149, 159, 172, 173, 200,
    211
Nayyar, Kuldip, 199
Nehru, B.K., 22
Nepal, 105, 115, 118, 119, 132, 201
Nepotism, 41, 42
Niazi, Lt. Gen., 173
Nilgiris, 23, 90, 206, 215, 249, 261
North Burma, 75
North East Frontier Agency, 108
North West Frontier Province, 39
November 28, 1962, Lt. Gen. BM
    Kaul took over 4 Corps, 10

Oberoi Intercontinental, 79
Ordnance Corps, 56, 81
Oxford Dictionary, 41

Padma Bhushan, 16

Padma Vibhushan, 200
Pakistan, 4, 7, 11, 76, 80, 81, 83,
    84, 85, 86, 123, 124, 125, 127,
    128, 129, 132, 133, 135, 140,
    141, 143, 144
Palam Airport, 74
Palampur, 22, 94, 95
Palit, Maj. Gen. Monty, 222
Panthaki, Behram, 161
Parade Commander, 46, 47
Paris, 7, 190
Parsi, 1, 41
Passing Out Parade, 258
Pathankot, 165, 166, 188
Patna, 164
Paul, Swaraj, 217
Pay Commission, 5
Pegu, 6
Peking, 189
Personal Assistants, 52, 202
Peshwari Chapplis, 118
Planning Commission, 207
Pokhra, 118, 119
police, 124, 150, 159, 262
Poonch, 164, 166, 167
Porter King, 146, 188
President, 48, 49, 60, 149, 153,
    159, 183, 192, 200, 206, 231,
    250, 254
Presiding Officer, 9
Prime Minister, 13, 41, 58, 125,
    126, 128, 129, 132, 135, 136,
    137, 154, 155, 156, 158, 173,
    174, 183, 191, 192, 200, 201,
    203, 206
Prime Minister's Relief Fund, 183
Principal Staff Officer (PSO), 34
PSO, 70, 71, 93

Public Relations Officer, 135
Pune, 125
Punjab Regiment, 166
Pushto, 169

Quarter Guard, 112
Quartermaster General, 68
Queen, 119, 231, 250

Rai Hav. Agan Singh, 48
Rajasthan, 164, 166, 189
Raj Bhavan, 22, 109
Rajesh Khanna, 182
Rajwade, Maj. Gen. M.R., 81
Rangoon, 6
Rao Maj. Gen. K.V. Krishna, 220
Rao, Narasimha, 217
Rashtrapati Bhavan, 16, 36, 96, 183, 192
Rawalpindi, 39, 195, 196
Rawlley, Naveen, 169
Red Cross, 217
Red Fort, 72, 127
Regiment, 4, 6, 8, 21, 30, 31, 48, 49, 57, 88, 96, 97, 111, 121, 166, 168, 213, 218, 230; Col. of, xii, 4, 8, 9, 19, 97, 232; Frontier Force, 3, 5, 6, 243
Republic Day Parade, 49
Research and Development Organisation, 98
Reviewing Officer, 258
Rifle Regiment, 28
Royal College of Defence Studies, 217
Royal Nepal Army, 119
Royal Scots, 3, 4, 209
Runn of Kutch, 147

sailors, 177
saloon, 120
Sam, 1, 2, 4, 5, 6, 7, 8, 9, 10, 11, 14, 15, 16, 17, 19, 23, 24, 25, 27, 39, 47, 50, 55, 57, 60, 61, 83, 93, 95, 104, 112, 130, 131, 132, 134, 135, 162, 163, 164, 174, 190, 199, 200, 211, 216, 217, 218, 219, 220, 221, 222, 225, 226, 227, 228, 229, 230, 231, 232, 233, 235, 241, 242, 243, 253, 260, 261, 262, 263
Sam Bahadur, 112
Sam Bahadur Room, 213
Santa Cruz Airport, 117
Sarkar, Maj. Gen. B.N., 140
Satpal, 52
Savile Row, 51
Scientific Adviser, 60
Scotch, 107
Secretariat, 33, 46, 58, 131, 145, 206, 207
Secretariat Staff, 45, 202
Security Forces, 14, 124, 141, 159
Selecus, Macedonian General, 178
Sena Medal, 202
Senior Cambridge, 33
Sepoy, 99
Service Chiefs, 27, 73, 131, 154, 156, 158, 183, 200
Service Headquarters, 38, 59, 159
Service Officers Quarters, Sardar Patel Marg, 68
Seth, 52

Sethna, Brig. Adi, 139
Shanti Bhawan, 26
Sherry, 19
Sherwood College, Nainital, 233
Shaha, Surendra Bahadur, 201
Shillong, 12, 13, 19, 21, 22, 41, 55, 213
Shiny Eighth, 97
Sialkot, 164, 166, 194
Sibal, Lt. Gen. H.K., 203
Sikhs, 54th, 196; Light Infantry, 204
Sind, 194
Sikkim, 13, 75, 79, 132, 218
Sikkim Guards, 218
Siliguri, 79, 128
Silchar, 147
Shimla, 11, 19
Simla Agreement, (Accord), 194
Singh, Lt. Gen. Kulwant, 15
Singh, Lt. Gen. Daulet, 9
Singh, Lt. Gen. K.K., 167
Singh, Maj. Gen. K.K., 218
Singh, L.P., 130
Singh, Lt. Gen. Sagat, 169
Singh, Lt. Gen, Sartaj, 165
Singh, Swaran, 7, 93, 239, 240
Sinha, Brig. S.K., 70
Sood, R.P., 56
South Asia, 173
South Block, 25, 45, 52, 73, 99, 125
South Korea, 97
Soviet Union, 136, 215
Sports Authority of India, 216
Srinagar, 106, 164, 188, 199
Stavka, 215
Straits of Malacca, 172

Sub-Area Commander, 25
Subramaniam, 52, 108
Suchetgarh, 194
Supreme Commander, 60
Swatantra Party, 113
Sweetheart, 16, 20, 37, 43, 93, 111
Sydney, 8

Tagore, Sharmila, 182
Tangkar La, 79
Taungdaw, 21
Thakochak, 194, 195, 197, 198, 199
Thapar, 46
Tehran, 197
Thimayya, Gen. K.S., 250
Thorat, Lt. Gen. S.P.P., 73
Tibet, 22, 132, 144, 145, 148, 167, 170, 172, 229
Tom Pocock, 210
Tripura, 128, 141, 223, 228, 240
Tuli Maj. Gen., 150

Udhampur, 165
UNDP, 173
USA, 101, 131, 146
Ukil, 52
United Kingdom, 4, 212
United Nations, 157, 173, 193
United States, 8, 173, 187
Uppal, 52
Urdu, 46, 169
Uri, 138
US Aid Mission, 55
USSR, 86, 101, 117, 142, 148, 171, 189, 229
Uttar Pradesh, 241

Vice Chief of Army Staff, 59,
139, 232
Vietnam, 172
Victoria Cross, 48
Vijay Chowk, 112
Vintage Car Rally, 209
VIP Flight, 117
Vohra, Maj. Gen. Vir, 217
Vishisht Seva Medal, 208

Wagah, 194
Walker, Lt. Gen. (now Gen.) Sir
Walter, 22
Watergate, 27
Wavell, Field Marshal, 23

Welfare Officer, 45
Wellington, 10, 17, 23, 90, 149,
215, 226, 230, 235, 246, 261
West Bengal, 11, 12, 228, 240
West Germany, 101
Western Army Commander, 9,
137, 155, 159, 160, 166, 176
Western Army, 168
World War, Second, 5, 21

Yadav, H.S. (Kim), 11
Yugoslav Army Chief, 75
Yugoslav Military Attaché, 39

Zia-ul-Haq, 197